# DISCOVERING OLD TESTAMENT ORIGINS

## The Books of Genesis, Exodus and Samuel

### MARGARET NUTTING RALPH

PAULIST PRESS
New York/Mahwah

Library of Congress Cataloging-in-Publication Data

Ralph, Margaret Nutting.
    Discovering Old Testament origins: the books of Genesis, Exodus, and Samuel/Margaret Nutting Ralph.
      p.   cm.
    Includes index.
    ISBN 0-8091-3322-9
    1. Bible. O.T. Genesis—Study and teaching. 2. Bible. O.T. Exodus—Study and teaching. 3. Bible. O.T. Samuel—Study and teaching. I. Title.
BS1239.R33   1992
222'.11061—dc20                              92-8494
                                                    CIP

Published by Paulist Press
997 Macarthur Boulevard
Mahwah, New Jersey 07430

Printed and bound in the
United States of America

# Contents

## Exodus

## 1 Samuel

# Preface

Have you ever been misquoted? Isn't it aggravating? I often think that God must feel the same way. When I hear what some people claim God has "said" it makes me cringe. But it also gives me pause. As a teacher of scripture do I sometimes misrepresent God too?

If you think about it, though, people who misquote others, ourselves included, seldom do so purposefully. The problem is not that we are malicious but that we have honestly misunderstood what another person intended to say.

Why do misunderstandings occur? There are many possible reasons. One is that we may not know the meaning of a word which someone has used. Another is that the speaker may have used an idiom with which we were unfamiliar. Perhaps we misunderstood the tone of a comment so we took seriously something intended to be a joke. Perhaps we walked into the middle of a conversation and misunderstood what we heard for that reason.

People misunderstand what God has "said" for many of the same reasons. Believing that scripture is a living word, and that one might hear God speak through scripture, many people then fail to actually read scripture. Instead they read random passages here and there, and somehow or other expect to understand what has been "said." The book which you now hold is based on the premise that before you can hope to understand what God "says" in the books of Genesis, Exodus, and 1, 2 Samuel, you must first read each book. Do not start your study of Genesis, Exodus, 1, 2 Samuel by reading this book. Instead pick up your Bible and read one book, Genesis for example, straight through as you would a novel. As you read, jot down every question that comes to mind. Do not stop to read

1

footnotes or commentaries. Allow your first impression to be, not what someone else says the Bible "says," but what the Bible actually "says" in context.

Obviously those who so carefully compiled our Old Testament books intended that a book be read as a whole, not chopped up—a paragraph here and a paragraph there—read in random order and out of context. There is no book on earth with a plot which you could possibly understand using such a haphazard method. The books of the Old Testament are no exception.

Over the years I have collected the questions which students ask when reading Genesis, Exodus, 1, 2 Samuel for the first time. This book is a collection of short articles written in response to those questions.

It is my experience that the content of these articles is appropriate and useful for juniors in high school and anyone older. I do not recommend this book for most younger students. I have found that one must have developed beyond the very "literal" way of thinking which is normal in the early teen years before one is able to understand the points made in these articles.

The quantity of material is appropriate for a variety of religious education settings. If two articles were discussed every class meeting, this book would be a one-quarter course for an in-school class that meets every day, a semester course for an in-school class that meets two to three times a week, and a yearlong course for an out-of-school class that meets once a week. One may, of course, go faster or slower, depending on how much time is spent on the review and discussion questions. The material is also appropriate for adult education groups.

The format of question and response may tempt the students to skip responses to questions which have not occurred to them. This would be a mistake. One question often leads to related questions which do not appear in the heading but which are addressed in the articles.

Despite the question and answer format, the short articles written in response to specific questions are not pat answers. I have tried to respond to questions in such a way as to teach a methodology so as to enable students to think. The goal is to equip students with the tools they will need to search out answers to questions which do not appear in these articles.

The fact that the responses deal with methodology is an additional reason to read the articles in order. Methodological points made in early articles are usually not repeated in subsequent articles.

It may be that a student will be unfamiliar with a word or concept in a given article which has been presumed known and so is not explained. The glossary in the back of the book has been designed to help the student in such a situation. Students should remember to use the glossary if unfamiliar words appear or to review concepts which were explained in earlier articles.

In addition to a glossary, the book contains an index of biblical passages. This will help both teacher and student locate comments on given passages.

The Appendix includes a list of the books of the Bible as they appear in the Hebrew, Protestant, and Roman Catholic Old Testaments, a map of Palestine, and a timeline that locates major people and events in chronological order.

Both teacher and students may expect, and even want, to read more introductory material before reading the specific Old Testament texts. This desire is purposely thwarted in this book in an attempt to let the texts themselves have the first word. Some background information is provided in various articles as the need arises. However, the student is urged to read the biblical text first so that questions are not explained away before the student has had an opportunity to ask them. All commentary is secondary to actually reading the Old Testament text.

Of course not all questions which students raise will be addressed in this book. This is all to the good. To grow in one's ability to raise the questions, to explore answers, and to live with mystery are goals in themselves. While it is wonderful to reach a degree of understanding as we read the Old Testament, not one of us will ever succeed in completely understanding the truth and wisdom which are to be found in Genesis, in Exodus and in 1, 2 Samuel.

# THE BOOK OF GENESIS

# ARTICLE 1

# Creation: God's Work

**Question: "How does the author know how the world was created? Is it just that the author is inspired?" (Gen 1:1–2:4)**

The author of Genesis 1:1–2:4, in which we read of the creation of the world in six days, is not addressing the question, "*How* was the world created?" Indeed, the author had neither natural nor supernatural knowledge on this subject. Rather, the author is teaching *that* the world was created, that all that exists was created by a loving God.

Many who read this story in the book of Genesis misunderstand it because they bring presumptions to the story, indeed to the Bible as a whole, which are false presumptions and thus lead to error.

One such false presumption is to assume that the author of Genesis 1:1–2:4 is writing as an historian or a journalist or a scientist would write. Obviously, if one approaches the story with such a misunderstanding one is confronted with many questions to which there are no answers. For instance: "How could there be light but no sun?" Or: "How could there be three days but no sun?"

The person who asks, "How does the author know *how* the world was created?" is going to have to completely change directions and approach the story with a completely different frame of mind. Such a person will also have to revise his or her idea of inspiration.

So let's try to drop any presumptions we bring to this story and let the story speak for itself. We have here a story in which God is pictured as creating all that exists. The organization of the story is very logical. It is organized around a work week.

This tells us that the author lived at a time when society was organized according to a work week. Otherwise the author would not have known about work weeks and could not have organized the story in this way.

"But wait!," many students object. "Isn't this story describing how the Sabbath started? Isn't the story explaining the reason for having a Sabbath—because God rested on the seventh day?"

The answer to this question is, "No." The story is not contemporary with the beginning of the Sabbath celebration, nor is it an ancient story. The author did not live at the dawn of creation. Rather, the author lived at a time when his society worked six days and honored the Sabbath day.

Perhaps this point can be made more clearly by drawing a comparison. Many of you have heard Bill Cosby retell the story of Noah. In Bill Cosby's account, God appears to Noah while Noah is in his rec room, Noah builds the ark in his driveway, and Noah asks God, "Are we on 'Candid Camera'?" So when someone hears Bill Cosby's story he or she knows that the author lived when there were rec rooms, driveways, and "Candid Camera." Otherwise these details could not have appeared in the story.

Just so, the author of this first story in Genesis lived when the work week and the Sabbath were well established. Otherwise these details could not have appeared in the story.

The organization of a work week is significant for another reason. This organizational scheme gives us a hint of the theme of the story. The author of Genesis 1:1–2:4 is teaching his audience that creation is God's work. So he chooses a work week as a way of organizing the story. God is pictured as having three days on which he separates things: light from darkness, the water above the dome from the water below, and the water from the dry land. Next come three days of populating what had been separated: the sun, moon and stars are placed in the dome of the sky, birds and fish are created, and finally animals and human beings are placed on the dry land.

By organizing the story around a work week the author is able to have his organization reflect his theme: Creation is God's work. All that exists exists because it was created by the hand of a loving God.

Once we understand that the author is teaching *that* God created the world, not *how,* we can better understand the kind of inspiration which the author had.

## HEAVEN AND EARTH WITH ALL THEIR ARRAY

### Heavens

God said, "Let there be a vault in
the waters to divide the waters
in two" (Gen 1:6).

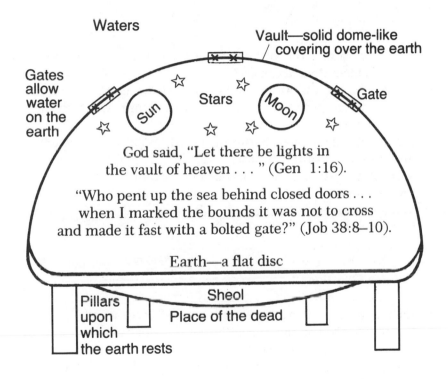

Waters

Vault—solid dome-like
covering over the earth

Gates
allow
water
on the
earth

Gate

Sun

Stars

Moon

God said, "Let there be lights in
the vault of heaven . . . " (Gen 1:16).

"Who pent up the sea behind closed doors . . .
when I marked the bounds it was not to cross
and made it fast with a bolted gate?" (Job 38:8–10).

Earth—a flat disc

Pillars
upon
which
the earth rests

Sheol

Place of the dead

The biblical authors' inspiration did not give them knowledge about science or any other subject which belongs to people of later generations. Rather, the biblical authors had spiritual insight. The biblical authors were able to perceive God's role in the lives of God's people.

Since spiritual insight is a gift from God, those who have written with spiritual insight are called "inspired" authors. Through these authors God has revealed God's self to God's people.

## Review Questions

1. What question is the author of Genesis 1:1–2:4 addressing?
2. What is the author teaching?
3. What false presumptions might someone bring to this story?
4. If one brings false presumptions to the story, what problem arises?
5. How is the story of creation organized? What does this tell us about the time of the author?
6. What relationship is there between the organization of the story and its theme?
7. What spiritual gift do inspired authors have? What do they not have?

## Discussion Questions

1. Did anything in this article surprise you? If so, what?
2. Is it obvious to you that the author of this story was not teaching science? Why or why not?
3. Is it obvious to you that the author did not live at the dawn of creation? Why or why not?
4. What does this sentence mean: "The biblical authors' inspiration did not give them knowledge about science or any other subject which belongs to people of later generations"?
5. What do you think "inspiration" means? Have you ever been inspired? Explain.

# ARTICLE 2

# Stories: Vehicles of Truth

**Question: "Wait a minute! Are you saying that this story of creation is just a story? Are you saying that it isn't true?" (Gen 1:1–2:4)**

Genesis 1:1–2:4 is not *just* a story. But it is a story, a story which teaches the truth.

Why does the questioner ask if the story of creation is *just* a story? And if it is a story, why does the questioner then say, "You mean it isn't true?"

Obviously the questioner has brought false presumptions to the Bible and in the process of having those presumptions challenged is having difficulty holding on to her belief that the Bible is "true." The questioner is evidently equating "truth" with scientific or historical fact.

The Bible has been treasured for two thousand years because people of faith have found that it speaks to the deepest and most important truths of our lives. These truths involve our relationship with God, who is the source of our existence. They involve the reason for our existence. Why are we alive? What is our purpose? Does God exist? What is God like? What would God have us be like? What behavior on our part pleases God? What behavior separates us from God and from each other? What is our final destiny?

While the answers to these questions are of utmost importance they are not easy to discern. When we ask such questions we enter the realm of mystery. Where might we find the answers to such questions?

Since we live after the time the Bible was written we might say, "Read the Bible. What the Bible teaches in answer to these questions is true." This answer reflects the belief of Christians and the

11

reason why we say the Bible is "revelation." The Bible teaches us the truth about God's nature, our own nature, our relationship with God and what we should be doing to build up God's kingdom rather than to tear it down.

But what about those people who lived before the Bible was written? Where would they look for answers to such questions? The people who lived before the Bible was written and the people who wrote what we read in the Bible looked to their own experiences to find answers to these most important questions. They looked to the experiences of their own lives, to the events in their own lives, to see how God was being revealed in these experiences and events.

For instance, the author of this first story in Genesis looked at the world around him. He experienced the variety and beauty of creation and he asked himself, "What is the source of all that exists?"

The author was an inspired person. He was open to God's presence in life and events and so became a person of spiritual perception. As an inspired person he was moved to pass on his spiritual insights to others. But how could he do this?

The author of Genesis 1:1–2:4 chose to pass on his spiritual insights in the form of a story. Indeed, he had few other choices. He could not choose to write as a scientist because he lived before the scientific age and was writing on a subject which included God. God does not fall within the parameters of scientific study. (Scientists study material forms and recurring phenomena.)

He could not choose to write as an historian because history is about those events which were witnessed and about which we have oral or written traditions. Creation is not an event which any human being witnessed.

"Maybe the event wasn't witnessed," students admit, "but maybe God told the first human beings about creation and so we do have an oral tradition."

Again, this is simply bringing presumptions to Genesis that can't be supported by the text. The author makes no such claim.

Rather, the author expects us to recognize that he has chosen to teach us a spiritual truth through a story.

This particular kind of story is referred to as a "myth." By "myth" we do not mean "something once believed to be true but now known to be false," although that is one meaning of the word "myth."

---

**MYTH: AN IMAGINATIVE AND SYMBOLIC STORY ABOUT A REALITY WHICH IS BEYOND COMPREHENSION.**

*Function:* To orient people in a moral universe.

*Creation Story*

*3 days of separation*

- Light/Darkness
- Water (firmament) Water
- Water/Dry Land

*3 days of population*

- Sun, Moon, Stars
- Birds, Fish
- Animals, Human Beings

*Story Teaches:*
- There is one God
- All creation is good, especially human beings
- Sun and Moon are not gods
- Human beings are made in the image of a loving God

---

When we say this story is a "myth" we are saying that the author is using symbols and images to speak of a reality which is really beyond comprehension. Since the truth is beyond comprehension the author must speak through images and symbols. The author has no other choice except to remain silent.

However, the fact that the author uses images and symbols does not mean that the story is "not true." Truth is not limited to scientific and historical fact. This story deals with reality and teaches a truth in relation to that reality. The story is a very serious attempt, and a very successful one, to teach the truth about the reality of all that exists. God made all that exists, and everything God made is good.

## Review Questions

1. The Bible speaks to truths about certain relationships in our lives. What are these relationships? What questions do we have about these relationships?

2. What do we mean when we say that the Bible is revelation?
3. Where did biblical authors look for answers to life's questions?
4. What experience lies behind the story of creation?
5. Why could the author of the creation story not pass on his spiritual insight in historical or scientific writing?
6. When we say that Genesis 1:1–2:4 is written in the literary form, "myth," what do we mean?
7. What truth about reality does the story teach?

## Discussion Questions

1. What is the difference between these two statements: "This is a story." "This is just a story." Why does the word "just" not belong if one is talking about the creation story?
2. Why is it difficult to answer this question: "What is God like?"
3. Have you ever experienced God's presence in the events of your life? Explain.
4. Does it surprise or upset you to read that Genesis 1:1–2:4 is a myth? Why or why not?
5. Can a myth be true? Explain.

# ARTICLE 3

# The Bible: A Library of Books

**Question: "Are you saying that the Bible is a myth?"**

No, we are not saying that the Bible is a myth. Behind this question is a presumption that what one says about one part of the Bible one has said about the whole Bible.

So far we have not discussed any part of the Bible except the first story in the book of Genesis. What we have said about that story we have said only about that story. What we have said about that story cannot be applied to the Bible as a whole, nor even to the book of Genesis as a whole.

Why is this? The reason that what is said about one part of the Bible cannot be said about the Bible as a whole is because the Bible is not just one book. The Bible is a collection of books, and these books contain a whole variety of kinds of writing.

Since you are just beginning to read the Bible we will not elaborate on the kinds of writing in the Bible just yet. We will have plenty of opportunity to do that as we continue to read.

However, before we proceed it will be useful to become comfortable with the fact that the Bible contains a wide variety of kinds of writing and to realize that we must always ask ourselves, "What kind of writing is this?" We have already seen that if we misunderstand the kind of writing we are reading we will misunderstand what the author is saying. If we misunderstand what the author is saying we will misunderstand the revelation which is contained in the work.

Many people are resistant to the idea that the Bible contains many kinds of writing. They say, "This is too complicated. I can read the Bible and get a lot out of it without asking questions about literary form." It may be true that you can "get a lot out of the Bible" without learning about the kinds of writing which the authors use. But it is also true that what you are getting may not be what the biblical authors are teaching. You will not be able to understand what the biblical authors are saying if you fail to consider the varieties of literary forms which they are using.

However, it is not difficult to determine one kind of writing from another. We all do this every time we read a newspaper. Newspapers contain a wide variety of kinds of writing. In front page stories the writers are trying to be objective. They are answering the question, "What happened?" Editorials are entirely different. Those who write editorials often present only one side of a question and try to persuade others to their point of view. Newspapers contain humorous writing in which authors try to picture reality in such a way that we laugh at our own experiences. Newspapers contain advice columns in which people who claim no expertise offer advice to others. They contain comic strips and editorial strips in which imaginary characters are sometimes in conversation with historical characters.

We read and enjoy this variety of literary forms every day. We can tell one from another simply by bringing our experience to our reading. If an author were to say, "George Washington and John Kennedy had the following conversation," we would know that the conversation which followed was the composition of the author, not the transcription of an historical conversation. We draw this conclusion because we know that George Washington and John Kennedy were not contemporaries.

But what if a person from another country who knows absolutely nothing about American history reads this introduction? Because such a person would not have the knowledge which the author is presuming on the part of the audience, such a person might well misunderstand the kind of writing he or she is reading.

Since we do not live in the culture of the biblical authors we might make just such a mistake. We might misunderstand a clue to the biblical authors' intent because we don't bring sufficient knowledge to the subject.

This is what happened to the person who asked the question,

## LITERARY FORM

Answers the question:    ——"What kind of writing is this?"

When we say a work is one    ——External Characteristics
particular form wo are                Poetry?
describing such things as              Prose?
                                      Number of Lines?
                                      Rhyme scheme?
                ——Internal Characteristics
                                      Attitude?
                                      Tone?
                                      Purpose?

Some possible forms are    ——Riddle      Epic

| | |
|---|---|
| Riddle | Epic |
| Poem | Mock Epic |
| Fiction | Sonnet |
| Myth | Elegy |
| Legend | Epigram |
| Parable | Blessing |
| Biography | Curse |
| Autobiography | Fable |
| Parody | Fairy Tale |
| Editorial | Romance |
| History | Satire |
| Letter | Proverb |
| Revelation | Midrash |
| Allegory | Oracle |
| Debate | Novel |

*If we misunderstand the form we misunderstand the meaning!*

"Are you saying that the Bible is a myth?" Her lack of knowledge that the Bible is a library of books rather than a single book led her to draw a false conclusion.

Understanding that the Bible is a library of different kinds of writing will help us avoid making this mistake ourselves.

## Review Questions

1. Why is it that what is said about one story in the Bible cannot be said about the Bible as a whole?
2. What is the danger of never asking, "What kind of writing am I reading?"
3. Name some literary forms which appear in a newspaper. How does one form differ from another?
4. How do we distinguish one literary form from another?
5. What might happen if we don't bring sufficient experience or knowledge to our reading?

## Discussion Questions

1. What is the difference between a library with a number of books and a book with a number of chapters? What relevance does this question have to the Bible?
2. Do you think that you are able to distinguish different kinds of writing? Why or why not?
3. How would you respond to a person who says, "I don't need to know about literary forms to understand the Bible."
4. Name all the varieties of literary forms with which you are familiar. How do they differ, one from another?

# ARTICLE 4

## The Bible:
## An Edited Arrangement of Stories

**Question: "Why does the author say that there were no plants on earth and no one to till the ground? (Gen 2:5) We already read that God had created plants and people." (Gen 1:1–2:4; 2:19 also discussed)**

The person who asked this question has accurately observed that the second story in Genesis, the story of the man and woman in the garden, is not simply a continuation of the first story.

In the first story everything has been created and everything is good. Starting with Genesis 2:5 we are reading a different story on a different subject. If one thought this second story was a continuation of the story of the creation of the world in six days one would be puzzled by obvious inconsistencies, as is this questioner. "Why does the author say people aren't created yet when they are?" "Why does the author say that man was created before animals and birds?" (see Gen 2:19). "Weren't people created last, the summit of God's creation?"

The reason for such discrepancies is that the Bible is an edited arrangement of stories which once existed independently of each other. The stories had various functions in the communities in which they existed. Editors, at various times in the history of the Hebrew people, collected the traditional stories of their people and arranged them in a certain order for their contemporary audiences.

Although the stories once existed independently of each other and had different functions, in the Bible they are placed next to each other. The editors who combined them made no attempt to completely reconcile them because the inconsistencies are irrelevant to the purposes of the authors.

19

For instance, these two stories disagree on the order in which material forms were created. However, neither story is teaching anything about the order in which material forms were created. As we already noted, the author of the first story is not teaching how the world was created or in what order. Rather, the author is teaching *that* the world was created by God and is good.

The author of the second story talks about creation not as the subject of his story but as a way to "set the stage." We will explore the teaching in this second story in a subsequent article.

It is important to understand that you are reading an edited text, not only because this knowledge helps you understand the reason for apparent inconsistencies, but also because it helps you realize that the order of the stories in the Bible is not the order in which the stories were written.

Imagine that you were going to write a family history. You might collect a number of materials including diaries and letters written by members of your family who are no longer alive. As you edited the materials you would arrange them in the order you wanted them thematically, not in the order in which they were originally written. You might write a chapter of introduction to your work. So the book would begin with a writing much more recent than that which appears later when the letters are included.

Something similar occurred with the Bible. The stories which you will be reading were edited a number of times. We will have occasion to describe these various editings and the characteristics of each as you read. However, the first story, the creation in six days, dates not to the earliest editing but to a more recent one.

Scripture scholars believe that one of the editings took place some four hundred years before Jesus' birth. The Jewish people had just returned from a traumatic experience, exile in Babylon. As they returned to the holy land those responsible for passing on religious traditions, the priests, edited inherited materials and added to them. Among the additions was this first story of creation.

Placed in this historical setting we see even more clearly what the author is teaching through the story. The author is reaffirming the traditional beliefs of the Hebrew people, beliefs which were not held by the Babylonians.

## TIMELINE

| | |
|---|---|
| 1850 B.C. | Abraham experiences God's call |
| | Isaac |
| | Jacob |
| | Joseph |
| | Slavery in Egypt |
| 1250 B.C. | Moses and the exodus |
| | Period of the Judges |
| | Saul |
| 1000 B.C. | David |
| | Solomon |
| 922 B.C. | Kingdom divides |
| | Prophets call the people to fidelity |
| 721 B.C. | Northern kingdom falls to Assyrians |
| 630 B.C. | Josiah's reform |
| 587 B.C. | Southern kingdom falls Beginning of Babylonian exile |
| 537 B.C. | Cyrus, a Persian, conquers the Babylonians and lets the Israelites return to the holy land |
| 450 B.C. | Time of reinterpretations in the light of events |

Time of P
Editing
Tradition

The Babylonians believed in many gods. This story reaffirms the traditional belief in one God. The Babylonians believed that the sun and the moon were gods. This story pictures the sun and moon as material creations that do not rule human beings. The Babylonians believed that spirit was good but not matter. This story affirms and reaffirms the goodness of material creation. After each day God says that what has been created is good. The Babylonian creation story pictures human beings as created from the corpse of a rebellious and defeated god. In this story man and woman are created in the image of a loving God. Human beings are capable of love and are "very good."

So we see that one more benefit of understanding that the Bible is an edited arrangement of stories is that this knowledge helps us place each story in its appropriate historical context. By doing this we can better understand what truths the author is emphasizing for a particular historical audience.

## Review Questions

1. What evidence is there that the story of the man and woman in the garden is not simply a continuation of Genesis 1:1–2:4?
2. What is the explanation for inconsistencies in the stories?
3. Why did the editors not attempt to reconcile these inconsistencies?
4. Why is it important to know that you are reading an edited text?
5. What is the historical setting for Genesis 1:1–2:4?
6. Name four specific teachings that are understood once Genesis 1:1–2:4 is placed in its historical setting.

## Discussion Questions

1. Do the inconsistencies in the first two stories in Genesis bother you? Why or why not?
2. Have you ever lived in a culture that challenged the beliefs which were a part of your upbringing? Explain. What was your reaction? What relevance does this question have to Genesis 1:1–2:4?

3. Do you think any of the beliefs which the story teaches in reaction to Babylonian beliefs need to be reemphasized today? Which ones? Why?
4. What do you think it means to say that human beings are created in God's image?

# ARTICLE 5

# Suffering: The Ramification of Sin

**Question: "Why did God punish the whole human race for one person's sin? I think this is mean." (Gen 2:4–3:24)**

God did not "punish" the whole human race for one person's sin. The story about Adam and Eve in the garden is not a story about "punishment" but a story about suffering and its causes. Among the causes of suffering is sin.

The person who wrote this story of Adam and Eve was not an historian writing about an historical event. As was true with the story of the creation of the world in six days, the author is writing in a literary form which does not claim that the events pictured are historical events.

The author gives us clear signals that we should not mistake the story for history by the obvious symbols which he uses: a tree of knowledge of good and evil, a tree of life, and a talking serpent.

Although the story employs symbols it deals with reality, the reality of suffering. What kind of suffering? The suffering we all know from experience. The story deals with the suffering that results from not having what we need ("By the sweat of your face you shall eat bread . . ." [Gen 3:19]), from physical pain (". . . in pain you shall bring forth children" [Gen 3:16]), from unjust social structures ("Your desire shall be for your husband, and he shall rule over you" [Gen 3:16]), and from physical death (". . . at the east of the garden of Eden he placed the cherubim, and a sword flaming and turning to guard the way to the tree of life" [Gen 3:24]).

The author knows that suffering exists from his own experience and from observing the lives of those people around him. These observations have caused the author to ask, "Why is it that people

24

suffer? Is the fact of suffering compatible with a belief in a loving and all-powerful God?"

It is this question which lies behind the story of Adam and Eve. Through the story the author is teaching his belief that the root cause of suffering is sin.

The man ("Adam" is a collective noun: this story is about each of us) and his wife live in a world of no suffering, a world of right relationships. Each loves the other so much that the man and woman are as one.

There is no self-alienation (naked but not ashamed). God comes to walk in the evening. The man and woman know the spiritual "order" (a pun in English) because God has revealed it to them. "You may freely eat of every tree of the garden; but of the tree of the knowledge of good and evil you shall not eat, for in the day that you eat of it you shall die" (Gen 2:17).

Freely choosing to act contrary to the spiritual order, the man and the woman do eat, and they do die. They die spiritually. All of their relationships are disrupted. They are ashamed of themselves, they blame each other and they hide from God.

The author does not picture God as all-knowing nor as punishing in this story. God comes for his walk, not knowing that the "sin" has been committed. God discovers the man's sin by the man's inability to respond to God's unchanging love. "Where are you?" (Gen 2:9)

God not only makes clothes for the man and woman, but he tells them the consequences of acting contrary to the spiritual order. Their lives will now be full of suffering.

The suffering is not a punishment inflicted by God but a consequence of sin. To understand the difference between a consequence and a punishment we need only look at our experience. Hunger, weakness and even death are consequences of not eating rather than punishments for not eating.

Why, then, does the author picture God as saying, "I will multiply your pains . . ."? Because biblical authors attribute all consequences to God. They speak of ultimate rather than proximate causes.

The story of Adam and Eve is accurately referred to as a "myth" because it is a symbolic and imaginative story about a reality beyond comprehension. The function of the story is to orient us in a moral universe. The story is "true" because it teaches something true in regard to the question which it addresses: Why do human beings suffer? One reason is that human beings sin, and suffering is always the consequence of sin.

The story of Adam and Eve will be misunderstood if its literary form is misunderstood, if it is thought to be history or science rather than a myth.

The story will also be misunderstood if it is taken to teach more than it does. The story is not saying that all suffering is due to sin, just that sin does always result in suffering.

It is because of this insight about the consequence of sin, a true insight regarding the spiritual order, that the story is recognized as containing revelation. Through this story an inspired author is teaching a spiritual truth: sin always causes suffering. Each of us suffers from our own and others' sins.

## Review Questions

1. How do we know that the story of the man and woman in the garden is not written as history?
2. With what reality does the story deal?
3. With what kinds of suffering does the story deal?
4. What questions has the author asked after observing human suffering?
5. What is the author teaching through the story?
6. How do we know that the story is about each of us?
7. In what way do the man and woman die when they eat of the forbidden fruit?
8. What relationships are disrupted by sin?
9. How does God discover the man's sin?
10. In what literary form is the story of Adam and Eve written?
11. Why is the story recognized as containing revelation?

## Discussion Questions

1. Do you think the fact that people suffer is compatible with the idea that God is all powerful and all loving? Why or why not?

## INTERPRETING A MYTH

Through concrete symbols and a concrete plot the author speaks about what is beyond comprehension.

| | |
|---|---|
| Adam | Each person—all of us |
| Eve | The other person whom we need to love and by whom we need to be loved |
| Garden | A place of no suffering |
| God's instructions | Moral and spiritual order |
| Tree of knowledge of good and evil | The possibility of acting contrary to the spiritual order |
| Tree of life | Avoid physical death—one kind of suffering |
| Naked but unashamed | Self-acceptance |
| Serpent | Temptation |
| Eating | Sin |
| Naked but ashamed | Self-alienation |
| Hiding | Loss of capacity to respond to God's love |
| Punishments | Suffering, known from experience, which is seen as the natural consequence of disobeying the spiritual order |
| Expelled from garden and unable to return | Man is powerless to undo the effects of sin |

PLOT: No suffering—sin—suffering

THEME: Sin causes suffering

2. Do you believe that sin always causes suffering? Why or why not?
3. What is the difference between these two sentences? "Suffering is punishment for sin." "Suffering is the consequence of sin."
4. Do you think sin hampers one's ability to respond to God's love? Why or why not?
5. What is the difference between these two sentences: "Sin always causes suffering" and "All suffering is due to sin"?

# Cain and Abel:
# A New Emphasis to an Old Story

**Question: "Why didn't God look with favor on Cain and his offering?" (Gen 4:1–16)**

The author does not tell us why God did not look with favor on Cain's offering. However, the question invites us to surmise why God did not accept Cain's offering, and, in the course of this "surmising," we will learn more about the way stories have been appropriated, edited, and arranged for a purpose in the book of Genesis.

Scholars suggest that the story of Cain and Abel had an entirely different purpose before it was appropriated and used by an early editor of biblical materials who is referred to as "J."

The J editor is called J because J is the first letter of the word "Yahweh" in German, and the J editor refers to God as Yahweh throughout his narrative. Other sources use other words for God, at least during the time before Moses, since God did not reveal God's self as Yahweh until the time of Moses. So a reference to God as Yahweh in a story in which the setting predates Moses is evidence that the narrative is from the J tradition.

The Yahwist editor lived during the time of the united kingdom under David and Solomon (tenth century B.C.). He understood the kingdom in which he lived to be the fulfillment of God's promise to Abraham.

As a background to the call of Abraham (Gen 12) the Yahwist editor appropriated stories which already existed in his culture and arranged them to demonstrate the need for God's intervention on humankind's behalf. These stories, as a group, could be called "sin

**TIMELINE**

1850 B.C. — — Abraham experiences
God's call
Isaac
Jacob
Joseph

Slavery in Egypt

1250 B.C. — — Moses and the exodus

Period of the Judges
Saul

Time of J
Editing        1000 B.C. — — David
Tradition        Solomon

922 B.C. — — Kingdom divides

Prophets call the people to
fidelity

721 B.C. — — Northern kingdom falls to
Assyrians

630 B.C. — — Josiah's reform

587 B.C. — — Southern kingdom falls
Beginning of Babylonian exile

537 B.C. — — Cyrus, a Persian, conquers the
Babylonians and lets the
Israelites return to the holy
land

Time of P
Editing        450 B.C. — — Time of reinterpretations in
Tradition        the light of events

stories." They include the story of the man and woman in the garden which we have already discussed, this story of Cain and Abel, the story of Noah and the flood, and the story of the tower of Babel.

Perhaps the story of Cain and Abel was originally a story about the animosity which existed between nomadic people, shepherds like Abel, and settled people, farmers like Cain. A natural animosity would have existed between these groups because those who tilled the soil would need to lay claim to it, at least temporarily, and would not want flocks grazing on their crops. Nomadic people would resent such claims and their exclusion from the land.

If this animosity lies at the core of the original story, the story was told from the point of view of the nomads, since God is pictured as favoring Abel over Cain.

However, the contradictory claims of nomads and tillers of the soil is not the point of the story as it is appropriated and used by the Yahwist editor. Rather, the Yahwist editor uses the story to illustrate how the effects of sin snowball.

As we saw in the story of Adam and Eve, sin disrupts all of the man and woman's relationships. Where they had originally been close to God and each other, they later hide from God and blame each other.

This estrangement caused by sin becomes worse in the story of Cain and Abel. Sin is "lurking at the door" (Gen 4:7), and Cain succumbs to it. While Adam blamed Eve, Cain kills Abel. We know that his sin is premeditated because Cain first invites his brother to go out into the field where the murder takes place.

While Adam hid from God, Cain lies to God. When God asks Cain where his brother is, Cain says, "I do not know; am I my brother's keeper?" (Gen 4:9). God knows that Cain has killed Abel because Abel's blood is crying out to God from the ground (see Gen 4:10).

As Adam and Eve were alienated from an ordered world, having been expelled from the garden, so is Cain. God explains this ramification of sin to Cain as he says, "When you till the ground, it will no longer yield to you its strength; you will be a fugitive and a wanderer on the earth" (Gen 4:12).

However, God is not pictured as deserting Cain. Just as God

---

**YAHWIST EDITING TRADITION**

*Cumulative Chart*

Dates to time of monarchy (1000 B.C.).

Refers to God as Yahweh throughout narrative.

Called J rather than Y because German scholars identified source and German word for Yahweh is *Jahve.*

Pictures God anthropomorphically.

Emphasizes growth in sinfulness of human race but offers hope.

---

continued to show his love for Adam and Eve by making them clothes, so does God continue to care for Cain. "And the Lord put a mark on Cain, so that no one who came upon him would kill him" (Gen 4:15).

This involved, caring God is another characteristic of the Yahwist editor. In the J tradition God is pictured as intimately involved in events. This is in contrast to another editor's work, the E tradition, which we will discuss soon, in which God is more transcendent.

The Yahwist editor pictures God "anthropomorphically," as though God were like human beings. God walks and talks with his people, wanting to save them, even as people choose to sink deeper and deeper into sin.

It is in order to set the stage for the beginning of salvation history that the J editor appropriates existing stories, such as the story of Cain and Abel, and retells them as sin stories. Because human beings are immersed in sin they need to have God intervene and save them.

## Review Questions

1. What is the J editor called? Why?
2. When did the J editor live?
3. What might we call the stories which the J editor used as background to the call of Abraham? Why did he use them?
4. What might the story of Cain and Abel have been about originally?
5. What does J use the story to illustrate?
6. How does the estrangement caused by sin become worse in Cain and Abel?
7. What will be the ramifications of Cain's sin?
8. How does God continue to care for Cain?
9. What picture of God is characteristic of the J editor?

## Discussion Questions

1. What does it mean to say that an author "appropriates" a story and uses it for religious purposes?
2. Do you agree that sin disrupts relationships with others? Why or why not?
3. What does it mean to say that God is described anthropomorphically? Give examples from the stories of Adam and Eve, and Cain and Abel.

# ARTICLE 7

# Genealogies: A Variety of Purposes

**Question: "Why is Lamech's song of vengeance in the Bible? (Gen 4:23–24) He certainly isn't a good example." (Gen 1:28; 2:4; 4:17–22; 5:1–32; 6:1–5; 6:9; 10:1; 11:10; 11:27; 25:12; 25:19; 36:1; 37:2 also discussed)**

Lamech is not a good example. As Lamech tells his wives, "I have killed a man for wounding me, a young man for striking me" (Gen 4:23), we see that sin has taken hold in Cain's descendants. This vengeful song is added to a genealogy of Cain's descendants (see Gen 4:17–22), precisely because it emphasizes the growing effect of sin on the human race.

Genealogies play important roles in the book of Genesis. Contrary to expectation, the tracing of blood lines is not their primary purpose.

Most of the genealogies in Genesis are the work of the P editors, the editing which took place after the Babylonian exile. In fact, the genealogies are a major organizational device of the P editor. In order to connect blocks of materials from other sources the P editors fill in the blanks with genealogies which begin: "These are the generations of . . ." This connecting device will appear over and over in the book of Genesis (see Gen 2:4; 5:1; 6:9; 10:1; 11:10; 11:27; 25:12; 25:19; 36:1; and 37:2). The genealogy which starts at Genesis 5:1 helps to fill in the gap between Adam and Noah.

While most of the genealogies in Genesis are the work of the P editors, the genealogy to which Lamech's vengeful song is attached is the work of the J editor. By comparing the J genealogy in Genesis

---

**GENEALOGIES**

*Function:* Not so much to trace blood lines as to emphasize a theme.

| Gen. 2:4 | 11:27 |
|----------|-------|
| 5:1 | 25.12 |
| 6:9 | 25:19 |
| 10:1 | 36:1 |
| 11:10 | 37:2 |

---

**PRIESTLY EDITING TRADITION**

*Cumulative Chart*

Dates to time after Babylonian exile (587–537 B.C.).

Called P after priests who did editing.

Uses genealogies as a structural device.

Responsible for "creation in six days" story.

Emphasizes that human beings are made in God's image, creation is good, God's blessing is coming to realization.

Uses repetitive formulas.

---

4:17–22 with the P genealogy in Genesis 5:1–32 (genealogies which include many of the same names although in different orders), we can see how the editors use similar genealogies for different purposes. The genealogies are used to emphasize particular themes.

The J editor uses his genealogy to emphasize the growth in sinfulness of the human race. Notice that Cain is pictured as the father of civilization in that he built a city (see Gen 4:17). Among Cain's descendants are those who "have livestock" (Gen 4:20), those who are musicians (see Gen 4:21), and those who make bronze and iron tools (see Gen 4:22). However, as civilization grows, so does sin, as Lamech's song reveals.

The descendants of Cain are not the only descendants of Adam. Adam also bears Seth, a son on whom Cain's curse does not fall. To Seth's son, Enosh, is attributed the beginning of religious practices. "To Seth also a son was born, and he named him Enosh. At that time people began to invoke the name of the Lord" (Gen 4:26).

While the J editor uses his genealogy to emphasize the growth of sin, the P editors use a similar genealogy to emphasize the fact that human beings continue to be made in the image of God. The genealogy begins with an allusion to the P creation story in which male and female are created in God's image. "When God created humankind, he made them in the likeness of God. Male and female he created them, and he blessed them and named them 'Humankind' when they were created" (Gen 5:1–2). This genealogy then names Seth as Adam's son and follows the line on from there. Through the genealogy the P editor is emphasizing the realization of God's blessing and God's command to humankind at the time of creation. "God blessed them, and God said to them, 'Be fruitful and multiply, and fill the earth . . .'" (Gen 1:28).

As was evident in the creation story, the P editors use a fixed formula which is repeated with each generation. First they tell how old the person is when he becomes a father. Next they name the number of years the person lived after the birth of his son. They mention that the person had other children and then say what age the person was when he died. This emphasis on blessing as well as the use of a repetitive formula are characteristics of the P editors. We will notice these traits recurring often in the book of Genesis.

Immediately after the P genealogy, however, we return to the J editor with his emphasis on the growth of sin. All order is ignored as "sons of God" marry "daughters of humans" (see Gen 6:1–4). "The Lord saw that the wickedness of humankind was great in the earth, and that every inclination of the thoughts of their hearts was only evil continually" (Gen 6:5). It is because Lamech's vengeful heart is an example of the truth of this statement that Lamech's song is appended to the J genealogy.

## Review Questions

1. To which editing tradition do most of the genealogies belong?
2. How do the P editors use the genealogies?
3. What purpose is served by comparing the genealogies of the P and J editors?
4. For what purpose does the J editor use the genealogy?
5. Are the descendants of Cain the only descendants of Adam? Explain.
6. For what purpose do the P editors use the genealogy in Genesis 5:1-32?
7. Name two characteristics of the P editors.
8. Why is Lamech's song appended to the J genealogy?

## Discussion Questions

1. If you were going to write a story and needed to pick one action or event in our society to symbolize our tendency to act outside the spiritual order, what would you pick?
2. If you needed to pick one action or event to symbolize the fact that human beings are made in God's image what would you pick?
3. Do you think evil exists? Why or why not?

# ARTICLE 8

# The Meaning Behind Adam's Age

**Question: "Did Adam and the generations after him really live to be so old?" (Gen 5:5)**

There are two mistaken presumptions behind this question, both of which we have already discussed. However, the question shows that sometimes the ramifications of facts are not understood and have to be explained. The two false presumptions behind the question are first, that Adam is an historical person, and second that the purpose of a genealogy is to be historically accurate.

When one asks, "Was Adam really so old?" the "really" in the question reflects a desire to have a factual account. Adam was "really" a certain age only if "Adam" is an historical person. In the second creation story "Adam" is not a masculine singular noun, naming an historical person. Rather "Adam" is a collective noun, and refers to each of us. As already noted, the story of Adam teaches that the human race has caused suffering for itself (ourselves) by choosing sin over the spiritual order.

However, as Genesis continues we see that Adam appears in genealogies. In our culture a genealogy is meant to trace blood lines. To say that an ancestor lived a certain number of years is to give an historical fact about that person's longevity.

When we read scripture we bring the presumptions of our culture to our reading, sometimes overlooking the fact that another culture may have entirely different presumptions.

However, we have already discovered that the genealogies in Genesis 4 and 5 have purposes other than to trace blood lines. This is evident from the fact that a comparison of the two reveals that similar names are listed, but in different sequences. Adam and

38

Noah, the first and last names on the list, are constant, but other names appear with different spellings in different sequences.

Each editor has appropriated a tradition and used it for his own purposes. Through this use of genealogies the editors are teaching spiritual truths through images. So the presence of "Adam," even in a genealogy, is not a claim to historicity.

Why, then, do the P editors use a tradition that ascribes specific ages to those they name?

Scholars give several explanations for these ages. One is that ascribing great ages to those who lived before the flood is a custom of the time. The same phenomena is present in a list of pre-flood Sumerian kings. The kings are said to have lived anywhere from 18,600 years to 43,200 years! Such extreme exaggeration was a way of attributing greatness to those ancient peoples.

The ages which appear in the P editors' genealogy may be used for a similar purpose. In the context of the Bible, greatness would be goodness. Remember, it is the P editors who emphasize that God's image and blessing remain with God's people through the generations. Perhaps the P tradition is ascribing goodness to the primeval ancestors by attributing such long lives to them.

However, when interwoven with the work of the J editor, who emphasizes that sin has become part of the fiber of things even as towns, civilization and music have developed (see Gen 4:17–22), the long life spans of the primeval ancestors have a different effect. The reading audience, of course, has a much shorter life span than nine hundred years. One of the consequences of sin in the Adam story was lack of access to the tree of life. So the reader might understand his or her own much shorter life span as one more example of how sin has become more and more pervasive.

"Did Adam really live to be so old?" We see now that the question gets us off on entirely the wrong track. The question we need to ask is, "Why did the editor ascribe such long lives to the primeval ancestors?" When worded this way the question can be answered. The editors appropriated a custom of the time and reinterpreted it to teach a spiritual truth. Our various interpretations hold two truths in tension: Human beings are made in God's image and are blessed, but sin continues to pervade our lives and causes a great deal of suffering.

## Review Questions

1. What two false presumptions lie behind the question, "Did Adam really live to be so old?"
2. What evidence is there in the genealogies that their primary purpose is not to trace blood lines?
3. Why were great ages ascribed to Sumerian kings who were said to have lived before the flood?
4. How might a reader with a normal life span interpret the suggestion that those who were first deprived of the "tree of life" lived many years longer than does the reader's generation?
5. How does the question with which we began this article need to be reworded to get us on the right track?
6. What is the answer to the reworded question?

## Discussion Questions

1. Name some ramifications of the fact that the references to Adam are not claiming historicity.
2. Do you feel you will lose anything crucial to your beliefs if you agree that the biblical authors are not claiming historicity for Adam? Why or why not?
3. Do you feel that you have access to the "tree of life"? Why or why not?
4. An American expression is, "The good die young." Do you think the biblical editors would agree with this idea?

# ARTICLE 9

# Noah and the Flood

**Question: "Is Noah supposed to take two of each animal or seven?"**
**(Gen 6:19; 7:2) There seem to be contradictory instructions." (Gen**
**1:2; 1:28; 6:5–6; 6:8; 7:11; 7:12; 8:3; 8:11; 9:1 also discussed)**

This questioner has not yet let it sink in that she is reading not
one but two accounts of a story which have been braided together.
She notices the evidence for such a conclusion but is still puzzled
by it.

Once we realize we are reading two stories braided together we
are no longer bothered by such inconsistencies. This knowledge
frees us to ask the more important question, "What spiritual truth
is being taught through the story of Noah?"

To answer this question we will first take a careful look at the
story as it stands with the J and P stories interwound. We will then
compare this combined story to a similar Babylonian flood story.
By comparing the Israelite version with the Babylonian version we
will be able to see the particular emphasis which is present in the
biblical account.

The core of the story of Noah and the flood is similar in both the
J and P traditions. We can separate the J and P strands of the story
by noticing contradictions and by noticing the characteristic interests of each editor as we have come to know them.

As we have seen, the J editor emphasizes the pervasive effect of
sin at the same time that he offers hope. These elements are present
in the J portion of the Noah story. Sin has spread throughout the
whole earth. "The Lord saw that the wickedness of humankind was
great in the earth and that every inclination of the thoughts of their

41

hearts was only evil continually. And the Lord was sorry that he had made humankind on the earth, and it grieved him to his heart" (Gen 6:5–6).

The J editor always describes God anthropomorphically, that is, as though God were a human being. This anthropomorphic description is one more piece of evidence that this passage is the contribution of the J editor.

Even as the J editor tells us that God grieves over humankind's sinfulness, he pictures God as planning to save the race through Noah. "But Noah found favor in the sight of the Lord" (Gen 6:8).

The J version continues with God telling Noah to take seven pairs of clean animals and one of unclean animals onto the ark (see Gen 7:2). As our questioner has noted, this is in contradiction to the instructions in the P version of the story in which God says, "And of every living thing, of all flesh, you shall bring two of every kind into the ark . . ." (Gen 6:19).

The laws about clean and unclean animals were promulgated during the time of Moses, around 1250 B.C. To picture God as instructing Noah in regard to clean and unclean animals is to include a detail that would have made sense in the time of the J editor (ca. 1000 B.C.) but is historically out of sequence when included in a primeval flood story.

The P editors refrain from doing this. The P editors have, from the story of creation, emphasized that all that God created was good. No mention of clean and unclean will appear in the P account until the time of Moses.

The P editors also refer back to the story of creation when they describe how the water from the flood appeared. ". . . on that day all the fountains of the great deep burst forth, and the windows of the heavens were opened" (Gen 7:11). In other words, the water above the dome and the water beneath the dome, which God had separated on the second day, no longer remained separated. The world returned to the unordered state in which it had been before God's creative work. The J editor, on the other hand, attributes the flood to rain (see Gen 7:12).

The extent of the flood is much worse in the P account. J has the rain last forty days and forty nights. P, on the other hand, says that the water does not recede for one hundred fifty days (see Gen 8:3).

## NOAH TRADITIONS

| J | P |
|---|---|
| ■ Emphasis on pervasive spread of sin and on hope<br>■ God described anthropomorphically<br>■ Instructions involve clean and unclean animals<br>■ Flood due to rain, lasts 40 days and 40 nights | ■ Refers back to creation story<br>■ "Be fruitful, multiply and fill the earth"<br>■ No mention of unclean animals (Creation good)<br>■ Flood due to waters above and beneath dome breaking forth. Doesn't recede for 150 days |

| Gilgamesh | J and P Combined Story |
|---|---|
| ■ There are many gods<br>■ People destroyed for no apparent reason<br>■ People given immortality | ■ There is one God<br>■ Sin is the reason that the destruction takes place<br>■ People in convenant relationship with God |

P once more refers to the creation story as he pictures a wind blowing over the earth as it did at the first creation (see Gen 8:1 and 1:2). After the waters have receded God blesses Noah with the identical blessing which he gave humankind at creation. "Be fruitful and multiply and fill the earth" (see Gen 9:1 and 1:28).

The particular emphasis of each editor, then, is the emphasis we have already noted. The J editor emphasizes sin's snowballing and increasingly detrimental effect even as he introduces a message of hope. The P editors emphasize that the blessing of God on his people, who are made in God's image, is not lost despite all that happens.

The J and P flood stories have a great deal in common even as they have these minor differences. As a unit they differ in several important aspects from a similar Mesopotamian flood story included in a longer narrative called *Gilgamesh.*

It seems that once more the biblical authors appropriated and revised a story from the surrounding culture, retelling it so that it embodies a spiritual message. First, the flood story in *Gilgamesh* presumes that there are many gods. In the biblical story there is only one God. In the flood story in *Gilgamesh* the gods decide to destroy humankind for no apparent reason. In the biblical story sin is the reason for the destruction. The flood story in *Gilgamesh* ends with the ancestor, Utnapishtim, and his family being given immortality. Noah and his family are not given immortality but they are pictured by the P editors as entering into a covenant relationship with God. We will learn a great deal more about covenant relationships as we continue to read Genesis.

For now, let us say that the biblical authors are, through the story of Noah and the flood, still setting the stage for salvation history. The story of Noah is one more sin story which illustrates humankind's need to be saved.

## Review Questions

1. Why are there contradictions in the story of Noah?
2. What question is more crucial than the question about these inconsistencies?
3. What characteristic interests of the J tradition appear in the Noah story?
4. What is a major emphasis of the P editors?
5. Name several details which differ in the J and P traditions.
6. Name three ways in which the combined J and P story of Noah differs from the Babylonian flood story in *Gilgamesh.*
7. In its context in Genesis, what is the story of Noah illustrating?

## Discussion Questions

1. Why do you think that a story about a flood would lend itself to be used as a story about sin? In what symbolic ways might the

"water" be used? Do we use water as a symbol in a ritual that has to do with sin? Explain.
2. The church is sometimes compared to Noah's ark. Why?
3. Would you invest your life savings in a group who wanted to search for the original ark? Why or why not?

# ARTICLE 10

# The Tower of Babel: An Etiology

**Question: "Why would God want to confuse peoples' language? I thought God wanted us to know and love each other." (Gen 11:1–9; Gen 1:28; 4:17, 21, 22; 6:4; 9:13; 9:20–23; 12:2 also discussed)**

At the root of this question is a misunderstanding of the kind of writing which one is reading when one reads the story of the tower of Babel. To explain the meaning of this story we need to understand a kind of writing called an "etiology."

An etiology is a story which is told to explain the origin of something which is well known to the listeners. The Bible contains etiologies that purport to tell the origins of the names of people and places, as well as the origins of institutions, ceremonies, nations and natural phenomena.

We have already read several etiologies in Genesis for the origins of cities (see Gen 4:17), of music (see Gen 4:21), of those who make bronze and iron instruments (see Gen 4:22), of a race of giant heroes called the Nephilim (see Gen 6:4) and of the rainbow (see Gen 9:13).

The Genesis editors appropriated etiologies, just as they appropriated other kinds of writing which were present in the contemporary culture, and used them to teach spiritual truths.

Just before the story of the tower of Babel we read an appropriated etiology, the story of Noah getting drunk and falling asleep naked in his tent. This story originally explained the origin of vineyards. Noah is pictured as the first to discover the inebriating effect of wine. "Noah, a man of the soil, was the first to plant a vineyard. He drank some of the wine and became drunk, and he lay uncovered in his tent" (Gen 9:20–21).

This story continues as an etiology that purports to explain why

46

one people, the Canaanites (descendants of Ham who failed to show his father proper respect; see Gen 9:22), became slaves to the Israelites (descendants of Shem who did show his father proper respect; see Gen 9:23). The story is not really so much about individuals as it is an etiology about peoples.

The story of the tower of Babel is another instance in which an etiology has been appropriated and used to teach another lesson entirely. As an etiology, the story accounts for the fact, known from experience, that people of different nations speak different languages. Etiologies are imaginative stories, not historical stories. So the answer to the question, "Why would God want to confuse peoples' language?" is that God didn't. The questioner has mistaken the literary form of the story and the purpose of an etiology.

We can see that it is the J editor who has appropriated this etiology. The J editor's characteristic anthropomorphic description of God is clearly present. God is pictured with human characteristics as he "comes down" to see the tower. "The Lord came down to see the city and the tower, which mortals had built. And the Lord said, 'Look, they are one people, and they have all one language, and this is only the beginning of what they will do; . . . come, let us go down, and confuse their language there, so that they will not understand one another's speech' " (Gen 11:5–7).

The J editor is using the etiology as one more sin story with which to set the stage for salvation history which will begin with the call of Abraham in Genesis 12. But why does the etiology lend itself for use as a "sin story"? What is the sin?

In its present position in the braided arrangement of the J and P traditions the sin seems to be the desire on humankind's part to stay in one place and to make a name for themselves. Humankind is pictured as not wanting to be scattered. "Come, let us build ourselves a city, and a tower with its top in the heavens, and let us make a name for ourselves; otherwise we shall be scattered abroad upon the face of the whole earth" (Gen 11:4).

To refuse to be scattered is to refuse to respond to God's command, since God told male and female, "Be fruitful and multiply and fill the earth" (Gen 1:28). To desire to make one's own name great is to refuse to recognize one's proper place in relation to God. After all, God will soon tell Abraham, "I will make your name great" (Gen 12:2).

**SINS' EFFECTS GROW**

Human beings' relationships are destroyed

| Relationship | Adam and Eve | Cain and Abel | Story of Noah | Tower of Babel |
|---|---|---|---|---|
| With self | Adam is ashamed | Cain must master sin—like a crouching beast hungering for him | Man's thoughts fashion wickedness | |
| With God | Adam hides from God | Cain leaves the presence of Yahweh | Yahweh regrets making man | Man powerless to reach God |
| With others | Adam blames Eve | Cain murders Abel | Man makes violence | Men cannot even speak to each other |
| With environment | Adam is expelled from the garden and must work by the sweat of his brow | Cain wanders as a stranger on the earth | The earth is corrupt | |

*Therefore, human beings need to be redeemed!*        "Yahweh said to Abraham . . ."

It is typical of the J editor to appropriate a narrative to account for the scattering of peoples over the face of the earth. The P editors accomplish the same purpose in their own typical way, with the list of nations which is found in Genesis 10.

So as we conclude the first eleven chapters of the book of Genesis we see clearly that the human race needs to be saved. The relationships which we saw disrupted in the story of Adam and Eve have become more and more strained until they are completely severed. Humankind cannot mend the broken relationship with God. In fact, peoples cannot even talk with each other. Human beings' only hope lies in God's lovingly taking the initiative to save God's people and to make it possible for us to once again love God and each other.

## Review Questions

1. What is an etiology?
2. What etiological interest is behind the story of Noah getting drunk?
3. What etiological interest is behind the story of Ham and Shem who found Noah naked in the tent?
4. What was the etiological interest behind the story of the tower of Babel?
5. What evidence is there that the story of the tower of Babel is from the J tradition?
6. What is the sin in the story of the tower of Babel?
7. How does the J editor account for the scattering of people over the earth? How do the P editors accomplish the same thing?
8. As chapter 11 concludes, what is the situation of humankind?

## Discussion Questions

1. Do you know any modern day etiologies? If so, what are they?
2. Why does the fact that people speak different languages lend itself to a sin story?
3. From a spiritual point of view what is wrong with the idea, "I will make a name for myself?"
4. Do you regard hostilities among nations as evidence of sin? Why or why not?

# ARTICLE 11

# Legends

**Question: "Why did God tell Abram that he would curse anyone who curses Abram? (Gen 12:3) This doesn't sound very loving of God."**

Once more a question forces us to ask, "What kind of writing are we reading when we read stories in the Bible?" Is the story about the call of Abraham the same kind of writing as were the stories of creation and of Adam and Eve? We named the kind of writing in those stories "myth." Are we still reading myth?

The answer to that question is "no." As we begin to read the stories of Abraham and the other patriarchs we are reading a different kind of writing than we have been reading thus far.

The story of the call of Abraham can accurately be called a legend. A legend differs from a myth in that a legend has, at its core, an historical person or event. Therefore, a legend can be defined as a symbolic and imaginative story with an historical base.

Legends and myths are both, then, imaginative stories that use symbols. But the functions of the stories differ. As we noted, the function of a myth is to orient people in a moral universe. The function of a legend is to pass on the traditions of a people in such a way that those traditions become meaningful for the audience. At the core of the legend are historical people and events.

"How can you tell the difference?" students often ask. How can you tell from reading the story that the accounts involving Abraham are more firmly based in history than is the story of Adam and Eve?

In the story of Adam and Eve, Adam is presented as the very first

> **MYTH:** An imaginative and symbolic story about a reality which is beyond comprehension
>
> **LEGEND:** An imaginative and symbolic story with an historical core

human being. We know nothing of an historical nature about the first human being because that person's life does not fall within the bounds of history. History by definition deals with those events which were witnessed and about which we have oral or written tradition. Any story about a first human being would be about a prehistoric event rather than an event which falls within the bounds of history. So no story about a first human being could accurately be called a legend.

On the other hand, the world of Abraham is a world that falls within the bounds of history. The Genesis accounts of the "nationality" of the patriarchs, the part of the world in which they lived, their movement to Canaan, their occupations, and their ways of relating to each other socially all have their roots in history. As we read about the patriarchs we are reading accounts which give us an accurate picture of the second millennium B.C.

Although the legends about the patriarchs have their roots in history we should not read them in the same frame of mind with which we would read the work of a modern historian. The legends in Genesis are folk history; that is, they are history which is based on oral tradition. In addition, the legends in Genesis have been appropriated and retold to emphasize religious teachings.

We will be exploring the ramifications of these two facts as we continue to read Genesis. But to answer the question, "Why did God say he would curse other nations," we must know a little about the ramifications of the fact that these legends are based on oral tradition.

Any literature which is based on oral tradition does not claim to have exact quotations. Hebrew, the language in which the Old Testament legends were originally written, did not have quotation marks. So when you see something in quotation marks in an English Bible, these are a way of attributing a composed speech to a character in the story, not a claim that you are reading an exact quotation.

With this fact in mind we see that the answer to the question, "Why did God say he would curse other nations?" is, "God didn't say that." The real question is, "Why does the legend picture God as saying this?"

The legend pictures God as expressing himself as human beings did at the time the storyteller lived. Blessings and curses were common among primitive peoples. That God is pictured as expressing himself in this way is one more example of the anthropomorphic way of describing God which we have seen is characteristic of the J editor.

More important than the mode of expression is the belief expressed. In this passage the author pictures God calling Abraham, promising Abraham land and descendants, and blessing Abraham. Out of all the scattered nations God has picked one person whom God will make a nation unlike any other nation, a nation that will be a blessing to all other nations. As God tells Abraham, in him "all the families of the earth shall be blessed" (Gen 12:3).

The fact that legends do not claim to have exact quotations is not the only fact about legends which we need to know. We will learn more about what to expect from legends as we continue to read Genesis.

## Review Questions

1. What kind of writing is the story of the call of Abraham?
2. Define this kind of writing.
3. How does a legend compare to a myth?
4. What is the object of historical study?
5. Do all events fall within the bounds of history? Explain.
6. What kind of history are the legends in Genesis?
7. What do quotation marks signify in literature which is based on oral tradition?
8. How might we reword the question with which this article began to make the question more pertinent?

9. Why does the author picture God as using a curse?
10. What important belief is expressed in God's words to Abraham in Genesis 12:3?

**Discussion Questions**

1. Do you know a legend about George Washington? What is it? What is the function of this legend?
2. Do you speak more than one language? Are there some things you can say in one language and not in another? Do you believe it is true that every translation is to some degree an interpretation? What does this question have to do with this article?
3. Have you ever felt particularly chosen or blessed? Explain.

# ARTICLE 12

## Legends and the Elohist Tradition

**Question: "Why didn't Abram (Abraham) trust God to take care of him in Egypt? Didn't he lack faith when he told Sarai (Sarah) to say she was his sister?" (Gen 12:10–20; Gen 20:1–18; 26:1–14 also discussed)**

The person who asked this question, one which reveals a moral sensitivity on the part of the questioner, shares this sensitivity with one of the editors whose work appears in the book of Genesis, one whom we have not yet discussed.

As we read various legends of the patriarchs we will read not only the work of the J and P editors whom we have already met, but the work of the E, or Elohist editor.

Most of the materials which we read in the stories of Abraham and Sarah are from the Yahwist source, as is this first story of Abraham and Sarah in Egypt. However, occasionally we will read a second account of a story, a "doublet." When we read a doublet we are most likely reading the work of the Elohist editor.

As it happens we do read a second account of the story of Abraham asking Sarah to say she is his sister in Genesis 20:1–18. By comparing the two accounts we can learn more about the Elohist editor and more about the literary form "legend."

When reading the Yahwist version of this legend (Gen 12:10–20) students are often shocked not only at the behavior of Abraham but at the behavior of God. It does seem that Abraham, who had enough faith to leave his homeland and head for the promised land, and who had received God's promise of protection, fails miserably when he asks Sarah to say she is his sister in order to insure his own

54

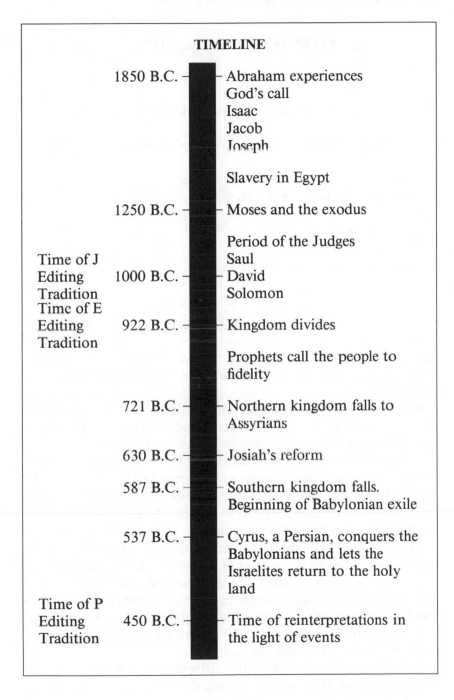

**TIMELINE**

| | | |
|---|---|---|
| | 1850 B.C. — | Abraham experiences God's call |
| | | Isaac |
| | | Jacob |
| | | Joseph |
| | | Slavery in Egypt |
| | 1250 B.C. — | Moses and the exodus |
| | | Period of the Judges |
| Time of J | | Saul |
| Editing | 1000 B.C. — | David |
| Tradition | | Solomon |
| Time of E | | |
| Editing | 922 B.C. — | Kingdom divides |
| Tradition | | |
| | | Prophets call the people to fidelity |
| | 721 B.C. — | Northern kingdom falls to Assyrians |
| | 630 B.C. — | Josiah's reform |
| | 587 B.C. — | Southern kingdom falls. Beginning of Babylonian exile |
| | 537 B.C. — | Cyrus, a Persian, conquers the Babylonians and lets the Israelites return to the holy land |
| Time of P | | |
| Editing | 450 B.C. — | Time of reinterpretations in |
| Tradition | | the light of events |

---

**ELOHIST EDITING TRADITION**

*Cumulative Chart*

Developed in North after division of kingdom (922 B.C.).

Calls God "Elohim" until time of Sinai revelation so referred to as E.

Appears most often in doublets.

Exhibits moral sensitivity.

God's presence is mediated by angels, dreams, etc.

Deemphasizes kings in favor of prophets.

---

safety. But even more distressing is God's behavior. Why would God inflict plagues on Pharaoh and his house when Pharaoh is innocent?

When we read the second account of this legend by the Elohist editor we can see that he must have had much the same moral sensibility that we bring to the story (Gen 20:1–18).

In the Elohist account, Abimelech asks God the very question we asked: "Lord, will you destroy an innocent people?" (Gen 20:4) While Abraham's behavior cannot be put in an entirely positive light he is somewhat exonerated in that Sarah is said to have been his half-sister. So Abraham's actions were not totally dishonest.

Moral sensitivity is not the only characteristic of the Elohist editor which appears in this legend of Abraham and Sarah. The Elohist editor is called "Elohist" because he uses the Hebrew word *Elohim* to refer to God up until the time of Moses (1250 B.C.). As you know, the Yahwist editor refers to God as Yahweh before and after Moses. In this translation (NRSV) we see that Elohim is translated as "God," "Yahweh" as "Lord."

In addition, the Elohist editor distinguishes himself from the Yahwist in his less anthropomorphic descriptions of God. In the

Elohist material God's presence is usually mediated. In this passage, you notice, God does not appear directly, but in a dream.

Scholars believe the Elohist tradition is a northern tradition which developed after the division of the kingdom (922 B.C.). Since the north broke away from Jerusalem and its king, the northern tradition emphasized the role of the king much less, preferring instead the role of the prophets. Notice Abraham is called a prophet in this account (see Gen 20:7).

In addition to learning about the Elohist tradition we can learn more about legends by comparing the two accounts. Notice that the setting for the two legends is different. While Abraham and Sarah are present in both, they are in Egypt and dealing with the Pharaoh in one account, in Gerar and dealing with Abimelech in the other. To complicate matters, we can read the same legend in still a different social setting in Genesis 26:1–14. In this account the patriarch is not Abraham but Isaac, the wife not Sarah but Rebekah. However, the location is once again Gerar and King Abimelech.

Thus we see that another characteristic of literature which comes through oral tradition (as do legends) in addition to the lack of exact quotations which we have already noted is that there is no claim to accuracy in exact social settings. Stories are told to teach something important to the contemporary audience, not to pass on exact historical settings.

This might be easier to understand if you think of stories about your own family which are passed on through oral tradition at family gatherings. These stories are important because they reveal something about your family unit and hold up values to succeeding generations. It is not so important whether a particular event happened to your great-grandmother or your great-great-grandmother, or whether that ancestor lived in one town or another at the time of the event.

Scholars believe the earliest version of this story is the one attached to Isaac and Rebekah. However, the story became attached to Abraham because it illustrates God's fidelity to his promise to Abraham, that God would protect him and bless other nations who bless Abraham.

This legend of Abraham does picture Abraham as failing in his faith in God. However, it pictures God as being faithful to his promise to Abraham. It is in order to teach this most important spiritual lesson that the legend was told to each generation, including our own.

## Review Questions

1. From what source are most of the materials about Abraham and Sarah which we read in Genesis?
2. What will be one sign that we are reading the work of the Elohist editor?
3. Name three characteristics of the Elohist tradition.
4. To what location and date do scholars attribute the Elohist tradition?
5. What is a second characteristic of legends in addition to no claim to exact quotations?
6. Why did this legend get attached to Abraham?

## Discussion Questions

1. Do you have some family legends? What are they? Do these legends have exact quotations? Exact social settings? Does it matter that they do not? Why do we tell family stories?
2. Do you tell jokes? Is your main source for jokes oral or written tradition? If oral, what can you say about literature which comes through oral tradition, based on your knowledge of jokes?
3. If you had a deeply religious experience of God's presence and wanted to write about it, would you describe God anthropomorphically or would you describe God's presence as mediated by dreams, visions, clouds, etc. Why? What does this question have to do with Genesis?

# ARTICLE 13

# God's Covenant with Abraham

**Question: "Why did God tell Abraham to cut all those poor animals in half?" (Gen 15:9; Gen 15:1–18; 17:11; 17:19; 21:22–34 also discussed)**

The Genesis editor pictures God as telling Abraham to cut animals in half because the editor is teaching his audience that God entered into a covenant relationship with Abraham.

In order to explain this answer we will first review why we have reworded the question. Then we will explain the concept "covenant" and the particular covenant celebration which involves cutting animals in half.

To ask, "Why did God tell Abraham . . ." is to assume that an historical conversation is being reported. To reword the question, "Why does the Genesis editor picture God as telling Abraham . . ." is to acknowledge the kind of writing we are reading. We are reading a legend, an imaginative story with an historical base. The conversation is the composition of the storyteller. Through the story the beliefs of the people are handed on orally from one generation to another.

As we read Genesis we are reading an arrangement of various traditions. Since we already know this we do not have to be concerned with inconsistencies in the story. We know that inconsistencies, such as the fact that night (Gen 15:5) seems to precede the sunset (Gen 15:12), are the result of the braiding of various traditions and are irrelevant to the editors' purposes.

The purpose in this passage is to describe the kind of relationship which existed between Abraham and God. This relationship is described as a "covenant."

## ONE STEP IN THE INTERPRETATION
## OF THE IMAGE "COVENANT"

| Experience | Mutual Responsibilities | | (Abstract beliefs become embodied and take on material, concrete expression in rituals, institutions, people, etc.) |
|---|---|---|---|
| | *God* | *The People* | *Signs* |
| Abraham experiences God's call | Will give protection, land, and descendants | Will have faith and obey | Rite of cut animals Circumcision Isaac |

A covenant is an unbreakable agreement entered into by two parties in which each has obligations to the other. A covenant is celebrated by a ritual and is expressed through concrete signs.

Covenant making was a normal part of Abraham's culture. As we read on in Genesis we will see Abraham make a covenant with Abimelech over a well (see Gen 21:22–34).

In Abraham's covenant with God each assumes obligations toward the other. God promises Abraham that God will protect Abraham as God says, "Do not be afraid, Abram, I am your shield" (Gen 15:1). In addition God promises Abraham descendants: "... 'no one but your very own issue shall be your heir.' He brought him outside and said, 'Look toward heaven and count the stars, if you are able to count them.' Then he said to him, 'So shall your descendants be' " (Gen 15:4–5).

Finally God promises Abraham that his descendants will have land. "To your descendants I give this land, from the river of Egypt to the great river, the river Euphrates" (Gen 15:18).

Abraham's obligation to God is that Abraham will have faith and obey. "And he (Abraham) believed the Lord, and the Lord reckoned it to him as righteousness" (Gen 15:6).

The covenant is celebrated through a ritual involving cut animals. This covenant ritual was not unique to this one occasion but was a customary way to celebrate covenant agreements in Abraham's world.

Animals would be cut in half and laid out so that the two parties agreeing to the covenant could pass between the halves. This ritual action symbolized the fact that the contracting parties would rather be cut in half themselves than break the covenant.

Notice that the Genesis legend pictures God as binding God's self to the covenant. "When the sun had gone down and it was dark, a smoking fire pot and a flaming torch passed between these pieces" (Gen 15:17). The fire passing between the halves symbolizes God's passing between the halves. We will see fire used as a symbol for God's presence again when we read the book of Exodus.

As we continue to read Genesis we will see the concrete signs of the covenant described by the P editor. One concrete sign is pictured as being circumcision. "Every male among you shall be circumcised. You shall circumcise the flesh of your foreskins, and it shall be a sign of the covenant between me and you" (Gen 17:11). Scripture scholars doubt that circumcision had such a clearly defined religious significance at the time of Abraham, but it certainly came to be a sign of the covenant.

Another sign of the covenant is Isaac, the child of the promise. ". . . your wife Sarah shall bear you a son, and you shall name him Isaac. I will establish my covenant with him as an everlasting covenant for his offspring after him" (Gen 17:19). As a sign of their new identities in covenant relationship, Abram's name is changed to Abraham, Sarai's to Sarah.

The idea of covenant is central to the Israelites' understanding of their special relationship with God. As we continue to read Genesis and Exodus we will see a growth in understanding of the concept of covenant as well as a variety of covenant celebrations. But the image "covenant" will remain firm through the entire 2000 years of salvation history and will continue right up to the present day.


**Review Questions**

1. Why did we reword the question with which this article began?
2. What is a covenant?
3. What three things does God promise Abraham?

4. What is Abraham's obligation to God?
5. What is the meaning of the ceremony involving cut animals?
6. How is God's binding God's self to the covenant symbolized?
7. Name two signs of the covenant.

## Discussion Questions

1. Are you aware of any relationships in our society which we refer to as covenant relationships? What are they? Why are they called covenant relationships?
2. In what ways are a mass and a wedding covenant celebrations?
3. Are you in a covenant relationship with God? What has God promised you? What is your response supposed to be? How is this covenant ritualized?

# ARTICLE 14

# Cultural Values and Human Faults

**Question: "Didn't people of Abraham's time have any respect for marriage? Why would Sarah let her maid sleep with Abraham?" (Gen 16:1–2; Gen 21:10; 21:12–13; 19:8 also discussed)**

One of the mistakes we often make when reading the Bible is to forget that we live in a culture very different from any of the cultures we encounter in the Bible. We tend to take our own values, priorities and customs, which have developed over thousands of years, and act as though these should be the values, priorities and customs of cultures which existed thousands of years ago. We must not assume that our point of view was shared by the Hebrews of 1850 B.C.

The patriarchal culture did respect marriage. However, the right to bear children had an extremely high priority. If a woman could not bear children it was customary for her to give her maid to her husband for the purpose of bearing children. The children from this union would belong to the husband and wife, not to the maid.

Perhaps the right to bear children had such a high priority because the Hebrews did not have our idea of life after death. Our idea that death is not really death, that life continues after life on earth, did not develop among the Israelites until about two hundred years before the birth of Jesus. So a great deal of the Hebrews' sense of purpose in life was tied in with childbearing.

To a modern reader the idea that a woman slave could be forced to bear another couple's child is just as shocking as the thought that the exclusivity of the marriage relationship could be violated. The woman slave was simply property. She could be told to sleep with

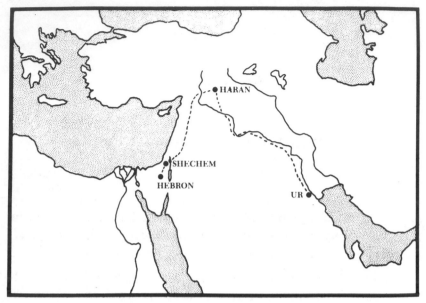

**The Journey of Abraham from Ur to Canaan**

her mistress' husband, and the child which she would bear would not be considered her own.

As it happens, Sarah becomes so jealous of Hagar after the birth of Isaac that she wants both Hagar and Ishmael sent away. Sarah says, "Cast out the slave woman with her son; for the son of this slave woman shall not inherit along with my son Isaac" (Gen 21:10).

Again the modern reader is shocked to see that God seems to support Sarah in her jealousy rather than Hagar in her distress, for God tells Abraham to do as Sarah wants. "But God said to Abraham, 'Do not be distressed because of the boy and because of your slave woman; whatever Sarah says to you, do as she tells you, for it is through Isaac that offspring shall be named for you. As for the son of the slave woman, I will make a nation of him also, because he is your offspring' " (Gen 21:12–13).

We see here another example of a story told to emphasize God's fidelity to his promises. God's promise to Abraham is through the child of the promise, through Isaac. Instead of trusting God to be faithful to his promise Sarah decided to take things into her own hands. She took the initiative to try to provide Abraham with a child. God's promises are not fulfilled through Sarah's initiatives, but through God's. So God assures Abraham not only that God's promise will be accomplished through Isaac, but that God will also take care of Hagar and Ishmael. Abraham should trust God and not be too distressed by Sarah's demands. As we read on we see that God does take care of Hagar and Ishmael.

We will also see, however, that an even more shocking episode involving the treatment of women will appear in Genesis 19. Here we read that the townspeople of Sodom ask Lot to send his male guests out "so that we may know them" (Gen 19:5). Rather than let his guests be sexually molested, Lot offers to send his daughters out instead. "Look, I have two daughters who have not known a man; let me bring them out to you, and do to them as you please; only do nothing to these men, for they have come under the shelter of my roof" (Gen 19:8). Lot is pictured as being so concerned with hospitality, with protecting his male guests, that he is willing to abandon his daughters to the crowd. In Lot's eyes he has a higher duty to his male guests than he does to his female offspring.

Neither Abraham, Sarah nor Lot consistently act in ways which we can admire. Some of their behavior seems reprehensible to us simply because our culture has a different value system than did theirs. Also, some of this behavior would have been considered equally wrong by those in their own culture. Old Testament people had their faults.

The Genesis editors do not hesitate to reveal the faults of their ancestors in the faith as they pass on their traditional stories. In fact, the weaknesses of these human beings make it all the more clear that it is God who saves.

## Review Questions

1. Why might the right to bear children have had such a high priority in the Hebrew culture?
2. Through whose initiative is God's promise to Abraham fulfilled?
3. What is shocking to us about the treatment of women in the 2nd

millennium B.C.? What rights or duties have a higher priority in
their culture than do the rights of women?
4. Why do the biblical editors not hide the faults of their ancestors
   in faith?


## Discussion Questions

1. Who do you think takes the initiative in spiritual relationships,
   God or us? Explain.
2. Do you think that there are "values and priorities" in our culture that might surprise or shock someone from another culture? If so, what are they and why?
3. What does this expression mean: "Let go and let God"? What
   does this question have to do with this article?

# ARTICLE 15

# Images of God's Presence

**Question: "Who appears to Abraham at Mamre and later to Lot? I can't figure out if it is God, men or angels." (Gen 18:1–19:1)**

The story of Abraham at Mamre is about Abraham's encounter with God, as we learn from Genesis 18:1. "The Lord appeared to Abraham" (Gen 18:1). However, God's presence is variously represented as the presence of the Lord, the presence of three men (Gen 18:2; 18:16), the presence of angels (19:1), and the presence of "two men and the Lord" (Gen 18:22).

Why does the Genesis editor (thought to be J) tell the story in this way? Scholars offer a variety of explanations. One explanation is familiar to us. We have already noted that inconsistencies in the narrative point to a variety of sources. Perhaps the J editor was dealing with several versions of the story, versions which were not consistent in the way in which they imaged God's presence. Perhaps early versions of the story reflected polytheism (a belief in many gods) rather than monotheism (a belief in one God), and the J editor saw no need to camouflage this fact. Certainly other cultures had similar stories in which heavenly visitors, disguised as humans, received hospitality from human beings who were later blessed for their goodness.

For the person who asked the question the various descriptions of God's presence were distracting. What effect might J have hoped these descriptions would have? One possibility is that the descriptions represent God's mysterious presence among his people. The God of Abraham is not only a transcendent God, but a God who dwells among the people.

The fact that the three men/angels represent God's presence

67

would have been clear to the audience. Abraham's behavior toward the guests would be one piece of evidence. While hospitality was certainly an enormously important virtue in Abraham's culture, Abraham's reaction to the visitors reflects his knowledge that he is in the presence of the divine. "When he (Abraham) saw them, he ran from the tent entrance to meet them, and bowed down to the ground" (Gen 18:2). Abraham then bustles around overseeing the preparation of a veritable feast.

The question which the guests ask next would probably have shocked and then amused the audiences who heard this story. We have already seen that Lot offered his daughters in hospitality. It would not have been unheard of for a wife to also be offered in hospitality. So when the guests, after accepting such exaggerated hospitality, ask, "Where is your wife Sarah?" the audience might well have thought, just for a moment, that perhaps this is not God's presence after all!

As the story continues the audience is reassured in their original understanding by the behavior of the guests themselves. One guest announces the fulfillment of God's promise to Abraham. "I will surely return to you in due season, and your wife Sarah will have a son" (Gen 18:9).

Once again the J editor refers to the guest as Lord, as he pictures him knowing what Sarah thinks and reaffirming the promise. "The Lord said to Abraham, 'Why did Sarah laugh, and say, "Shall I indeed bear a child now that I am old?" Is anything too wonderful for the Lord? At the set time I will return to you, in due season, and Sarah shall have a son' " (Gen 18:14).

Not only is the "Lord" able to know what others are thinking, but the Lord chooses to let Abraham know what he is thinking. "The Lord said, 'Shall I hide from Abraham what I am about to do, seeing that Abraham shall become a great and mighty nation, and all the nations of the earth shall be blessed in him?' " (Gen 18:17–18). The J editor then pictures an anthropomorphic God telling Abraham that God must go down and see if Sodom and Gomorrah are as evil as he has heard.

In chapter 19 the two men who represent God's presence are referred to as angels. These angels, too, act as only God can act, saving those who have been chosen, revealing God's will, and exercising God's righteous judgment. These "angels" say that God has sent them. ". . . the Lord has sent us to destroy it" (i.e., Sodom and Gomorrah; Gen 19:13).

Who appears to Abraham at Mamre? God does. However, in the development of these legends, God's presence is described in a variety of ways.

### Review Questions

1. In what ways is God's presence represented in the story of Abraham at Mamre?
2. Why might the J editor have told the story in this way?
3. What effect might the J editor have hoped the description would have?
4. What about Abraham's behavior reflects that he knew he was in the presence of the divine?
5. What about the visitors' behavior reflects that they represent God's presence?
6. How does the editor picture the fact that God has chosen to reveal God's self to Abraham?

### Discussion Questions

1. Do you feel that you are in relationship with God? Describe the relationship. What images have you used in your description?
2. Do you find the changing image of God's presence in Genesis effective? Mysterious? Ineffective? None of the above? Explain.
3. Does it seem disrespectful to you to describe God anthropomorphically? Why or why not?

# ARTICLE 16

# God's Justice and God's Saving Power

**Question: "After God promises Abraham that he wouldn't destroy the city if ten good men were found there, Lot and his family are removed and the city is destroyed. Why didn't God leave them there and spare the city?" (Gen 18:23–19:28)**

The person who asked this question is presuming that the story of Abraham's bargaining with God (Gen 18:23–33) is primarily about the fate of Sodom and Gomorrah, when in fact the story is primarily about God's justice.

Is God just? If so, one would think that the fate of the innocent person and the fate of the guilty person would not be the same. At the beginning of their confrontation Abraham puts the question bluntly: "Will you indeed sweep away the righteous with the wicked? Suppose there are fifty righteous within the city; will you then sweep away the place and not forgive it for the fifty righteous who are in it? Far be it from you to do such a thing, to slay the righteous with the wicked, so that the righteous fare as the wicked! Far be that from you. Shall not the judge of all the earth do what is just?" (Gen 18:23–25)

The fact that the story is so obviously concerned with God's justice causes many scholars to date this legend later than the J editor (1000 B.C.). The story deals with questions which were very much on the Israelites' mind during and after the Babylonian exile (587–537 B.C.).

Although we will not attempt to conclusively date this legend, we mention the opinion about its late date because it reminds us that when we read scripture we are reading a process of revelation. In other words, early insights about God and God's will for God's

70

people may obviously be more primitive than later insights. Is the thought that God would not destroy the innocent along with the guilty contemporary with the thought that hospitality demands the offer of one's daughters to an unruly mob? Obviously not. *OK, but not the same story!*

If the legends we read in the Bible appeared in the order in which they were written it would be much easier to trace the process of revelation which the Bible contains. However, we know that we are reading a much edited text. One ramification of this fact is that early and later insights may well appear side by side.

The question of suffering and how suffering relates to God's love, power and justice has previously been raised in the book of Genesis. As we noted, the story of the man and woman in the garden addresses this problem. This story attributes suffering to sin. But is all suffering due to sin?

The Israelites believed that suffering *was* due to sin. This belief left God's love, power and justice unchallenged because if all suffering is due to sin then all suffering is deserved.

The belief that all suffering is due to sin came under careful scrutiny after the Babylonian exile. Ezekiel, a prophet of the time, questioned this belief (see Ezek 18:1–4), as did the author of the book of Job. The debate on this issue appears to be a post-Babylonian exile debate.

The fact that Sodom and Gomorrah are destroyed is further evidence that the story of Abraham bargaining with God is not a picture of Abraham's attempting to save the city, but of Abraham's attempting to learn more about God's justice. After all, Abraham has become God's chosen instrument to teach God's justice. ". . . for I (God) have chosen him (Abraham) that he may charge his children and his household after him to keep the way of the Lord by doing righteousness and justice" (Gen 18:19).

One might answer our original question by saying that God felt free to destroy the city because God had removed the just people from it. However, this statement does not prove to be true. Lot and his family are not virtuous, as is obvious from the story of Lot's wife (a story told to teach the dangers of "looking back" from one's commitment to God, with an etiological component which probably accounts for the presence of a rock formation known to the audience [Gen 19:26]), and the story of his daughters (an etiology casting aspersions on the origins of the Israelites' enemies, the Moabites and the Ammonites [see Gen 19:30–37]). Lot and his family are removed, not because they are virtuous, but because they are related to Abraham. "So it was that when God destroyed the cities of the Plain, God remembered Abraham, and sent Lot out of the midst of the overthrow, when he overthrew the cities in which Lot had settled" (Gen 19:29). Once more we see that God is being faithful to his promise to Abraham. Others are blessed because of their relationship to him. In this edited order the stories of Abraham's bargaining with God and of the destruction of Sodom and Gomorrah hold in tension God's justice and God's power to save. We have seen this tension constantly present in the book of Genesis, and we will continue to see it not only in Genesis but in the Bible as a whole.

### Review Questions

1. What is the story of Abraham's bargaining with God in Genesis 18:23–33 primarily about?
2. Why do scholars suggest that the story of Abraham's bargaining with God is not contemporary with the J editor?
3. What effect does editing have on our ability to trace a process of revelation in the book of Genesis?
4. Why does a belief that all suffering is due to sin "protect God's reputation"?
5. At what point in Israel's history do the Israelites seem to doubt that all suffering is due to sin?
6. Does God remove the just people from Sodom and Gomorrah? Explain.
7. In what ways are the stories involving Lot's wife and daughters etiologies?
8. Why are Lot and his family removed?
9. What two truths are held in tension in the stories of Abraham's bargaining with God and the destruction of Sodom and Gomorrah?

**Discussion Questions**

1. Why is the idea that the good might suffer the same fate as the evil incompatible with our idea of God?
2. Why are scripture scholars interested in knowing *when* something was written?
3. What exactly do we mean when we talk about a process of revelation?
4. What are the dangers in "looking back" once one has become a disciple? What does this question have to do with this article?

# ARTICLE 17

# Does God Want Child Sacrifice?

**Question: "Why did God tell Abraham to sacrifice Isaac in the first place?" (Gen 22:1–18; 2 Kings 16:2–3; Ex 34:19–20 also discussed)**

To answer this question we will first reword it. "Why did Abraham think that God wanted him to sacrifice Isaac?" But before we answer the reworded question we will explain why the rewording was necessary.

The story of the sacrifice of Isaac is a legend. A legend is a story with an historical base which has been passed on through oral tradition, generation after generation. The fact that the story is a legend means that there is no claim to exact quotations. The story is not claiming that God said these words. The dialogue between God and Abraham is a narrative device used by a masterful storyteller to set the stage for a spiritual struggle which ends with a profound religious insight.

Abraham thought that God wanted child sacrifice because child sacrifice was practiced in the Canaanite culture at the time Abraham lived. However, Abraham was so open to God's love and God's will that he came to the realization that his God was not a God who wanted child sacrifice.

While it may seem obvious to us that child sacrifice is wrong, this was not obvious to earlier cultures. We see that by the time of Moses (1250 B.C.) child sacrifice was expressly forbidden. The first-born of most animals was still sacrificed to Yahweh, but the first-born of donkeys and of human beings was redeemed. "All that first opens the womb is mine, all your male livestock, the firstborn of

74

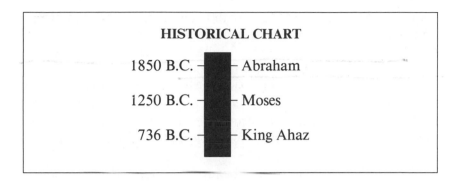

**HISTORICAL CHART**

| 1850 B.C. | — Abraham |
| 1250 B.C. | — Moses |
| 736 B.C. | — King Ahaz |

cow and sheep. The firstborn of a donkey you shall redeem with a lamb, or if you will not redeem it you shall break its neck. All the firstborn of your sons you shall redeem" (Ex 34:19–20).

Even after child sacrifice was forbidden it was still occasionally practiced. We read in 2 Kings that King Ahaz (736 B.C.) sacrificed his son in fire. "He (i.e., King Ahaz) did not do what was right in the sight of the Lord, his God, as his ancestor David had done, but he walked in the way of the kings of Israel. He even made his son pass through fire, according to the abominable practices of the nations whom the Lord drove out before the people of Israel" (2 Kings 16:2–3).

The story of the sacrifice of Isaac was originally a legend about Abraham's realizing that child sacrifice was not what God wanted. However, the story continued to be told after the question of child sacrifice was no longer an issue. The story's emphasis changed from the problem of sacrifice to the problem of trusting God in the face of a terrible moral dilemma.

In the form in which we read the story, Abraham's ordeal is described as "a test." "After these things God tested Abraham" (Gen 22:1). To introduce the story in this way is to make it more relevant and more gripping to the generations of audiences who have heard it.

Abraham was a man whose trust in God grew slowly. We noticed how Abraham was pictured as not trusting God in his early travels in Egypt. But with the birth of Isaac, distrust has disappeared. God has done what one would think would have been the impossible in

providing Abraham and Sarah with a son, just as God had promised. The fulfillment of God's promise rests on the survival of this
son. How could the promise be fulfilled if the son were sacrificed?
Still, is anything too wonderful for God?

Abraham trusts God. In the story, Abraham's trust is rewarded
because a sacrifice other than Isaac is provided. At a deeper level,
what Abraham had learned to trust was God's love. Abraham came
to the insight that God's love was of a kind that did not want child
sacrifice.

Abraham's complete trust is beautifully pictured in the narrative. When God calls Abraham, Abraham responds, "Here I am"
(Gen 22:1), words which reflect his total openness to be present
before his God and to do God's will. The same "Here I am" is
Abraham's response to his son when Isaac calls Abraham (see Gen
22:7), and to the Angel when the Angel calls Abraham (see Gen
22:11). Abraham is struggling through his moral dilemma, always
open, walking forward with complete faith.

By describing Abraham's ordeal as a "test," the storyteller high-
lights that part of Abraham's experience which is most relevant to
those who are listening. The introduction takes the focus away
from the question of child sacrifice. In fact, it relieves the audience
of any fear that Isaac might be going to die. So instead of focusing
on the horror of child sacrifice the audience can focus on the love
and faith which enables Abraham to reach a new level of understanding about the nature of his God. God is too loving to want
child sacrifice, but God does want all of his people, including the
audience of each generation, to walk in love and faith when we
must face moral dilemmas, as did our father in faith, Abraham.

### Review Questions

1. Why do we need to reword the question with which this article
   began?
2. Why did Abraham think that God wanted child sacrifice?
3. When was child sacrifice expressly forbidden in the law? Did all
   kings obey this law? Explain.

4. To what common experience did the emphasis in the story change after child sacrifice was no longer an issue?
5. What exactly was Abraham's dilemma?
6. What is it that Abraham finally learns to trust?
7. What spiritual posture did Abraham have that enabled him to solve his moral dilemma?

## Discussion Questions

1. Have you ever faced a moral dilemma in which you had to search out God's will? How did you discern God's will?
2. Have you ever had to discard a belief you were taught and once accepted because you came to believe it was wrong? Explain.
3. Do you think God is more pleased if you "offer up" a great suffering or a great joy? Why?

# ARTICLE 18

# The Promise of Land

**Question: "Why did Abraham tell his servant that Isaac was never to go back to Abraham's homeland for any purpose?" (Gen 24:6, 8; Gen 12:1; 15:7–9; 15:18; 24:7; 23:6; 23:17–18; 25:9; 35:27–29; 49:29–33 also discussed)**

Abraham is adamant that Isaac must not return to Abraham's homeland because Abraham wants Isaac to be an instrument through whom God's promise of land can be fulfilled.

Remember, God's promise to Abraham included not only descendants but land. God's first command to Abraham was, "Go forth from the land of your kinsfolk and from your father's house to a land that I will show you" (Gen 12:1).

The ceremony involving the cut animals ritualized a covenant promise of land. "He (God) then said to him (Abraham) 'I am the Lord who brought you from Ur of the Chaldeans to give you this land as a possession.' 'O Lord God,' he asked, 'how am I to know that I shall possess it?' He answered him, 'Bring me a three year old heifer, and three year old she-goat . . .' " (Gen 15:7–9).

After the smoking brazier and flaming torch had passed through the cut halves God says, "To your descendants I give this land . . ." (Gen 15:18).

Abraham wants Isaac to be present in the land to receive the fulfillment of the promise. Abraham's motivation is made clear as he tells his servant, "The Lord, the God of heaven, who took me from my father's house and the land of my kin, and who confirmed by oath the promise he then made to me, 'I will give this land to your descendants,' he will send his messenger before you . . ." (Gen 24:7).

Abraham's instructions to his servant regarding the selection of a wife for Isaac are the last words we hear from Abraham. The arranging for his son's marriage is Abraham's last official duty.

However, Abraham has already come into ownership of one small part of the promised land. The importance of this purchase is almost lost on the reader since the purchase is for a burial ground for Sarah, and the story of its purchase is not somber, as one might expect, but humorous in its realistic details of oriental bargaining. While each of the bargainers, Abraham and the Hittites, are sharp bargainers, each maintains an aura of complete dignity and appears to be trying to outdue the other not in shrewdness but in generosity.

Abraham approaches the Hittites, acknowledges that he is an alien and a stranger, but asks to buy property nevertheless. Evidently Abraham's acknowledgment is simply false modesty for the Hittites respond, "Hear us, my lord; you are a mighty prince among us. Bury your dead in the choicest of our burial places; none of us will withhold from you any burying ground for burying your dead" (Gen 23:6).

Abraham does not let the flattery deter him from his goal of owning the land. He has a particular cave in mind. Ephron the Hittite, the owner of the cave, tries to give Abraham not only the cave but the field that it is on.

Abraham is adamant that he must purchase the land. He does not want to receive it as a gift but wants to pay full price for it.

The price Ephron the Hittite mentions is probably high. One would expect Abraham to make a counteroffer but he does not. Abraham not only secures his land but he "outdoes" the Hittite in generosity.

One can hear the relish of the storyteller as he concludes the story, since both the storyteller and the audience know just how important the purchase really is. "So the field of Ephron in Machpelah, which was to the east of Mamre, the field with the cave that was in it, and all the trees that were in the field, throughout its whole area, passed to Abraham as a possession in the presence of the Hittites, in the presence of all who went in at the gate of his city" (Gen 23:17–18).

Scripture scholars think that the storyteller is the P editor and that the "relish" in telling the story stems from the fact that the land had been lost during the Babylonian exile and had only recently been regained.

This plot of land became the burial place not only for Sarah but for Abraham (Gen 25:9), Isaac (Gen 35:27–29), Rebekah (Gen 49:31), Jacob, and Leah (Gen 49:29–33).

Since this tiny "toe hold" in the land was only the beginning of the fulfillment of God's promise to Abraham and his descendants, it is no wonder that Abraham wanted to make sure that Isaac stayed in Canaan. Otherwise Abraham's descendants might not be in the land so that God's promise could be fulfilled through them.

## Review Questions

1. What, in addition to descendants, did God's promise to Abraham include?
2. Why does Abraham not want Isaac to return to Abraham's homeland?
3. What is the first land which Abraham owns in Canaan?
4. To which editing tradition do scripture scholars attribute the story of the purchase of the land? Why would the story bear special significance at the time of this editing tradition?

## Discussion Questions

1. Are you tied emotionally to any land? Explain.
2. Are there cases in your family where the dream of one generation has been fulfilled in the next generation? Explain.
3. Of all that you and/or your family own, what is most important to you? Why?
4. Do you think that God has promised you anything? If so, what? Why do you think this?

# ARTICLE 19

## Jacob: The Deceiver
## and the Deceived

**Question: "Since Jacob lied to Isaac, why did the blessing count? Why didn't Isaac just take it back?" (Gen 27:27–29; Gen 24:2–4; 25:23; 25:34 also discussed)**

In Jacob's culture a blessing, once given, could not be taken back. The blessing was like an arrow shot from a bow. Once given it had a life, a power of its own.

We have already noted that blessings, as well as curses, were common in the Canaanite culture. Originally blessings and curses were related to magic words and actions. People believed that the words and actions caused the good or bad which they expressed. As with many elements of the Canaanite culture, the Israelites appropriated the custom, but interpreted it differently. For the Israelites the power of blessings and curses lay not in magic but in God. God was seen as powerfully present and as carrying out the blessing or curse.

Modern readers very often object to Jacob's succeeding in obtaining the blessing since he lied to do it. In our culture the most serious vows which bind us for life in covenant relationships are not binding if, in hindsight, it is discovered that at the time the vow was made one party was deceiving another. This is simply one of a myriad of ways in which the presumptions of our culture differ from the presumptions of the Israelites' culture.

The blessing which Isaac gave Jacob was a particularly important and powerful blessing because it was a deathbed blessing. Isaac was, in effect, passing on his life to his descendant. Scripture scholars believe the significance of the meal before the blessing is that food affects vitality. Isaac wanted to be full of life as he handed life on to his son.

This same sense of the seriousness of handing on life appeared in another custom foreign to us in chapter 24. When Abraham was old he was concerned with handing on life through Isaac, and so he made arrangements for Isaac to marry. When Abraham gave his servant instructions about finding Isaac a wife Abraham said, "Put your hand under my thigh and I will make you swear by the Lord, the God of heaven and earth, that you will not get a wife for my son from the daughters of the Canaanites, among whom I live, but will go to my country and to my kindred and get a wife for my son Isaac" (Gen 24:2–4).

"Put your hand under my thigh" is a euphemism. Abraham is telling the servant to put his hand under Abraham's genitals, the source of life. The instructions which Abraham gives the servant are of the utmost importance and so the servant is asked to bind himself in the most serious of oaths. To pass on life is a sacred duty.

Even as a modern reader objects to the deceit practiced by Rebekah and Jacob, we can see the inevitability of Jacob's success. Jacob has become the child of the promise. We know this because God has said so. After God healed Rebekah's sterility, she conceived twins who fought in the womb. When Rebekah asked God about this God is pictured as saying, "Two nations are in your womb, and two peoples born of you shall be divided; the one shall be stronger than the other, the elder shall serve the younger" (Gen 25:23). When Jacob is born second, gripping Esau's heel we know that the die is cast.

Although we may think poorly of Jacob because he lied in order to steal the blessing from Esau, we still cannot admire Esau. After all, Esau sells his birthright to Jacob for some bread and lentil stew (see Gen 25:34). Although the narrator of this story does not join us in making moral judgments about the characters in the story, he does make a disparaging remark about Esau. "Thus Esau despised his birthright" (Gen 25:34).

The fact that God's chosen instrument is not worthy to be chosen is not a new theme in Genesis. Remember we didn't always admire Abraham or Sarah either. God's plans succeed not because God's

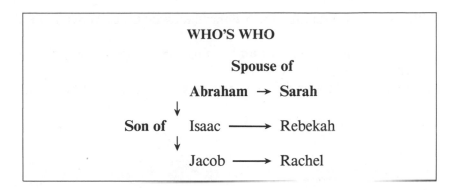

**WHO'S WHO**

Spouse of

Abraham → Sarah

Son of    Isaac ⟶ Rebekah

Jacob ⟶ Rachel

chosen instruments are great and holy people. God's plans succeed because God is great and holy.

As we continue to read Genesis we will continue to see deceit, next between Jacob and Laban. Although the narrator does not judge Jacob in a negative way, nor camouflage Jacob's importance as the inheritor of the promise, he does, as we will soon see, picture Jacob as not only the deceiver but the deceived.

### Review Questions

1. To what were blessings and curses originally related? How were they reinterpreted by the Israelites?
2. What presumption do we have about the binding power of agreements that Jacob's culture did not have?
3. What do scripture scholars think is the significance of the meal at the time Isaac gave his blessing?
4. Why does Abraham ask the servant to "put your hand under my thigh" when he swears the oath?
5. How do we know that Jacob has become the child of the promise?
6. Does it matter that God's chosen instruments are not faultless? Explain.

### Discussion Questions

1. Do you think agreements should be binding even if deceit is present at the time of the agreement? Why or why not?

2. Do you feel sympathetic for either Jacob or Esau? Why or why not?
3. Do you sometimes feel that blessings and curses have power? Why or why not?
4. Do you sometimes feel that certain people are "destined" for greatness? Why or why not?

# ARTICLE 20

# Laban: The Trickster and the Tricked

**Question: "The relationship between Jacob, Leah, and Rachel seems awfully strange. Why would Jacob have to sleep with Leah because Leah's son had given mandrakes to Rachel?" (Gen 30:16; Gen 29:26; 30:22–24; 30:39; 31:7–9; 31:32; 31:35 also discussed)**

To a modern reader the relationship between Jacob, Leah and Rachel seems preposterous. In our culture men do not have more than one wife, so a man could not be married to sisters. However, given the culture, the story is not only believable but poignant and ironic.

Jacob has gone to the home of his mother's brother, Laban, to choose a wife. Laban and his sister, Rebekah, have a great deal in common. Each is willing to practice deceit so as to trick an unwilling benefactor into acting on a child's behalf.

With Rebekah, Isaac was the unwilling benefactor who unwittingly gave Jacob the blessing that he wanted to give to Esau.

With Laban, Jacob is the unwilling benefactor who unwittingly takes Leah as his wife when he thought he was taking Rachel.

The irony in the situation is made perfectly evident as Laban explains to Jacob why he was given Leah as his bride instead of the younger Rachel. "This is not done in our country—giving the younger before the firstborn" (Gen 29:26). Jacob is forced to observe the appropriate honors due to a firstborn, the very convention which he had refused to observe when he stole his brother's blessing.

Although Laban undoubtedly thought he was doing something good for Leah, he put Leah in a terribly painful situation. Leah is

85

her husband's first wife but she knows perfectly well that her husband does not love her.

Rachel is in an equally painful situation. Like Sarah and Rebekah before her, Rachel is sterile.

It is because she is sterile that Rachel wants the mandrake roots. The roots were believed to be an aphrodisiac and were thought to cause fertility. In order to get the roots Rachel agrees that Jacob will return to Leah's bed.

Once again we see a folk belief appropriated but reinterpreted. Although Rachel does finally conceive and bear a child (Joseph), God and not the mandrake root is given credit for her fertility (see Gen 30:22–24).

The belief that a mandrake root causes fertility is not the only folk belief which appears in the story. After Laban had once again tricked Jacob by removing all the speckled and spotted goats, even though he had agreed that these very goats would be Jacob's wages, Jacob breeds the goats so as to produce more who are speckled and spotted. Jacob takes rods of poplar and almond and strips them so that the white inside is exposed. ". . . the flocks bred in front of the rods, and so the flocks produced young that were striped, speckled, and spotted" (Gen 30:39). This explanation reflects a folk belief that breeding could be influenced by whatever the flock saw at the time the breeding took place.

Once again, the power behind the magical effect is attributed to God. As Jacob tells his wives, ". . . your father has cheated me and changed my wages ten times, but God did not permit him to harm me. If he said, 'the speckled shall be your wages,' then all the flock bore speckled. . . . Thus God has taken away the livestock of your father and given them to me" (Gen 31:7–9).

Just as Jacob, the deceiver, is likewise deceived, so Laban, the trickster is likewise tricked. When Jacob flees Laban with his wives, children and livestock, he is unaware that Rachel has stolen Laban's household gods.

Laban is extremely angry at the theft. Jacob himself considers it such a serious matter that he promises the death penalty to whoever is found guilty (see Gen 31:32).

The guilty party is Rachel, who had been denied the opportunity to be Jacob's first wife by Laban's trickery. Rachel has stolen Laban's gods, put them in a saddle and sat on them. When her father enters to search for the gods Rachel says, "Let not my lord be angry that I cannot rise before you, for the way of women is upon me" (Gen 31:35).

The Israelites considered women unclean during the time when they were having their menstrual period. Anyone who came in contact with a menstruating woman was also considered unclean. So for Rachel to be sitting on Laban's household gods was the greatest of insults. What kind of god is it who would allow himself to be sat upon by a woman who was menstruating? Surely this is no god at all!

*funny!*

Every single relationship pictured in the Jacob-Laban cycle of stories is painful. The story is told in such a way that we understand the human situations of the characters as well as some of their folk beliefs. But no matter who the character or what the folk belief involved, God is always seen as the main actor, working through the people even with all their faults and all their folk beliefs. Nothing can prevent God from accomplishing God's will for God's people.

## Review Questions

1. What do Laban and his sister Rebekah have in common? Explain.
2. What is ironic about Laban's forcing Jacob to give appropriate honor to a firstborn child?
3. Why is Leah's situation so painful?
4. Why is Rachel's situation so painful?
5. Why did Rachel want the mandrake roots?
6. What folk belief regarding breeding appears in this story?
7. How are Laban's gods ridiculed by the storyteller?
8. How is the God of the Israelites built up by the storyteller?

## Discussion Questions

1. Do you feel sympathetic for Rachel or Leah? Why or why not?
2. Do you know of any culture in today's world where marriages

are arranged and the bride and groom do not know each other? Explain.

3. Does our culture still have folk beliefs? Do you know some? Explain.
4. Does our culture still have taboos? Can you name some?
5. Do you attribute the cause of events to God? Why or why not?

ARTICLE 21   *oracles at exiting & entering the land*

# Jacob's Encounters with God

**Question: "What changes Jacob? He seems to be a different person by the time he reconciles with Esau." (Gen 33:1–16; Gen 28:12–14; 28:17; 31:13; 32:9–12; 32:26; 32:30 also discussed)**

Jacob and Esau both act differently than one fears, even expects, when they meet again after a twenty-year separation.

Jacob reveals the reason for his changed behavior when he says to Esau, ". . . if I find favor with you, then accept my present from my hand, for truly to see your face is like seeing the face of God—since you have received me with such favor. Please accept my gift that is brought to you, because God has dealt graciously with me, and because I have everything I want" (Gen 33:10–11).

It appears that God's treatment of Jacob is behind Jacob's changed treatment of Esau. To understand Jacob's experiences of God we should look at the descriptions of Jacob's encounters with God as they appear in Genesis.

When Jacob was first fleeing Esau, while he was at Bethel, Jacob had a dream in which he experienced God's presence. "And he dreamed that there was a ladder set up on the earth, the top of it reaching to heaven; and the angels of God were ascending and descending on it. And the Lord stood beside him and said, 'I am the Lord, the God of Abraham . . . ' " (Gen 28:12–13).

The ladder represents the fact that there is a link between heaven and earth. That is why Jacob refers to the spot as "the gate of heaven" (see Gen 28:17), a holy place where God has made God's presence known. God makes the same promise to Jacob that God had made to Abraham. God promises Jacob the land, that his offspring will be like the dust of the earth, and that others will be blessed because of them (see Gen 28:13–14). God also promises Jacob protection.

We have already seen that Jacob does prosper in Haran, despite Laban's constant attempts to cheat him.

Jacob returns home because the Lord instructs him to. "I am the God of Bethel, where you anointed a pillar and made a vow to me. Now leave this land at once and return to the land of your birth" (Gen 31:13).

But Jacob returns full of fear. Despite God's promise to protect him, and despite God's promise to make his descendants as numerous as the sand, Jacob fears that Esau will kill them all. Jacob realizes that he should not doubt God, but he can't help it. Jacob reveals his struggle with God in prayer (see Gen 32:9–12).

Jacob then sends gifts to his brother, sends his family on ahead, and spends a night alone where he continues to wrestle with God. This time the struggle is not revealed in the form of a prayer but in a mysterious story. A man, who is later identified with God (Gen 32:30), wrestles with Jacob all night. The "man" does not prevail but does dislocate Jacob's hip. The "man" then says, " 'Let me go for the day is breaking.' But Jacob said, 'I will not let you go unless you bless me' " (Gen 32:26). When the "man" asks Jacob's name Jacob tells him. The man renames Jacob "Israel." Jacob asks the "man" his name. While the "man" refuses to give his name he does bless Jacob.

Scholars debate the levels of meaning of this story. Perhaps the story originally existed in folklore as a story about a demon who could only operate at night. This would explain why the man asked to be let go because day was breaking. Obviously the story contains a number of etiologies as it explains the meaning of the name "Israel," the reason for the name "Peniel," and the reason why Israelites do not eat the thigh muscle. This food taboo, however, wasn't actually observed by the Israelites and does not appear in the law.

One cannot fail to notice that Jacob is wrestling for a blessing on the eve of the day when he will meet his brother, from whom he stole a blessing. In the struggle, Jacob does receive the blessing.

While we may not figure out all of the possible significances of this strange story, we do know that it describes Jacob as having a profound experience of God's presence. This experience causes Jacob to say that Esau's welcome was like "seeing the face of God." Why? Because Esau's welcome was a confirmation of God's promise. Jacob experienced God's presence and protection in the changed attitude of his brother.

What changes Jacob? The experience of God's promise, and the experience of God's promise being fulfilled in the events of his life changed Jacob. Jacob no longer has to steal blessings or wrestle for a blessing. Jacob now lives in the knowledge that he truly is blessed.

## Review Questions

1. What is behind Jacob's changed treatment of Esau?
2. In Jacob's dream what did the ladder represent?
3. What does God promise Jacob?
4. Why does Jacob return home?
5. In what two ways do we see Jacob "struggle" with God?
6. What etiological elements are present in the story of Jacob's wrestling with God?
7. Why was Esau's welcome like "seeing the face of God" for Jacob?

## Discussion Questions

1. Is there anything, any ritual, any place in your life that con-cretely represents a link between heaven and earth? Explain.
2. Have you ever "wrestled" with God? Explain.
3. Have you ever felt God's protection through an event? Explain.
4. In what person's face do you most clearly see the face of God? Why?

# ARTICLE 22

# Stories Not of Individuals but of Tribes

**Question: "This story of Dinah's rape and her brothers' cruelty doesn't seem to fit. What is the point of this story?" (Gen 34:1–31; Gen 38:1–30; 49:5–7 also discussed)**

Very often in Genesis stories which appear to be about individual people are really about groups of people, about tribes and their subsequent relationships to each other.

Scripture scholars suggest that the story of Dinah's rape and her brothers' revenge may have been told to explain the relationship between Israel and Shechem which existed years later, or to explain why the tribes of Simeon and Levi declined. If these etiological explanations are accurate, then we would expect the story to put both Shechem and Dinah's brothers, Simeon and Levi, in a negative light.

On close reading, though, it is difficult to be sure who is put in the worst light. Jacob is pictured as acting in a very passive way. He doesn't seem to be outraged by his daughter's rape as are her brothers. "When they heard of it, the men were indignant and very angry, because he (i.e., Shechem) had committed an outrage in Israel by lying with Jacob's daughter, for such a thing ought not to be done" (Gen 34:7). With this last comment the narrator of the story seems to justify the anger of the brothers and to criticize Jacob's passivity.

The picture we get of Shechem and his father, Hamor, is certainly very negative. Not only does Shechem rape Dinah, but when the two speak to the men of their city, asking them to be circumcised, they reveal that their motive is economic. "Will not their

---

**WHO'S WHO**

**Dinah:** Jacob's daughter

**Simeon and Levi:** Jacob's sons who seek revenge for their sister's rape

**Shechem:** Raped Dinah

**Hamor:** Shechem's father

---

livestock, their property, and all their animals be ours? Only let us agree with them and they will live among us" (Gen 34:23).

When Jacob corrects his sons after the massacre he doesn't correct them because their actions were wrong but because their actions have made Jacob vulnerable to attack. Their only response is once again to find fault with Jacob for his lack of action. "Should our sister be treated as a whore?" (Gen 34:31).

Since the brothers do not seem to be put in a very negative light it is difficult to determine if the story was meant to account for the lack of prominence of the tribes of Simeon and Levi. A much clearer condemnation of the brothers' behavior will come in Genesis 49 when Jacob is pictured as speaking of the future destinies of the tribes.

> Simeon and Levi are brothers;
>    Weapons of violence are their swords.
> May I never come into their council;
>    May I not be joined to their company—
> For in their anger they killed men
>    and at their whim they hamstrung oxen.
> Cursed be their anger, for it is fierce,
>    and their wrath, for it is cruel!
> I will divide them in Jacob,
>    and scatter them in Israel (Gen 49:5–7).

A second story which seems out of place may also function primarily as an etiology. This is the story of Judah and Tamar in chapter 38.

---

**WHO'S WHO**

**Judah:** Jacob's son

**Er:** Judah's son

**Tamar:** Er's wife/widow

**Onan:** Judah's son who did not fulfill his obligation to his
        dead brother and to Tamar, his brother's widow

---

Judah is one of Jacob's sons. Judah has three sons of his own. Er,
the oldest son, marries Tamar. After his marriage but before any
children are conceived Er dies.

Among the Israelites, if a man dies childless his brother must
marry the widow in hopes that she will bear a son who will be the
heir of her first husband. Although Judah instructs his second son
to fulfill this obligation, the son, Onan, refuses to do it. "But since
Onan knew that the offspring would not be his, he spilled his semen
on the ground whenever he went in to his brother's wife, so that he
would not give offspring to his brother" (Gen 38:9). Onan's failure
to fulfill his duty to his dead brother resulted in his death.

Tamar then went to live in her father's house, and Judah failed to
arrange for his third son to marry her. So, in order to bear a son,
Tamar tricked and seduced Judah himself. She conceived twins
who, like Jacob and Esau, fought in the womb.

The story of Judah and Tamar seems to be out of place. It seems
simply to interrupt the stories of Joseph. Scripture scholars suggest
it functions as an etiology of the tribe of Judah. Had Tamar not
done as she did, Judah's line would have ended. But Judah's line
became more and more important. King David himself was born
of the house of Judah.

It is helpful when reading Genesis to keep in mind that the stories
are all told in hindsight, formed in the light of subsequent events,
often to explain why things are as they are for the storyteller's
audience. Both the stories of Dinah and of Tamar may not be
primarily about Dinah and Tamar at all but about Israel's relation-

ship with Shechem and about the tribe of Judah. It is for this reason that they do not fit perfectly smoothly into the much edited arrangement of stories in Genesis.

## Review Questions

1. What two etiological purposes might be behind the story of Dinah's rape and her brothers' cruelty?
2. What is Jacob's response to his daughter's rape?
3. How do Shechem and his son reveal their characters?
4. What obligation did Onan fail to fulfill?
5. What etiological purpose might the story of Judah and Tamar have?

## Discussion Questions

1. What effect does hindsight have on stories like the story of Dinah and her brothers or the story of Judah and Tamar?
2. Why do we tend to belittle or picture as evil our political foes?
3. Do you know of animosities that have lasted generations? Name some.

*This chapter doesn't cut it — no real explanation at all — even if we grant that groups, not individuals, are the topics, nature or the point of the stories are not made clear here —*

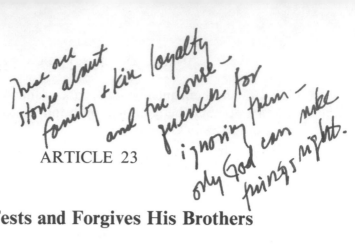

*These are stories about family + kin loyalty and true [course] — punishment for ignoring them — only God can make things right.*

ARTICLE 23

# Joseph Tests and Forgives His Brothers

**Question: "Why did Judah tell Joseph that they were guilty of stealing the cup when they weren't?" (Gen 44:16; Gen 37:4; 37:7; 37:21–28; 39:22; 40:4; 41:41; 42:6; 42:21; 42:27–35; 43:33; 44:33; 45:5; 50:15–17 also discussed)**

Actually, Judah does not say that they are guilty of stealing the cup, only that they are guilty. "What can we say to my lord? What can we speak? How can we clear ourselves? God has found out the guilt of your servants; here we are then, my lord's slaves, both we and also the one in whose possession the cup has been found" (Gen 44:16). It is the old guilt of mistreating Joseph to which Judah refers.

In fact, it is to see if Judah and his brothers have repented of the sin that had caused this guilt, and have had a change of heart, that Joseph plants the cup in Benjamin's bag in the first place. He wants to see if the brothers will abandon Benjamin as they had him.

From the interconnectedness of these plot elements we can see that the stories of Joseph and his brothers form a more cohesive whole than does any other cycle of stories which we have read in Genesis. At the same time, however, the stories clearly demonstrate the fact that the editors were working with a variety of traditions. For instance, who defended Joseph? Reuben (Gen 37:21) or Judah? (Gen 37:26). Is Joseph sold to the Ishmaelites (Gen 37:28), or carried off by the Midianites? (Gen 37:28) What position did Joseph have in jail? Was he in charge of all the prisoners (Gen 39:22), or a slave to two? (Gen 40:4). What position did Joseph have in Egypt? Was he in charge of the palace (Gen 41:40), or in charge of the land? (Gen 41:41). When did the brothers find the money in

96

their sacks? Was it on the first day of their journey home (Gen 42:27), or when they arrived home? (Gen 42:35).

Despite these inconsistencies the stories form a cohesive whole and can only be understood as a whole. Joseph's testing of his brothers can only be understood in the light of what Joseph's brothers had done to him.

Remember, Joseph was Jacob's favorite child. In at least one tradition, Joseph's favored status is the reason for his brothers' hatred. "But when his brothers saw that their father loved him more than all his brothers, they hated him, and could not speak peaceably to him" (Gen 37:4). Their crime against Joseph was also a crime against Jacob because Jacob was inconsolable in his grief.

If one is unaware of these early plot elements one is unable to understand why Joseph tests his brothers as he does. What does Joseph want to discover? He wants to know if his brothers have changed, or if they would once again be willing to sacrifice the favored brother, now Benjamin, and cause their father inconsolable grief in order to benefit themselves.

When the brothers first approach Joseph in Egypt we recognize the fulfillment of Joseph's dream (see Gen 37:7) because the "brothers came and bowed themselves before him with their faces to the ground" (Gen 42:6).

Joseph, of course, recognizes them and begins the test, which involves accusing them of being spies, and manipulating events so that the brothers must bring Benjamin to him. Early in the test, even though the brothers do not recognize Joseph, they interpret their difficulties as being the result of their sin. "Alas, we are paying the penalty for what we did to our brother; we saw his anguish when he pleaded with us, but we would not listen. That is why this anguish has come upon us" (Gen 42:21).

When the brothers return to Egypt with Benjamin, Joseph treats Benjamin with obvious favoritism. Although the brothers were seated "the firstborn according to his birthright and the youngest according to his youth" (Gen 43:33), the firstborn was not treated preferentially. Instead, Benjamin was given five times as much as his older brothers.

Joseph then arranges to plant his cup in Benjamin's sack, thus creating a situation that will test the brothers. Will they once more

---

**THE PATRIARCHS**

Abraham
Isaac
Jacob
Joseph

---

abandon the favored youngest brother? Or will they sacrifice themselves instead?

It is at this point that Judah admits guilt even though he didn't steal the cup. The brothers once again interpret their difficulties as God's punishment for their sin against Joseph.

Now that the brothers are thoroughly trapped, Joseph gets his answer. Judah pleads eloquently for Benjamin's safety, not just for Benjamin's sake but for Jacob's sake as well. Judah explains to Joseph that Benjamin is their father's favorite without any bitterness. Judah offers himself in Benjamin's place. "Now therefore, please let your servant remain as a slave to my lord in place of the boy; and let the boy go back with his brothers" (Gen 44:33).

Only after Joseph is sure that his brothers are no longer the evil people they had been does he reveal his identity to them. "I am your brother Joseph, whom you sold into Egypt" (Gen 45:5).

Although Joseph reminds his brothers of their mistreatment of him and immediately treats them kindly we do not hear the brothers ask forgiveness for their sin until after Jacob dies. "Realizing that their father was dead, Joseph's brothers said, 'What if Joseph still bears a grudge against us and pays us back in full for all the wrong that we did to him?' So they approached Joseph saying, 'Your father gave this instruction before he died, "Say to Joseph: I beg you, forgive the crime of your brothers and the wrong they did in harming you . . ." ' " (Gen 50:15–17).

Joseph's brothers need not have used their father's memory in this way. Joseph had already forgiven his brothers from his heart.

## Review Questions

1. To what guilt does Judah refer when he admits guilt to Joseph?
2. Why does Joseph plant the cup in Benjamin's bag?
3. What evidence is there that the editors were working with a variety of traditions?
4. What is one reason given for Joseph's brothers' hatred of him?
5. How do the brothers interpret their difficulties?
6. Have the brothers changed? How do you know?
7. Did Joseph's brothers believe they had been forgiven? How do you know?

## Discussion Questions

1. Do you think guilt is good or bad? Why?
2. Do you think it is good or bad to have "favorites"? Why?
3. Do you think God uses dreams to communicate with people? Do you have any personal experience that has lead you to this conclusion?
4. Do you agree with this statement: "Love no more sweetly lives than when it has something dreadful to forgive"? What does this question have to do with this article?

# ARTICLE 24

# Wisdom Discerns God's Ways

**Question: "Why does Joseph attribute his brothers' evil behavior to God?" (Gen 45:5–8; Gen 50:15–21; Gen 41:15–16 also discussed)**

The person who asked this question is referring to the interpretation Joseph puts on past events when he says, "And now do not be distressed, or angry with yourselves, because you sold me here, for God sent me before you to preserve life . . . God sent me before you to preserve for you a remnant on earth, and to keep alive for you many survivors. So it was not you who sent me here, but God" (Gen 45:5, 7–8).

At the psychological level we might say that Joseph's words are meant to calm his brothers' fears and to help them overcome their guilt, now that they are changed people. Joseph wants to be in right relationship with his brothers. He has forgiven them. So, even though they did sell him into Egypt, they should put all that behind them now.

At a deeper level, though, Joseph's words are only comforting if they are true. The words express the theological beliefs of the editor.

Underlying the Joseph story is the theological perspective that God is constantly at work in the events of everyday life, not just when people intend God's will to be accomplished, but even when they do not. God is at work not just when people are aware of God's power and presence in their lives, but even when they are not.

The story of Joseph is not the only place in the Bible where this theological perspective is expressed. One finds it particularly in wisdom literature.

100

Wisdom literature originally developed in courtly settings and was, of course, not limited to Israel. Its main emphasis was on courtly conduct: how to behave well, speak well, order relationships well, and handle time and money well.

When the Israelites appropriated wisdom literature they expanded the concept of wisdom beyond "worldly wisdom." For the Israelites, "The fear of the Lord is the beginning of knowledge" (Prov 12:7). All other order, order in relationships and in the proper use of time and goods, flows from a right relationship with God.

So, wisdom literature expresses a belief that God is present in the nitty-gritty of everyday living more subtly than does other literature. Notice in the Joseph story that God is never pictured as appearing directly to Joseph and telling him what to do. God does not say, "Go to Egypt," or "Go to the Pharaoh," or even "Forgive your brothers." Yet it is clear to the reader that behind each person's actions, the good and the bad, a provident God is at work ordering all for good.

Joseph, as a character, is a perfect model of a person who has received the gift of wisdom. Joseph's conduct is constant evidence of wisdom as he orders events to bring about right relationships. He refuses the advances of his master's wife. He knows how to handle himself in a courtly setting. In addition, Joseph's ability to interpret dreams is evidence that he has the gift of wisdom.

Dreams and their interpretation are central to the plot of the Joseph story. Remember, one of the reasons given for the brothers' hatred of Joseph is that they resent Joseph's dreams. While the editor does not attribute the dreams directly to God, the reader knows that the dreams are from God because we realize, in hindsight, that they accurately foreshadow events. The reader is also persuaded, since the events were foreseen, that they were foreordained.

It is because Joseph is able to interpret dreams that he comes to the notice of the Pharaoh and rises to a position of great power. Joseph attributes his ability to interpret dreams directly to God. The Pharaoh says, " 'I have heard it said of you that when you hear a dream you can interpret it.' Joseph answers Pharaoh, 'It is not I; God will give Pharaoh a favorable answer' " (Gen 41:16).

---

**PRIESTLY EDITING TRADITION**

*Cumulative Chart*

Dates to time after Babylonian exile (587–537 B.C.).

Called P after priests who did editing.

Uses genealogies as a structural device.

Responsible for "creation in six days" story.

Emphasizes that human beings are made in God's image, creation is good, God's blessing is coming to realization.

Uses repetitive formulas.

Emphasizes importance of circumcision.

Interest in God's promise of land, in God's justice as it relates to innocent people, and in the role of wisdom.

---

Were it not for his dreams and his ability to interpret dreams, for his gift of wisdom, Joseph would not have been in Egypt, would not have become powerful, and would not have used that power to save his family.

So, while Joseph's claim that "it was not you (his brothers) who sent me here, but God" (Gen 45:8) was meant to comfort them, it was also meant to teach them of God's provident love. Joseph, the model of wisdom, is pictured as teaching his brothers exactly what is taught in the book of Proverbs. "The human mind may devise many plans, but it is the purpose of the Lord that will be established" (Prov 19:21).

Joseph is telling his brothers that God's purpose was to save their family.

**Review Questions**

1. At the psychological level, what might Joseph's words in Genesis 45:5–8 mean?
2. What theological belief underlies Joseph's words in Genesis 45:5–8?
3. How do the Israelites expand the concept of wisdom?
4. From what does all order flow?
5. How is Joseph's conduct a model of wisdom?
6. What role do dreams play in the Joseph story?
7. What does Joseph think is the reason for all that has happened?


**Discussion Questions**

1. What does this expression mean: "God writes straight with crooked lines"? Do you agree with this statement? Why or why not? What does this statement have to do with this article?
2. Do you believe that order in relationships, in business, etc., all flow from a right relationship with God? Explain.
3. Have you ever had to forgive something serious? Why is it essential to forgive, no matter what?

# ARTICLE 25

# The Promised Land

**Question: "Why does Jacob insist on blessing Ephraim with his right hand rather than Manasseh?" (Gen 48:14–20; Gen 48:3–4; 49:10; 50:12–13; 50:24–25 also discussed)**

The scene in which Jacob blesses Ephraim with his right hand rather than Manasseh is a scene that directs the reader's attention both to the past and to the future. In fact, this same "past and future" point of view is present in Jacob's whole deathbed scene. Because the deathbed scene recapitulates the promise made to Abraham and directs the reader's attention to the future fulfillment of that promise, the scene serves to draw the book of Genesis toward a fitting conclusion.

The blessing of Ephraim and Manasseh, in which a younger son is given preference over an older son, reminds us of similar scenes which appeared earlier in the book of Genesis. We remember that Abel was preferred to Cain, Isaac to Ishmael, Jacob to Esau, and Joseph to his older brothers. As we have noted before, the stories of such preferences reflect an etiological purpose. The tribe of Ephraim was to become more powerful than the tribe of Manasseh. This fact is symbolized and foreshadowed by the account of Jacob's crossing his hands so that the younger child, who is on his left, receives the blessing with Jacob's right hand, evidently the preferential blessing.

Just as the blessing recalls the past and foreshadows the future, so does the deathbed scene as a whole. When Joseph first arrives with his sons, Jacob reminds them of God's promise, which had origi-

104

---

**WHO'S WHO**

**Jacob:** (Israel) Father of 12 sons

**Joseph:** One of 12 sons who saved the family in Israel

**Ephraim and Manasseh:** Joseph's sons after whom tribes were later named. The tribe of Ephraim would become more powerful than the tribe of Manasseh.

---

nally been made to Abraham. "God Almighty appeared to me at Luz in the land of Canaan, and blessing me, he said, 'I will make you fertile and numerous and raise you into an assembly of tribes, and I will give this land to your descendants after you as a permanent possession' " (Gen 48:3–4).

Jacob then adopts Joseph's two sons as his own. In fact, the tribe of Joseph did split into two tribes, the tribe of Ephraim and the tribe of Manasseh. So while the blessing accounts for the presence of one tribe over another, the adoption scene itself accounts for the fact that there would be two tribes rather than one.

As Jacob blesses Ephraim and Manasseh he specifically recalls the earlier patriarchs. "The God before whom my ancestors Abraham and Isaac walked, the God who has been my shepherd all my life to this day, the angel who has redeemed me from all harm, bless the boys; and in them let my name be perpetuated, and the name of my ancestors Abraham and Isaac; and let them grow into a multitude on the earth" (Gen 48:15–16).

Before Jacob dies he is pictured as drawing his sons around him so that "I may tell you what is to happen to you in days to come" (Gen 49:1). What follows is not a description of what will happen to the sons themselves but what will happen to the tribes. This collection of sayings, blessings, and curses describes the tribes as they were before the establishment of the kingdom. However, the ascendancy of the tribe of Judah, the tribe from which David will come, is clearly stated:

---

**TRIBES NAMED IN JACOB'S BLESSING**

| | |
|---------|---------|
| Reuben | Dan |
| Simeon | Gad |
| Levi | Asher |
| Judah | Naphtali |
| Zebulun | Joseph |
| Issachar | Benjamin |

---

The scepter shall never depart from Judah,
  or the mace from between his legs,
While tribute is brought to him,
  and he receives the peoples' homage (Gen 49:10).

Before Jacob dies he makes Joseph promise that Joseph will take him back to Canaan for burial. He wants to be buried in the only piece of land that the Israelites own in Canaan. After Jacob dies Joseph fulfills this promise. "Thus Jacob's sons did for him as he had instructed them. They carried him to the land of Canaan and buried him in the cave in the field of Machpelah, facing on Mamre, the field that Abraham had bought for a burial ground from Ephraim the Hittite" (Gen 50:12–13).

Joseph, on his deathbed, instructs his brothers differently than did Jacob. First, he once again tries to comfort them, reminding them of God's provident care and that God's promise to Abraham would some day be fulfilled. "But God will surely come to you and bring you up out of this land to the land that he swore to Abraham, to Isaac, and Jacob" (Gen 50:24). Joseph asks his brothers to bury him in Canaan, not when he dies, but when God fulfills this promise. "When God comes to you, you shall carry up my bones from here" (Gen 50:25).

So the book of Genesis ends with God's promise only partially fulfilled. God has saved Abraham's descendants, but as Joseph dies those descendants do not have a land to call their own. When the story continues, some 400 years later, in the book of Exodus, the descendants of Abraham, Isaac, Jacob and Joseph will be leaving Egypt for the land which they have been promised.

## Review Questions

1. How does Jacob's deathbed scene direct our attention both to the past and to the future?
2. What etiological purpose is behind the story of the blessing of Ephraim and Manasseh?
3. What etiological purpose is behind Jacob's adoption of two of Joseph's sons?
4. What is Jacob's long deathbed collection of sayings really about?
5. What is Jacob's last request?
6. Does Joseph ask to be buried in Canaan? When?
7. As the book of Genesis concludes are God's promises to Abraham fulfilled? Explain.

## Discussion Questions

1. Why do you think it mattered to Jacob where he was buried? Do you care where you are buried? Why or why not?
2. We have read about four generations in the book of Genesis. Do you know anything about four generations in your family? What do you know about your great-great grandparents? Which generation decided that you would live in this country? Do you think family histories are important? Why or why not?

# Summation and Transition
# from Genesis to Exodus

As we leave the book of Genesis we leave a story begun but not finished. A promise has been made but not yet fulfilled. So, from the point of view of plot, we need to have read Genesis to understand Exodus, to understand who these people are who are to leave Egypt and who are to go to the promised land.

However, a knowledge of the plot is not the only knowledge which we have gained while reading Genesis which we will find helpful while reading Exodus. In addition we have learned the characteristics of literature which is the edited arrangement of several inherited traditions.

So far in Genesis we have identified at least three traditions. We have seen that the Yahwist or J tradition dates to the tenth century B.C. This editor refers to God as "Yahweh" even before this name is revealed to Moses. The Yahwist editor describes God anthropomorphically. He emphasizes the effect sin has had on the human race even as he holds up hope.

We have noted that the P editor's point of view is from a later time, after the Babylonian exile (587–537 B.C.). We have seen that the P editor uses genealogies as a structural device. He likes fixed formulas. The P editor emphasizes that human beings are created in God's image. He is concerned with issues of his day such as the importance of circumcision, the question of God's justice as it relates to the suffering of innocent people, and the role of wisdom.

We found that the third tradition, that of the Elohist editor, was written from the point of view of the northern kingdom after the kingdom divided. This editor emphasizes the role of prophets over kings, and exhibits a moral sensitivity. He calls God "Elohim"

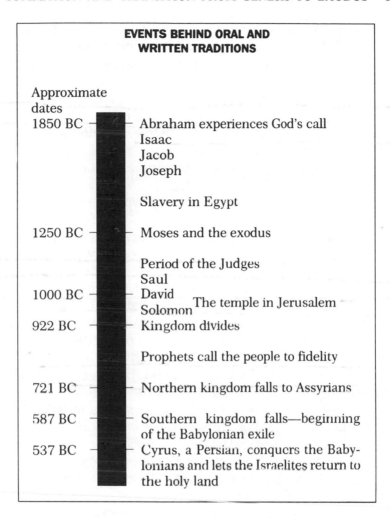

**EVENTS BEHIND ORAL AND
WRITTEN TRADITIONS**

Approximate
dates

1850 BC — Abraham experiences God's call
Isaac
Jacob
Joseph

Slavery in Egypt

1250 BC — Moses and the exodus

Period of the Judges
Saul
1000 BC — David
Solomon   The temple in Jerusalem
922 BC — Kingdom divides

Prophets call the people to fidelity

721 BC — Northern kingdom falls to Assyrians

587 BC — Southern kingdom falls—beginning
of the Babylonian exile
537 BC — Cyrus, a Persian, conquers the Babylonians and lets the Israelites return to
the holy land

rather than "Yahweh" until God reveals himself to Moses, and describes God's presence as mediated by angels, dreams, and so forth. So far we have recognized the work of the Elohist editor in doublets.

The effect that this weaving together of traditions has on the text is that the text contains inconsistencies and contradictions even as it maintains a clear plot and a clear theme. No attempt has been made to "clean up" the final manuscript, to make details in the various traditions consistent with each other. Rather, the various points of view are valued. Each tradition's point of view results in its contributing insights to the story which another point of view lacks.

Remember, each editor is speaking about events in hindsight, in the light of subsequent events. The Elohist editor will not speak so highly of kings because the northern kingdom has revolted against the king. The P editor will emphasize God's blessing because he is offering hope to those who have experienced the Babylonian exile. So stories are molded not to answer the question, "What exactly happened?" but to answer a more important question, "What do events tell us about God and our relationship with God?"

Since God's role in the course of events is the main theme, stories about events from other cultures which did not emphasize God's role are appropriated and retold by the Israelites to teach God's role. We have seen blessings, curses, etiologies, folklore and legends all appropriated and reworked so that they have become stories about God's power and presence in the lives of God's people.

We have also noted characteristics of legends. Although at their core legends are about historical events and people, legends are very different from what our culture considers historical writing. A legend is an imaginative story with an historical core. The story does not contain exact quotations or exact social settings. Rather, it contains dramatic elements, exaggerations, magical details—all elements that make the story more interesting and entertaining to a contemporary audience.

So as we read the book of Exodus we want to bring with us not only our knowledge of the plot of Genesis, but also all we have learned about the text. Armed with this information, we will find that many of the puzzling aspects of the book of Exodus will no longer be puzzling.

# ■ THE BOOK OF EXODUS ■

# ARTICLE 1

# The Israelites: Fruitful but Oppressed

**Question: "How long was it between the time Joseph died (Ex 1:6) and the time the new king who knew nothing of Joseph (Ex 1:8) came to power? It must have been several generations for the Israelites to have become so numerous." (Ex 1:7; 1:11; Gen 1:25 also discussed)**

Scholars have not reached complete consensus on the historical setting of the book of Exodus, but the majority opinion would place the beginning of the story of Exodus during the reign of Ramses II (1290–1224 B.C.).

Ramses II was a great builder. He founded the city of Rameses, an accomplishment that is referred to in the account of the Israelites' oppression. "Therefore they set taskmasters over them to oppress them with forced labor. They built supply cities of Pithom and Rameses for Pharaoh" (Ex 1:11).

If this historical setting is accurate, then the exodus occurred around 1250 B.C., after the Israelites had been in Egypt for over four hundred years.

Just how numerous the Israelites had become is another question. As we begin the book of Exodus we read a genealogy from P. Remember, "fruitfulness" has been a theme of the P editor all along. In the creation story P pictured God as saying, "Be fruitful and multiply, and fill the earth" (Gen 1:28). P has constantly emphasized that God's blessing and God's promise are still in effect.

We also know that the P editor uses genealogies as a literary

113 $\longrightarrow$ 149

device to fill gaps in the narrative. In Exodus 1:1–7 we see both P's fondness for genealogies and his emphasis on fruitfulness as he names the "sons of Israel who came to Egypt with Joseph." P says, "But the Israelites were fruitful and prolific; they multiplied and grew exceedingly strong, so that the land was filled with them" (Ex 1:7).

For the Egyptian king the growth in the population of the Israelites was both a threat and an opportunity. On the one hand the king did not want the Israelites to become so numerous that they could join forces with an enemy, defeat the Egyptians, and leave. On the other hand, the king saw the advantage in a large work force. One cannot build cities without men to do the labor.

The Israelites, who were people of the land and semi-nomadic, hated the life of slave laborers. The situation for the Israelites in Egypt became unbearable.

In addition to oppressing the Hebrew labor force the king of Egypt is pictured as ordering the death of all Hebrew newborn boys. This story, while it accounts for the Israelites' desire to leave, and sets the scene for Moses' birth, seems somewhat inconsistent with the idea that the Pharaoh needed the Israelites as slave labor. Certainly the labor force would be short-lived if all of the male babies were killed.

Scripture scholars deduce that the account of using the Hebrews for slave labor comes from the J editor while the story of the Pharaoh ordering the midwives to kill all male babies comes from the E tradition. Remember, in the E tradition a certain moral sensitivity is evident. We noticed this in the doublet of the story of Abraham saying his wife was his sister in Genesis 20:1–17. We find it again here where the midwives, because of their "fear of God" (see Ex 1:17), disobey the king and refuse to kill the Hebrews' baby boys, thus enabling the people to multiply and become strong.

How numerous had the Hebrews become? We can't answer this question with any precision. Not only does the text not say, but the literary form would not allow us to draw such a conclusion even were a number mentioned. The P editor emphasizes the fruitfulness of the people not in order to describe a large population but in order to show that God's will, that the people be fruitful, is being fulfilled.

## Review Questions

1. What date do scholars assign to the exodus?
2. How long had the Israelites been in Egypt?
3. What two characteristics of P are apparent in the genealogy in Exodus 1:1–7?
4. Why was the growth in population of the Israelites both a threat and an opportunity for the Egyptian king?
5. Why do scripture scholars think that the story of the midwives is from the E tradition?

## Discussion Questions

1. Why do you think the Bible remains silent about the four hundred years between Joseph and Moses?
2. The P editor emphasizes that God's blessing and God's promise were still in effect for his generation. Do you think that God's blessing and God's promise are still in effect for our generation? Why or why not?

# ARTICLE 2

# Stories Which Foreshadow Greatness

**Question: "If the midwives were brave enough to disobey the king why wasn't Moses' mother? I think it is terrible that she left him in the basket." (Ex 2:1–4)**

The person who asked this question is misunderstanding the kind of writing she is reading. The story of Moses' origins is not comparable to a story one might read in the newspaper about an abandoned baby.

Rather, the story of Moses' origins is comparable to the stories of the origins of other heroes, Jesus' included. The purpose of the story is not to describe a literal event but, in the light of subsequent events, to tell the story in such a way that the audience sees that truths which were actually understood later are foreshadowed.

So the storyteller is not faced with the problem, "How do I describe this birth exactly as it happened?" but with the problem, "How do I describe this birth so that the audience understands just how great this person really became?"

A traditional legend to describe the birth of one who became a great ruler already existed. In this legend, a king named Saigon, who became a great ruler in the 24th century B.C., is said to have been placed in a basket and allowed to float down the river.

By adapting a traditional motif known to be associated with a great ruler the storyteller is foreshadowing Moses' destiny as a great leader of his people. This foreshadowing of the role to which Moses will eventually be called continues as we read of the reason for his flight to Midian.

Moses, despite having been raised in the Egyptian court, feels an

---

**PURPOSE OF BIRTH NARRATIVES**

Author not addressing question: "How do I describe this birth exactly as it happened?"

Author is addressing question: "How do I describe this birth so that the audience understands just how great this person really became?"

---

affinity for his own people. When he sees an Egyptian abuse one of the Hebrew laborers, Moses kills the Egyptian (Ex 2:12). However, when he sees two Hebrews fighting with each other, he does not kill the Hebrew who was in the wrong but asks him a question: "Why do you strike your fellow Hebrew?" (Ex 2:13).

It is at this point that the Hebrew asks Moses a question central to the book of Exodus and one which the storyteller is answering even as he tells the story: "Who made you a ruler and judge over us . . . ?" (Ex 2:14).

Although a specific answer to that question will come soon, a subtle answer comes even as Moses flees Pharaoh and goes to the land of Midian. Moses' actions are foreshadowing what will soon be the actions of the Israelite people under Moses' leadership. The land of Midian is a desert area. So Moses is fleeing the Pharaoh and going to the desert, where he will later lead the people to safety.

We see this "saving" motif as we read that the seven daughters of Jethro, the priest of Midian, are unable to draw water because some shepherds come and drive them away. Moses defends the daughters and makes it possible for them to water their flock.

It is while Moses is tending the flock of his father-in-law, Jethro, that he goes to Mount Horeb and encounters God (Ex 3:1ff.). As we will read, the Israelites will also encounter God on this mountain, also called Sinai, during their time in the desert.

Who made Moses a ruler and judge over his people? Even as we hear the story of Moses' birth, of his being left in the basket, found by the Pharaoh's daughter, and nursed by his own mother, we know, from the way that the story is being told, that the answer to the question is, "God made Moses the ruler and judge over his people." Since the storyteller knows that this is, in fact, what happened, he tells the story of Moses' birth in a traditional way so that Moses' eventual greatness is foreshadowed for his audience.

## Review Questions

1. What is the purpose of the story about Moses' origins?
2. On what traditional legend might the story of Moses' birth be based?
3. What question, central to Exodus, is asked by the Hebrew laborer?
4. How do Moses' actions in Midian foreshadow his later actions with the Israelites?
5. Who did make Moses ruler over his people?

## Discussion Questions

1. What is the difference between the account of Moses' birth in Exodus and a story you might read in a newspaper about an abandoned baby?
2. What nationality are you? Do you feel a special affinity for "your own"? Why or why not?
3. Have you ever asked anyone "Who made you ruler and judge?" Have you ever wanted to? Explain.

# ARTICLE 3

# I Am Who I Am

**Question: "What does God mean when God says, 'I Am who I Am?' Is God telling God's name or refusing to tell?" (Ex 3:14; Ex 3:11–15; 4:1–10; 4:14–17; 6:3 also discussed)**

God is telling God's name when God says to Moses, "I Am who I Am." That God is entering a time of greater intimacy with his people will soon be stated explicitly by the P editor when God is pictured as saying, "I appeared to Abraham, Isaac and Jacob as God Almighty, but by my name 'The Lord' (i.e., Yahweh) I did not make my name known to them" (Ex. 6:3).

However, when we read God saying, "I Am who I Am" in chapter 3, we are not reading the account of the P editor but the account of the E editor, and we are reading an all-important scene. Remember the E editor is called E because he has refrained from referring to God as Yahweh until this scene, using instead the word "Elohim."

So there is no question that for both the Elohist tradition and the P tradition the revelation of God's name as "Yahweh" is a real revelation. But what does it reveal?

In Hebrew, the revelation of God's name consists of four letters: YHWH. Since the name was so holy Jews refrained from pronouncing it, saying "Adonai" (i.e., "Lord") instead. Even to add the vowels "a" and "e" to YHWH so that it becomes "Yahweh" is to begin to interpret the meaning of the revelation.

"Yahweh" is a form of the verb "to be," a third person form. "I Am who I Am" is a first-person form of the same verb "to be," "*hayah*" in Hebrew.

---

**"I AM WHO I AM"**

*Yahweh*

First person form of the verb "to be."

*Possible meanings:*
- I cause to be all that exists.
- I cause to be all that happens.
- I am always with you.

---

Many scholars suggest that the meaning of "Yahweh" must be "He causes to be." So "I Am who I Am" would mean, "I cause to be."

Given the root meaning of the word, several interpretations are offered for the meaning of "I Am who I Am." The first is that God causes to be all that exists, that God is the creator of all. A second is that God causes to be what is presently happening. God causes the events which will result in the Jews being saved. Still a third possible understanding for "I Am" is "I am the God who is always with you." Each of these meanings would appropriately fit the context. Perhaps the words "I Am who I Am" are meant to imply all three meanings as they remind us that total knowledge of God is far beyond our meager abilities to comprehend.

Notice that the revelation of God's name is part of a larger whole, the scene of Moses' call. Although we are reading a combination of traditions in chapter 3, both the J and E traditions, we see that both use the same basic structure, a structure traditionally used for the call of a prophet. First God appears to Moses because God has heard the cry of God's people and now plans to do something about it. Next God commissions the prophet, in this case, Moses. Then Moses objects. In our present account Moses objects not once but four times. First Moses says, "Who am I that I should go to Pharaoh and lead the Israelites out of Egypt?" (Ex 3:11). Next Moses says, ". . . when I go to the Israelites and say to them, 'The

---

**STRUCTURE FOR CALL OF A PROPHET**

God appears in response to people's need.

God commissions the prophet.

The prophet offers objections.

God responds to the objections.

---

God of your fathers has sent me to you,' if they ask me, 'What is his name?' what am I to tell them?" (Ex 3:13). It is at this point that God reveals God's self as "I Am." These two objections are thought to be from the E tradition.

The J tradition also has Moses offer two objections. First Moses says, "Suppose they will not believe me nor listen to my plea? For they may say, 'The Lord did not appear to you' " (Ex 4:1). Next Moses says, "If you please, Lord, I have never been eloquent, neither in the past, nor recently, nor now that you have spoken to your servant . . ." (Ex 4:10).

To the objections in the E tradition God first promises Moses that when he has brought the people out of Egypt they will worship God on this same mountain (Ex 3:12), and then, as we have seen, God reveals God's name to Moses (Ex 3:14–15).

To the objections in the J tradition God first gives three signs: the rod which turns into a snake, the hand which turns leprous and then clean, and the water, which turns to blood (Ex 4:2–9). To Moses' second objection God gives him Aaron, who will be Moses' spokesperson (Ex 4:14–17).

Although the traditions do not agree on details they nevertheless teach the same message. By using the form traditional to the call of a prophet, each tradition is teaching that Moses is a prophet, one chosen by God to speak for God. The crucial assurance which Moses needs and receives is knowledge of who God is: God is Yahweh who created all, who is responsible for the course of

---

### MOSES' OBJECTIONS AND GOD'S RESPONSES

**In E:** "Who am I that I should go to Pharaoh and lead the Israelites out of Egypt?"

"WHEN YOU HAVE BROUGHT THE PEOPLE OUT OF EGYPT THEY WILL WORSHIP ON THIS SAME MOUNTAIN."

"If they ask me, 'What is his name?' what am I to tell them?"

"I AM WHO I AM. I AM HAS SENT ME TO YOU."

**In J:** "Suppose they will not believe me."

GOD GIVES MIGHTY SIGNS: THE ROD WHICH TURNS INTO A SNAKE . . .

"I don't speak well."

GOD GIVES MOSES AARON AS A SPOKESPERSON

---

events, and who will be with Moses as Moses leads God's people out of Egypt.

**Review Questions**

1. Why is the E editor called "E"?
2. From what Hebrew verb is the word "Yahweh" derived?
3. Name three possible meanings of "I Am who I Am."
4. What structure is traditionally used for the call of a prophet?
5. What two objections is Moses pictured as making in the E tradition? How does God respond?

6. What two objections is Moses pictured as making in the J tradition? How does God respond?
7. What message is being taught by using the structure for the call of a prophet?

## Discussion Questions

1. Of the possible meanings for Yahweh, which appeals to you most? Why?
2. Why do you think prophets always resist their calls?
3. Do you ever object to God's call? Explain. Has God responded? Explain.

# ARTICLE 4

# Marked as God's Own

**Question: "What is this about God almost killing Moses? (Ex 4:24) Isn't Moses God's chosen one? Had Moses failed to circumcise his son?" (Ex 4:22–26; Gen 32:24–32)**

No one could read Exodus 4:24–26 and not be puzzled by it. The passage offers difficulties in every way. First we must ask, "What is the story line?" That is, "What does the text describe as having happened?"

Second we must ask, "What is the source of the story?" That is, "Is the story appropriated from folklore and retold with a new theme?"

And finally we must ask, "What is this new theme?" In other words, "In its present position in Exodus, what is the story teaching?"

Depending on the translation you are reading you may come away from the story with varying ideas of the plot. The verse on which translations differ is verse 25. The NRSV translates this verse, "But Zipporah took a flint and cut off her son's foreskin, and touched Moses' feet with it, and said, 'Truly you are a bridegroom of blood to me!' " (Ex 4:25). The New American Bible says, "But Zipporah took a piece of flint and cut off her son's foreskin and touching his person, she said, 'You are a spouse of blood to me' " (Ex 4:25).

What did Zipporah do with the foreskin? Did she touch her son or Moses with it? In the second translation it seems that the incident involves only her son yet she refers to the person as a "spouse." Was it her son or Moses whom she circumcised?

These questions cannot be answered with certainty. The most

---

**YAHWIST EDITING TRADITION**

*Cumulative Chart*

Dates to time of monarchy (1000 B.C.).

Refers to God as Yahweh throughout narrative.

Called J rather than Y because German scholars identified source and German word for Yahweh is *Jahve.*

Pictures God anthropomorphically.

Emphasizes growth in sinfulness of human race but offers hope.

Moses' objection: Suppose they don't believe me? Rod turns to snake . . . Aaron.

Appropriates and reinterprets folklore (i.e., Moses and Zipporah).

---

likely explanation seems to be that Zipporah circumcised her son and touched Moses' "feet" (most likely a euphemism for "penis") with the foreskin.

What does all this have to do with the story which we are reading in the book of Exodus? God all of a sudden seems to have turned into a threatening demon of the night (see Ex 4:24), not the "I Am" whom we recently met.

Scholars believe this strange story comes from the J tradition. It reminds us of a previous story which we read in Genesis 32:24–32 and discussed in Article 21, in which Jacob has a nighttime encounter with a man, later identified as God, and wrestles with him. This man/God tells Jacob to let him go because day is breaking. We suggested that perhaps this story originally existed in folklore as a story about a demon who could only operate at night. The story was appropriated and retold with an entirely different meaning.

Here, too, God appears as a threatening power at night. Zipporah saves Moses from this threat, evidently by putting blood on his penis. Perhaps, once more, we are dealing with a story which originally existed in folklore about a night demon who was warded off by the presence of blood. (We will see a similar belief behind a nomadic celebration of an early passover feast when we discuss the Passover celebrations.)

Without knowing the original source of the story or its intent we can see that it was appropriated and placed here in the book of Exodus to reinforce the fact that Moses and his son belong to God, not to Pharaoh, and that Jewish males are marked as belonging to God by circumcision.

Since Moses had been raised as an Egyptian and his sons born to a non-Jewish woman in Midian, it is possible that neither father nor sons were circumcised. Now, as Moses sets off for Egypt to fulfill God's command, the son is circumcised and the father is addressed as " 'a spouse of blood' in regard to circumcision" (Ex 4:26). Both are marked as God's.

Since in this scene God spares Moses after he has been marked with blood, the scene foreshadows the tenth plague (Ex 12:29–32) which will be visited upon the Egyptians. In this plague the firstborn of the Egyptians is slain but the firstborn of the Israelites is spared because of the blood which has been placed on the lintel.

That the scene is meant to foreshadow this plague is emphasized by the fact that it is inserted immediately after God warns that the firstborn will be killed. "Thus says the Lord: Israel is my son, my firstborn. Hence I tell you: Let my son go, that he may serve me. If you refuse to let him go, I warn you, I will kill your son, your firstborn" (Ex 4:22–23).

Moses, like Israel, is God's "firstborn son." Moses is not only spared, but chosen. Moses belongs to God and this belonging is symbolized by circumcision, his own and his son's.

### Review Questions

1.  What three questions do we need to ask in reference to the story in Exodus 4:24–26?

2. Why is even "the plot" difficult to determine?
3. What seems "folklorish" about the story?
4. In its present position in Exodus what is the story teaching?
5. In what way does this scene foreshadow the tenth plague?

## Discussion Questions

1. How are we marked as God's own? Do we consider someone to be in "danger" if they do not have this "mark"? Why or why not?
2. Did you read stories from folklore when you were a child? Do you remember any of them? Do any ideas from folklore still have some meaning in your imagination or some power in your life? Explain.

# ARTICLE 5

# Pharaoh's Hardened Heart

**Question: "How could anyone blame Pharaoh for not believing Moses and Aaron the first time they meet? (Ex 5:1–5) After all, God is the one who hardened Pharaoh's heart (Ex 4:21), and Moses and Aaron didn't use their mighty signs. Why didn't they?" (Ex 4:8–9; 4:29–31; 5:1–29; 7:3, 13, 14, 22; 8:15, 32; 9:7, 12, 35; 10:1, 20, 27 also discussed)**

This question illustrates the fact that even though someone is perfectly aware that the book of Exodus is an arrangement of various traditions and that many of the units of these traditions can fairly be called "legends," nevertheless it is sometimes difficult to understand the ramifications of these facts.

First let us deal with the observation that Pharaoh is not at fault because God is the one who hardened Pharaoh's heart. Then we will discuss why, in this first confrontation with Pharaoh, Moses and Aaron did not use any of their mighty signs.

It is true that in Exodus 4:21 God is pictured as saying, ". . . but I will harden his (i.e., Pharaoh's) heart, so that he will not let the people go" (Ex 4:21). Should this statement be interpreted literally so that one should think of Pharaoh as a person who lacks free will? Obviously the answer to that question is, "no." We already know that when we are reading a legend we are not dealing with exact quotations. We are dealing with an imaginative story built around an historical core.

The historical core in this story is that in the time around 1250 B.C. the Egyptian Pharaoh really was using Hebrew laborers to build cities. Moses was an historical person who, against all odds,

128

successfully led a band of his own people out of bondage in Egypt. Moses and his people experienced great hardship and great resistance to their leaving at the hands of Pharaoh. But, nevertheless, events resulted in the Israelites making a successful escape. Those who experienced these events experienced them as the result of God's power and presence in their lives.

In telling and retelling the story of God's mighty power and presence a variety of stories grew up. In some of these stories it is said that God hardened Pharaoh's heart (see Ex 7:3; 9:12; 10:1, 20, 27). In other stories Pharaoh is said to have hardened his own heart (see Ex 8:15, 32). And in some accounts the statement is simply made that Pharaoh's heart was hardened (see Ex 7:13, 14, 22; 9:7, 35). None of these accounts is in contradiction to another. None is meant to seriously engage the reader in a meditation on free will. Rather, we see a variety of narrative expressions, all of which describe the fact that the Pharaoh did not willingly let God's people go.

It is also true that Moses and Aaron are not pictured as using their mighty signs to persuade Pharaoh to do God's bidding in this first encounter (Ex 5:1–29). You may remember that we read of these mighty signs when Moses was objecting to his call and God was reassuring him and giving him signs. The signs of staff/snake, clean and leprous hand, and water turned to blood were all signs given in the J tradition when Moses objected because he feared he would not be believed by his own people (see Ex 4:1). The signs were given him for the purpose of persuading the Israelites that God had truly sent Moses (see Ex 4:8–9).

We are once again reading the J account when we read that Moses and Aaron appeared before Pharaoh for the first time. Just before they go to Pharaoh they use the signs to persuade their own people that they truly have been sent by God. "Then Moses and Aaron went and assembled all the elders of the Israelites. Aaron spoke all the words that the Lord had spoken to Moses, and performed the signs in the sight of the people. The people believed; and when they heard that the Lord had given heed to the Israelites and that he had seen their misery, they bowed down and worshipped" (Ex 4:29–31).

Later when we read that Moses and Aaron use the mighty signs to persuade Pharaoh we will be reading the P tradition. P adapts J's signs and puts them to an additional use in his narrative.

Is the Pharaoh to blame for his hard heart? Our narratives don't allow us to answer that question because they never do address the question. Instead the legends we are reading illustrate the fact that even human resistance does not prevent God's will from being accomplished.

### Review Questions

1. What is a legend?
2. What is the historical core in the story of the Israelites leaving Egypt?
3. In the J tradition why are the "mighty signs" given to Moses?
4. What lesson is being taught through Pharaoh's "hardened heart"?

### Discussion Questions

1. Did God harden Pharaoh's heart? Explain.
2. Do you think one person's "hardened heart" can completely obstruct God's plan for God's people? Why or why not?

# ARTICLE 6

# P's Commissioning Story

**Question: "Exodus 6:2–9 seems out of place. Here the people don't seem to believe Moses (Ex 6:9) but earlier they did believe (Ex 4:31). Why?" (Ex 6:2–7:7; Gen 23; 34:1–31; 49:7 also discussed)**

The reader, in noting this inconsistency, has picked up one of the "seams" that reveal where traditions have been joined. So far we have read the call and commissioning of Moses from two traditions which have been braided together, J and E. Now, in Exodus 6:2–7:7 we are reading the call and commissioning of Moses as it appears in the P tradition.

Remember, the P tradition dates to the time when the people had experienced the Babylonian exile (587–537 B.C.) and were trying to rebuild once more in their own land. Remember, too, that the role of priests had grown in importance in the post-exilic period and was of primary importance and interest to the P editors, priests themselves.

In addition, you may remember that we have previously noted the P editor's interest in God's promise of land. We remarked on this emphasis in Article 18 when the P editor recounted Abraham's purchase of his burial plot (Gen 23).

It is interesting to note that while the P tradition uses the same basic form which we have already noted in the J and E traditions, the form for the calling and commissioning of a prophet, it nevertheless emphasizes those points which are of particular interest to P's contemporary audience. When God speaks to Moses to say that he has heard the "groaning of his people" and plans to do something about it, God first says, ". . . I also established my covenant with them (i.e., Abraham, Isaac and Jacob) to give them the land of

131

Canaan, the land in which they resided as aliens" (Ex 6:4). Then, as God promises that he intends to save the people, God says, "I will bring you into the land that I swore to give to Abraham, Isaac and Jacob; I will give it to you for a possession. I am the Lord" (Ex 6:8).

For the P editors this promise had only recently been fulfilled. For some fifty years the Israelites had been exiled from this land which God had promised Abraham. Now they were home again and going over their traditions in the light of their own very painful experience.

The P editor does say that the people would not listen to Moses (Ex 6:9), as our questioner noted. This is a telescoping of the situation which we have seen in the J and E traditions, in which the people believe but then lose faith in the face of increased mistreatment.

The P tradition also mentions Moses' objection that he does not speak well, as well as God's response to this objection. Aaron will be with Moses.

This statement serves as an introduction to a genealogy which P has inserted. We have noted P's interest in genealogies throughout the Genesis-Exodus narrative, as well as the fact that genealogies, too, are used to emphasize certain themes.

In this genealogy the P tradition shows its special interest in the tribe of Levi. This is most understandable since the tribe of Levi is the tribe of priests. Notice that both Aaron and Moses are said to be descendants of the tribe of Levi.

We are not unfamiliar with the tribe of Levi. You may remember that in Article 22 we suggested that the story of the rape of Dinah and her brothers' cruel revenge may have been an etiology to explain why the tribes of Simeon and Levi declined (Gen 34:1–31). We also noted that the tribe is as much as condemned in Jacob's deathbed speech. "I will divide them in Jacob, and scatter them in Israel" (Gen 49:7).

In Exodus the tribe appears to be a priestly tribe. Scholars debate the actual history of the "Levites" since in some Old Testament passages they appear to be priests, in some they appear to be those associated with priests who do menial chores, and in some they appear to be a group of poor people who, along with widows, need special care.

Although we do not know the precise history, it nevertheless seems clear that in the post-exilic time priests had become very important. For this reason the P editor is interested in emphasizing the tribe of Levi and the fact that Moses and Aaron descended from this tribe.

After the inserted genealogy the P editor concludes the account of the call and commissioning of Moses, repeating a condensed version of the commission, Moses' objections and God's reassurance (Ex 6:24–7:5). The stage is now set, in all three traditions, for the stories of the plagues.

### Review Questions

1. What is the contemporary setting of the P editor?
2. What special interests of the P tradition are revealed in the story of Moses' call and commissioning?
3. What special interest of the P tradition is revealed in the genealogy?
4. What do we know about the tribe of Levi?

### Discussion Questions

1. Why do you think the final editors of the Bible included the J, E, and P traditions of Moses' call rather than choosing only one?
2. Have you ever been present for an event and then, in hindsight, had a very different understanding of the event than you had had originally? Why does this happen? What does this question have to do with the Bible?

# ARTICLE 7

# Characteristics of Legends

**Question: "How could the Egyptian sorcerers turn their staffs into snakes? Wasn't Aaron able to do it only through the power of God?" (Ex 7:8–12; Ex 4:2–9; 5:2; 8:6–7; 12:29 also discussed)**

If one begins to read the stories of the plagues with the frame of mind which this reader brings to the stories one will meet with constant frustration and find many inconsistencies. The person who would ask this question would also ask such questions as, "How could you tell that the magicians covered the land with frogs since the land was already covered with frogs?" (Ex 8:6–7). Or: "If all of the livestock were killed in the fifth plague (Ex 9:6) then how could the firstborn of the livestock die in the tenth plague?" (Ex 12:29).

Even before asking these questions such a person might ask, "Did Aaron's rod really turn into a snake?" The person who asks such questions wants the book of Exodus to answer the question, "What exactly happened?" He or she wants the literary form of the book to be factual and descriptive writing.

Instead we have a variety of legends. Legends, as we have said, are imaginative and symbolic stories built around an historical core. We have also noted various characteristics of legends: They do not contain exact quotations. They do not claim accuracy in social setting. They have been edited to emphasize a theme and to include a religious interpretation of the original event. In addition to these characteristics we have seen that legends often contain etiologies as well as folk customs which have been appropriated for religious purposes. Legends also incorporate magical details. These, too, function as story elements which contribute to the religious interpretation of the original event.

Remember that when we read about the call of Moses in the J and E traditions we noticed that in each tradition Moses protested his call, and in each God responded with promises or signs to encourage Moses. Only in the J tradition were these signs of a magical nature (Ex 4:2–9). In other words, a perfectly valid tradition tells the story without incorporating the magic rod. We have also noted that the P editor picks up this "magic rod" and incorporates it for a new role—to persuade Pharaoh rather than to persuade Moses' own people. With all of this background we should be able to read this legend for the masterful dramatic account which it is, and not bring to it inappropriate expectations and irrelevant questions. We should be able to understand that magical elements have been incorporated into the legend for the purpose of emphasizing a theme.

Years of teaching have taught me that the next question is, "Are you saying that this story is not true?" Rods don't turn into snakes. The author is not expecting the reader to suspend his or her experience of reality and accept as a literal fact what is obviously an imaginative detail. Nevertheless, the story is in the Bible because generations of Jews and Christians not only believe that what the story teaches is true but also believe that the story shapes their (our) own identities.

What is true is that a present and powerful God who loves his people made his presence and power known through a series of events which resulted in the Israelites escaping from slavery in Egypt.

Were the events natural or supernatural? This question would not have been posed by those who experienced the exodus or by those who passed on the stories from one generation to another. They did not use words like "supernatural" or "miracle." Rather, they used the word "sign" to name an event in which God's power and presence were experienced.

As we read the accounts of the plagues, then, we are reading imaginative and dramatic accounts of a confrontation between God, who had chosen Moses and Aaron as God's spokespersons, and Pharaoh, who claims that he himself is god in Egypt.

As the story progresses we will see that Pharaoh, his sorcerers, and everyone else involved grow in their understanding of the an-

---

**LEGENDS**

I.   Have an historical base

II.   Have an oral history
   A.  Not quotations
   B.  Not exact historical chronology
   C.  Not exact historical social setting
   D.  Some information presumed known

III.   Are edited narratives
   A.  Emphasize a theme
   B.  Reflect growth in moral sensitivity
   C.  Include religious interpretation

IV.   Are characterized by:
   A.  Exaggeration
   B.  Magical details
   C.  Etiologies
   D.  Folk customs appropriated for religious purposes

V.   Can be the vehicle for revelation
   A.  Revelation about God
   B.  Revelation about our relationship with God

---

swer to the question which Pharaoh had asked God's prophets, Moses and Aaron: "Who is the Lord, that I should heed him and let Israel go?" (Ex 5:2).

As we read the legends about the plagues, and as we learn to understand this literary form we, too, will grow in our understanding of the answer to this crucial question, "Who is God?" Revelation about God, and not about magic, is the subject of the book of Exodus.

**Review Questions**

1. Name four characteristics of legends.
2. Why are magical elements incorporated into the story?

3. Which tradition incorporated these magical details?
4. Instead of "miracle" what word would the Israelites have used to describe an event in which God's presence was experienced?
5. What question is at the core of the power struggle between Moses and Pharaoh?

## Discussion Questions

1. What does this sentence mean: Legends incorporate magical details in such a way that these story elements contribute to the religious interpretation of the original event?
2. What conclusion can you draw from the fact that a perfectly valid tradition of the plagues exists which does not include magical details?
3. Is the story of the plagues true? Explain.

# ARTICLE 8

# Who Is God in Egypt?

**Question: "The account of the plagues seems terribly drawn out and the Pharaoh unbelievably slow to learn. Is there a reason for this?" (Ex 7:14–10:28; Ex 4:21–23; 7:4–5 also discussed)**

At first reading one probably does find the account of the plagues "drawn out." On closer look, however, one can see the hand of a skilled craftsman in the story as it now stands, a blend of the J, E, and P traditions.

The cast of characters are God and his representatives, Moses and Aaron, against Pharaoh and his allies, the magicians. When the characters are seen in this configuration it is obvious why Pharaoh holds out so long. Pharaoh is pictured as God's adversary and is not easily defeated.

The arrangement which we now have is, as one might expect, a combination of traditions. Scripture scholars believe that the J tradition did not have plagues 3 and 6 (i.e., the gnats and the boils) while the P tradition did not have plagues 4, 5, 7, 8, and 9 (i.e., the flies, the pestilence, the hail, the locusts, and the darkness). Both J and P had plagues 1, 2, and 10 (the blood, the frogs and the death of the firstborn).

In this final editing the traditions have been combined in three groups of three, with the tenth plague standing alone.

The first plague in each group begins the same way. God tells Moses to rise early in the morning, to go to Pharaoh as he is going to the water, and to tell him that the God of the Hebrews says, "Let my people go" (Ex 7:16, 8:20; 9:13).

The second plague in each group still pictures Moses being sent

## STRUCTURE OF COMBINED TRADITIONS
## ABOUT THE PLAGUES

| | | |
|---|---|---|
| 1. Blood | 4. Flies | 7. Hail |
| 2. Frogs | 5. Pestilence | 8. Locusts |
| 3. Gnats | 6. Boils | 9. Darkness |

10. Death of firstborn

For the first plague in each group God tells Moses to rise early, go to Pharaoh as he is going to the water, and say, "Let my people go."

For the second plague in each group God tells Moses to go to Pharaoh.

For the third plague in each group Pharaoh is not to receive any warning.

to the Pharaoh to warn him, but there is no mention of the early morning hour.

The third plague in each group pictures God telling Moses and/or Aaron to cause a plague without the Pharaoh having received any warning at all.

In addition to this repetitive pattern there is some pattern to the gradual defeat of both the magicians and of Pharaoh himself. For the first two plagues the magicians seem as powerful as Moses and Aaron. They, too, can turn water to blood and can cause frogs to cover the land.

However, by the third plague the magicians are unable to duplicate the signs. When they cannot produce gnats they warn Pharaoh, "This is the finger of God" (Ex 8:19).

The magicians move from being ineffective to being victims of the plagues themselves. They, too, suffer from the boils of the sixth plague.

By the eighth plague Pharaoh's officials are begging him to let the Israelites go. "Let the people go so that they may worship the Lord their God; do you not yet understand that Egypt is ruined?" (Ex 10:7).

It is more difficult to see any progress in the defeat of the Pharaoh since each plague ends with the mention of Pharaoh's hardened heart. Nevertheless, one can see that Pharaoh is becoming more desperate, more willing to bargain. The Pharaoh moves from being unwilling to negotiate at all, to saying that the Israelites may sacrifice to their God as long as they don't leave the land (Ex 8:25), to saying that they may go as long as they don't take their children (Ex 10:10–11), to saying that they may go with their children but not with their livestock (Ex 10:24). The ninth plague ends with the Pharaoh telling Moses that if he sees Moses' face again Moses will die.

While all of this gradual buildup does result in dramatic tension, the reader is never really in doubt about what will happen. The omnipotent God had told Moses and Aaron exactly what would happen before any of these plagues occurred. "When Pharaoh does not listen to you, I will lay my hand upon Egypt and bring my people the Israelites, company by company, out of the land of Egypt, by great acts of judgment. The Egyptians shall know that I am the Lord, when I stretch out my hand against Egypt and bring the Israelites out from among them" (Ex 7:4–5).

More than suspense, the prolonged plagues build dread in the heart of the reader. For God had also told Moses ". . . I will harden his heart, so he will not let the people go. Then you shall say to Pharaoh, 'Thus says the Lord: Israel is my firstborn son. I said to you, "Let my son go that he may worship me." But you refused to let him go. Now I will kill your firstborn son' " (Ex 4:21–23).

The stage is set in all three traditions for the terrible last plague, the deaths of the firstborn, which will result in the Pharaoh summoning Moses and Aaron and begging them to leave quickly with their people and their herds (Ex 12:31–32). The Pharaoh has finally learned who really is God in Egypt.

## Review Questions

1. Why is Pharaoh pictured as holding out for so long?
2. What narrative characteristics allow us to say that the plagues are presented in three groups of three plagues each?
3. Is there a gradual change in the power of the magicians? Explain.
4. Why does the narrative build dread rather than suspense in the reader?

## Discussion Questions

1. Do you think God is more present in what we would call a "supernatural event" than in what we would call a "natural event"? Why or why not?
2. Do you know anyone who has had a total "change of heart," a real conversion? Was this a sudden or a gradual process? Explain.

# ARTICLE 9

# Appropriated Feasts

**Question: "Why is this long instruction about the Passover right in the middle of the account of the last plague?" (Ex 12:1–29; Ex 11:1–8; 12:29–39 also discussed)**

As you might suspect, the "long instruction about the Passover" is an insertion by the P editors, who are always interested in rubrics, into the middle of the J tradition's account of the announcement (Ex 11:1–8) and the fulfillment (Ex 12:29–39) of the last plague.

The description of the Passover celebration as it appears in the P tradition reveals the fact that two separate celebrations, which existed independently of Passover in the Israelites' culture, were later appropriated and assigned religious significance. These celebrations were reinterpreted to recall the Passover so that succeeding generations could remember and re-member ("once again join themselves to") God's mighty acts of salvation as they were experienced at the time of the exodus.

The first feast, the Passover, was a nomadic feast celebrated by shepherds before they passed over to their new spring pastures. During the first full moon they would have a meal, sacrifice an animal, and smear the blood of the sacrificed animal on the entrance to the tents. The intention behind this ceremony was to ward off any evil spirits who might affect adversely the fertility of the flock or the lives of the newborn sheep.

This ritual was appropriated and used to celebrate another passover, the passover in which the Israelites themselves were saved. The Passover meal was to be eaten with "loins girded, your sandals on your feet, and your staff in your hand" (Ex 12:11), the garb of shepherds ready to move to new fields, as well as the garb of the

142

---

### PRIESTLY EDITING TRADITION

*Cumulative Chart*

Dates to time after Babylonian exile (587–537 B.C.).

Called P after priests who did editing.

Uses genealogies as a structural device.

Responsible for "creation in six days" story.

Emphasizes that human beings are made in God's image, creation is good, God's blessing is coming to realization.

Uses repetitive formulas.

Emphasizes importance of circumcision.

Interest in God's promise of land, in God's justice as it relates to innocent people, and in the role of wisdom.

Adopts J's mighty signs to be used to persuade Pharaoh.

Interested in the tribe of Levi and the role of priests.

Interest in rubrics. Inserts Passover instructions.

Sees Israel as a worshipping people. Israel must, through liturgical celebrations, give witness to God's saving power.

---

Israelites ready to leave Egypt. The blood on the door posts was reinterpreted to recall the warding off of danger to Israel's firstborn. "For I will pass through the land of Egypt that night and I will strike down every firstborn in the land of Egypt, both human beings and animals; on all the gods of Egypt I will execute judgments: I am the Lord. The blood shall be a sign for you on the houses where you live: when I see the blood, I will pass over you, and no plague shall destroy you when I strike the land of Egypt" (Ex 12:12–13).

The second feast was an agricultural feast, also celebrated in the spring, to mark the first of the new spring harvest, the harvest of the barley crop. For seven days everyone was to eat bread newly made from the first crop. All of the previous harvest would be discarded, including old yeast. So the bread of the barley feast was always unleavened.

The Israelites would obviously not have celebrated this feast in the desert because they were not at that time farmers. However, when they became farmers they did celebrate this feast. This spring celebration was also eventually appropriated and integrated into the celebrations of Passover. We see this in the P tradition's instructions. "This day shall be a day of remembrance for you. You shall celebrate it as a festival to the Lord. Throughout your generations you shall observe it as a perpetual ordinance. Seven days you shall eat unleavened bread; on the first day you shall remove leaven from your houses, for whoever eats leavened bread from the first day until the seventh day shall be cut off from Israel" (Ex 12:14–15).

The connection of unleavened bread to the occasion of the Passover is a natural one. As the J tradition tells us, as the Israelites hurriedly departed from Egypt, "the people took their dough before it was leavened, with their kneading bowls wrapped up in their cloaks on their shoulders" (Ex 12:34).

Scripture scholars believe that by the seventh century both of these feasts had been integrated into the Passover celebration. Obviously the purpose of the celebration was to incorporate each succeeding generation into the exodus experience. This purpose is clearly stated as Moses is pictured giving instructions to the elders. "You shall observe this rite as a perpetual ordinance for you and your children. When you come to the land that the Lord will give you, as he has promised, you will keep this observance. And when your children ask you, 'What do you mean by this observance?' you shall say, 'It is the Passover sacrifice of the Lord, for he passed over the houses of the Israelites in Egypt, when he struck down the Egyptians but spared our houses' " (Ex 12:24–27).

By appropriating feasts, both nomadic and agricultural, and reinterpreting them so that they reminded each generation of the exodus experience, the Israelites were able to make their core experience present and effective in the lives of successive generations.

## Review Questions

1. From which tradition is the instruction about Passover taken?
2. As a nomadic feast, what did the Passover involve?
3. How were the garb and the blood from the nomadic feast reinterpreted to remind the Israelites of God's saving power?
4. Why was unleavened bread part of the feast involving the harvest of the barley crop?
5. How was the unleavened bread reinterpreted to remind people of the exodus experience?
6. By what century had these feasts been integrated into the Passover celebration?
7. What is the purpose of the Passover celebration?

## Discussion Questions

1. Can you think of agricultural celebrations that have been appropriated and reinterpreted in our Easter celebration? Name some.
2. Why do we celebrate Easter? Does our purpose compare to the Israelites' purpose in celebrating Passover? Explain.
3. Have you ever celebrated Passover? If so, what did the ceremony involve?
4. What is your favorite yearly celebration? Is the celebration a remembering and a re-membering? Explain.

# ARTICLE 10

# The Tenth Plague

**Question: "I just can't believe that God would be so cruel as to kill all the firstborn of the Egyptians in order to free the Israelites. Isn't it true that God made and loved the Egyptians too?" (Ex 11: 4–8, 29–30)**

This question is a very difficult one to handle but it is asked so often that we should do our best to respond. Our response will not be entirely satisfactory because we do not yet completely understand the mystery of suffering. Still we can offer some insights which may be of help to the questioner.

First, the questioner knows something which the J editor, whose account we are reading in Ex 11:4–8, 29–30, did not know. This is revealed by the question, "Isn't it true that God made and loved the Egyptians too?"

The time when the J tradition was being compiled (1000 B.C.) was a time of great national pride. In fact, the existence of the nation and the reign of the king had become the visible signs of the covenant relationship which the people understood they had with God. If someone had said to the J editor, "You know, God loves the Egyptians as much as God loves the Israelites," the J editor would have been sure that that person was wrong.

It was not until after the Babylonian exile (587–537 B.C.) that the Israelites started to come to terms with the fact that God loves other nations. So, as you read the account of this last plague, remember that you are reading an editor's point of view, not God's point of view.

We have noted in our previous article that the P editor, who

146

wrote from the point of view of 500–400 B.C., insists that the Passover be celebrated in a prescribed way. One might assume that the Passover had been celebrated according to these prescriptions all along from the time of the exodus. We noted, however, that the celebration prescribed by the P editor probably took shape in the seventh century B.C. This was a time of reform for the Israelites under King Josiah. One of Josiah's reforms was to reinstitute the Passover celebrations as the way of recalling God's covenant love. For some years this celebration had given way to feasts which celebrated the king and the temple. So it is perfectly evident that the concept of a "chosen nation" was central to the J tradition's concept of covenant love. The two were as one in the J tradition.

Are we saying, then, that the J tradition is not inspired, that it misrepresents God? Obviously, since the J tradition is in the canon it is and has been considered inspired for centuries. However, to say that the author is inspired is not to say that the author is all-knowing, that the author has a total grasp of God's mind and motives. Rather, it is to say that the author has some spiritual insights which speak to the actual experience of his people.

What was the experience? As we have already discussed, it is impossible to answer this question precisely when we read about the experience in the literary form, "legend." At the very least I think we could say this: A number of catastrophes occurred, including an epidemic, that were timed in such a way that the Israelites were able to leave Egypt.

Did the Israelites escape or were they expelled? Different traditions tell the story in different ways, but each tradition is told so that it is clear to the reader that the Israelites experienced the events as God saving them. This is the core religious experience. God saves.

Around this core experience we find what we always find in legends. We find dialogue which is the composition of the storyteller, not a direct quotation from God. We find exaggeration to emphasize a point: God, not Pharaoh, is God in Egypt. We find that the perspectives of the authors of the stories are bound by the centuries and the cultures within which they lived: J did not understand God's love for Egyptians. We find inconsistencies, since the legends from different traditions and different centuries are braided

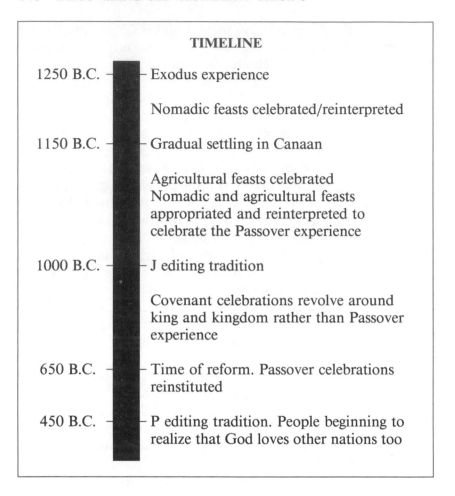

**TIMELINE**

1250 B.C. —— Exodus experience

Nomadic feasts celebrated/reinterpreted

1150 B.C. —— Gradual settling in Canaan

Agricultural feasts celebrated
Nomadic and agricultural feasts
appropriated and reinterpreted to
celebrate the Passover experience

1000 B.C. —— J editing tradition

Covenant celebrations revolve around
king and kingdom rather than Passover
experience

650 B.C. —— Time of reform. Passover celebrations
reinstituted

450 B.C. —— P editing tradition. People beginning to
realize that God loves other nations too

together. An example: Why, after nine plagues, were all the Egyptians so well-disposed toward Moses and the people? (See Ex 11:3.) The answer lies in the literary form, in the kind of writing we are reading, and not in the plot of the story.

Once we understand the limitations inherent in the J editor's perspective and we understand the characteristics of the literary form "legend" we still are left with the question, "Why would a loving God let all those people die?"

This is the question with which we still struggle. As New Testament people we have more insight into this question than did Old Testament authors, but we still struggle with the problem of suffering.

However, it still remains true that when people experience "a close call" and emerge unscathed they often say things which seem to reflect the J editor's limited point of view. For instance, a few years ago tornadoes went through our part of Kentucky. Lexington experienced very little damage while surrounding areas were devastated. One person said to me, "I think God saved Lexington." Is it possible to agree that God saved you without seeming to imply that God loves you more than God loves others who were adversely affected by what we would call "a natural disaster"?

Such questions bother us, but they didn't bother the J editor. The J editor's ancestors had experienced "being saved," and this experience continued to shape the self-concept of the nation.

## Review Questions

1. When did the Israelites start to realize that God loved other nations as much as God loved them?
2. How do we know that for the J editor the idea of "a chosen nation" was central to the idea of covenant love?
3. What might we be able to say about the core historical experience behind the story of the tenth plague? What can we say was the core religious experience?
4. Name four characteristics of these stories that reveal that we are reading legends.

## Discussion Questions

1. What does this statement mean: "To say that the J editor is inspired is not to say that the J editor is all-knowing"? Do you agree with this statement? Why or why not?
2. Why can we not define exactly what the Israelites experienced?
3. What does this statement mean: "As New Testament people we have more insight into the mystery of suffering than did the author of Exodus"? Do you agree with this statement? Why or why not?

# ARTICLE 11

# Israel: A Worshipping People

**Question: "What does it mean to say that the Israelites are to 'redeem' a firstborn son?" (Ex 13:13; Ex 13:1–16; Gen 22:1–19; Num 3:44–47 also discussed)**

To "redeem" a firstborn son meant to set him free by making an alternative sacrifice rather than killing him.

It was the tradition among many ancient people to offer to God the firstborn of both people and animals. However, the Israelites came to the realization that their God did not want child sacrifice. We see this realization dramatized in the story of the sacrifice of Isaac (Gen 22:1–19). In that story Abraham is pictured as at first understanding that God wanted him to sacrifice Isaac, but then coming to the realization that God did not want him to kill his son but to offer an animal, a ram, in place of the son.

In the Israelites' culture all firstborn males of both people and animals were understood to belong to God. Usually this fact would be ritualized by slaughtering the animal as a sacrifice to God. However, as we read here, a firstborn ass and a firstborn son were to be "redeemed."

The redemption of the firstborn son was accomplished in one of two ways: either through the dedication of the Levites to Yahweh (the Levites in this instance are the priests of the tribe of Levi), or through the offering of a sum of money.

We read about Yahweh giving instructions to Moses on how to redeem a firstborn son in the book of Numbers. "Then the Lord spoke to Moses, saying: 'Accept the Levites as substitutes for all the firstborn among the Israelites, and the livestock of the Levites as

⫞/⫝2

substitutes for their livestock; and the Levites shall be mine. I am the Lord. As the price of redemption of the two hundred seventy-three of the firstborn of the Israelites, over and above the number of the Levites, you shall accept five shekels apiece..." (Num 3:44-47).

This custom of offering the firstborn to Yahweh preceded the exodus experience. What we see here is that this custom is appropriated and redefined to remind the people of the exodus experience.

"When the Lord has brought you into the land of the Canaanites, as he swore to you and your ancestors, and has given it to you, you shall set apart to the Lord all that first opens the womb. . . . Every firstborn male among your children you shall redeem. When in the future your child asks you, 'What does this mean?' you shall answer, 'By strength of hand the Lord brought us out of Egypt, from the house of slavery . . ." (Ex 13:11-12,14).

Notice that inserted in this instruction to redeem the firstborn in remembrance of the Passover (Ex 13:1-2, 11-16) is a repetition of P's instructions to celebrate the feast of unleavened bread as a Passover celebration (Ex 13:3-10). We already know that this agricultural feast developed after the time of the exodus, when the Israelites became farmers, and was later appropriated and redefined as a Passover celebration.

We see in these passages, and in the P editor's earlier insertions of Passover instructions into the middle of the account of the last plague, that the P tradition incorporates rituals that developed much later into the accounts of events. In other words, as we read about an event we also read of the liturgical celebration of the event which developed long after the event.

With this observation we key in on a characteristic of the P tradition that will become more and more evident as we continue to read the book of Exodus. The P tradition views Israel as a worshipping people. For P this is the reason Israel has been chosen by God. As chosen people Israel must, through liturgical celebrations, give witness to God's redemption of God's firstborn, the nation Israel, by recalling and reclaiming God's saving action as it was experienced in the exodus and is celebrated in the Passover liturgies.

## Review Questions

1. What did "to redeem" a firstborn son mean to the Israelites?
2. In what two ways might a firstborn son be redeemed?
3. How was the sacrifice of the firstborn appropriated and redefined after the exodus experience?
4. From the point of view of the P tradition, why has Israel been chosen by God?
5. What duty rests on the Israelites because they have been chosen by God?

## Discussion Questions

1. Why do you think Abraham thought that he should sacrifice Isaac? Do you think there are ideas in our culture which you have accepted as pleasing to God which in fact are not? Can you think of any?
2. What does this sentence mean: "As we read about an event we also read of the liturgical celebration of that event which developed long after the event"? Do you think anything of a similar nature might be present in the New Testament accounts of the last supper?
3. Do you think we are a worshipping people? Why or why not? Do you think we should be? Why or why not?

# ARTICLE 12

# "What Happened?" "God Saved!"

**Question: "What actually happened at the Red Sea? This miracle that Moses worked is really amazing!" (Ex 14:10–30; Ex 13:17–22 also discussed)**

Oh, dear. With this question we are right back to square one. However, despite all that already has been learned about the characteristics of legends and the effects on the narrative of the interweaving of several traditions, this question inevitably comes up. So, it seems best to answer it as best we can.

First, scholars think the "Red Sea" should be translated as the "Reed Sea." The Hebrew words are *Yam Suph*. *Yam* means a sea or inland body of water. *Suph* means "reed" or "papyrus." The words have been translated "Red Sea" since the time of the Septuagint (a Greek translation of the Old Testament begun around 250 B.C.) and reached our English translations through the Vulgate (Jerome's Latin translation, based on the Septuagint, and dating to A.D. 383–384). One need only glance at a map to see that the Red Sea would not have been on the described route.

Scripture scholars debate about the description of the route as it appears in Exodus 13:17–22. Some of the cities mentioned seem to support a northern route. However, the accounts of the crossing of the Reed Sea and the arrival at Sinai demand a southern route (see map). Perhaps some took a northern route and their tradition has not been completely lost. However, our interest will remain with those who took a southern route under the leadership of Moses.

What actually happened when this group reached the Reed Sea? Obviously we cannot speak of the event except as we understand it

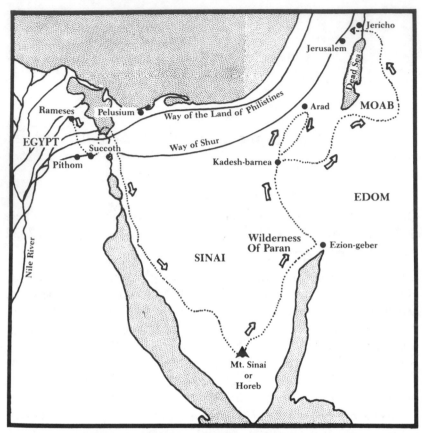

**The Traditional Exodus Escape Route**

through the eyes of those who have passed on the traditional stories. We can say that the core event was an overwhelming experience of God's saving power. Notice, we are not speaking of an experience in which the Israelites felt that they were fighting for God. Rather, the Israelites felt that God was fighting for them. Moses says exactly this when he tries to calm the Israelites' fear. "Do not be afraid, stand firm, and see the deliverance that the Lord will accomplish for you today; for the Egyptians whom you see today you shall never see again. The Lord will fight for you, and you have only to keep still (Ex 14:13–14).

We have a description of this overwhelming experience of God's saving power from several traditions. By comparing the J and P traditions we can grow in our understanding of the literary form we are reading, "legends."

While each tradition understands the crossing of the Reed Sea as God's direct action on Israel's behalf, the J tradition uses less "marvelous" details in its description. In the J tradition God uses wind and tide to save the Israelites. ". . . The Lord drove the sea back by a strong east wind all night, and turned the sea into dry land. . . . at dawn the sea returned to its normal depth" (Ex 14:21b; 27b).

The P tradition, into which details from J have been inserted, uses much more marvelous imagery to describe the event. In P Moses raises his hand to divide the water, and raises his hand again, causing the waters to drown the Egyptians. "Then Moses stretched out his hand over the sea . . . and the waters were divided. The Israelites went into the sea, on dry ground, the waters forming a wall for them on their right and on their left" (Ex 14:21a, 22) . . . "Then the Lord said to Moses, 'Stretch out your hand over the sea, so that the water may come back upon the Egyptians, upon their chariots and chariot drivers.' The waters returned and covered the chariots and the chariot drivers . . ." (Ex 14:26, 28a).

What really happened at the Reed Sea? J tells us exactly what happened, although this is probably not the answer for which the questioner was looking. This is what happened: "The Lord saved Israel that day from the Egyptians. . . . Israel saw the great work that the Lord did against the Egyptians. So the people feared the Lord and believed in the Lord and in his servant Moses" (Ex 14:30–31).

## Review Questions

1. What do scholars believe would be a correct translation of the "Red" Sea?
2. What is the Septuagint?
3. What is the Vulgate?
4. What route did Moses and his group take?
5. How do the J and P traditions differ in their descriptions of the Red Sea incident?
6. What really happened at the Reed Sea?

## Discussion Questions

1. Why does the question with which this article begins put us back to square one?
2. What is the difference between believing that you are fighting for God, and believing that God is fighting for you? Which do you think is the better "spiritual posture"? Why?
3. Have you ever had a personal experience in which you knew God was involved? Have you ever tried to explain this experience to someone else? If so, were you successful in communicating the meaning of the experience? Explain.

# ARTICLE 13

# A Song of Praise and Thanksgiving

**Question: "Isn't this poem out of place? (Ex 15:1–18) It makes it sound like the people are already settled in Canaan." (Ex 15:13–18)**

The poem has been placed here, as a conclusion to the account of the marvelous escape through the Reed Sea, because the first part of the poem (Ex 15:1–12) is a song of thanksgiving in response to God's mighty action on Israel's behalf. However, the questioner is right in pointing out that the second half of the poem (Ex 15:13–18) praises God for leading the people to Canaan.

Scholars date the bulk of this poem to the period after the Israelites had reached Canaan (1200 B.C.) but before the establishment of the monarchy (1000 B.C.). This would place the bulk of the poem during the period of the Judges, thus predating the oldest tradition which we have so far identified, the J tradition which dates to the time of the kingdom (1000 B.C.).

Perhaps even older than the bulk of the poem is the "refrain" which is repeated after the poem and attributed to Miriam. "Sing to the Lord, for he has triumphed gloriously; horse and rider he has thrown into the sea" (Ex 15:21). Scholars suggest that these might be the oldest lines in the Bible. They could well date to the time immediately after the event.

One way in which scholars date passages is to look at the imagery which is used. An image is "a mental representation of something not present to the senses." Two common types of images are similes and metaphors. Each of these is a comparison. A simile describes something by a comparison which uses the words "like" or

---

**TIMELINE FOR SONG**

| 1250 B.C. | Refrain |
|-----------|---------|
| 1150 B.C. | Poem |
| 1000 B.C. | J editing tradition |

---

"as," as in, "God is like a mighty warrior." A metaphor also is a comparison, but it does not use the words "like" or "as." The comparison is implied by a statement such as, "God is a mighty warrior."

So, in our examples, the words "mighty warrior" are used as an image of God. However, I might also describe God as a "king," as a "loving Father," as a "nuturing mother," or as a "knowing friend." To some extent, the image one chooses says something about God, but it also says something about the person who chose the image and about the times in which that person lives.

Notice that in this poem it is the image "warrior" which is used:

> The Lord is a warrior;
> The Lord is his name (Ex 15:3).

This warrior God is pictured almost as we would imagine a dragon:

---

**SIMILES AND METAPHORS:**
**COMPARISONS WHICH USE IMAGES**

**Simile:** A comparison that uses "like" or "as."
*Example:* God is like a mighty warrior.

**Metaphor:** A comparison that does not use "like" or "as."
*Example:* God is a mighty warrior.

---

> At the blast of your nostrils the waters piled up,
>     the floods stood up in a heap;
>     the deeps congealed in the heart of the sea (Ex 15:8).

This warrior God uses the wind as his weapon:

> You blew with your wind, the sea covered them;
>     they sank like lead in the mighty waters (Ex 15:10).

In addition to picturing God as a warrior, the poem pictures the land to which God led the people as God's holy "mountain":

> You brought them in and planted them on the
>     mountain of your own possession,
>     the place, O Lord, that you made your abode,
>     the sanctuary, O Lord, that your hands have
>     established (Ex 15:17).

This mountain is not Mount Sinai, about which we hear nothing in the poem. Nor is the "sanctuary" the temple which had not yet been built. Rather, this "mountain" is an image, a way of conceptualizing the place where God dwells.

Both the image of the "holy mountain" and of the "warrior God" who defeats his enemies with a storm help to date the poem. The imagery reflects the ways of "imaging" the power and presence of gods in the Canaanite culture.

However, the Israelites' God is superior to those other gods:

> Who is like you, O Lord, among the gods?
> Who is like you, majestic in holiness;
>     awesome in splendor, doing wonders? (Ex 15:11).

By proclaiming God's mighty works the Israelites are thanking and praising God for choosing them as God's own, for saving them from their enemies, and for leading them to the promised land.

## Review Questions

1. To what period in Israel's history do scholars date the poem in Exodus 15:1–18?
2. What lines do scholars think might be the oldest in the Bible?
3. What is an "image"?
4. What is a simile? A metaphor?
5. What image for God is used in this poem?
6. What image is used for the promised land?
7. Why do these images help to date the poem?

## Discussion Questions

1. Do you have a favorite image of God? If so, what is it?
2. Do your images of God date you in any way? Explain.
3. Have your images of God changed in your lifetime? Explain.

# ARTICLE 14

# Learning to Trust God's Providence

**Question: "Why were the people allowed to gather only enough manna for one day? Was it because it spoiled? If so why didn't it spoil before the Sabbath?" (Ex 16:4–35; Ex 15:26 also discussed)**

Although the P tradition does say that the manna spoiled if stored (Ex 16:21), this fact is not the primary reason behind God's being pictured as saying, "I will now rain down bread from heaven for you. Each day the people are to go out and gather their daily portion . . ." (Ex 16:4a).

In order to answer the question we will first describe the experience which lies at the core of the story. Then we will sort out how, in interpreting the experience, various traditions emphasize various themes.

Scholars believe that while the Israelites were in the desert they avoided starvation by eating quail and manna. Quail was a possible food supply because these birds would be completing their migration from Europe in the area where the Israelites were camped. Because of the quail's fatigue they could be caught.

Manna is a substance which drops from tamarisk trees due to the fact that two insects who live in the trees suck a sweet substance from the tree. Their secretions drop from the tree and harden. This substance has a sweet taste and is considered a delicacy. So the manna is provided daily.

The Israelites, as we have already discussed, did not make the distinction we make between natural and supernatural. They looked, rather, at events as signs of God's power and presence in their lives. So the Israelites understood that God had provided the quail and the manna for their daily food.

Given this core experience, various traditions recount the story in order to emphasize a variety of theological points of view. The J tradition's main interest seems to be to emphasize the fact that God can be trusted to take care of God's people. God's providence was seen in God's mighty acts at the Reed Sea, but it is also experienced in God's daily nurturing, in God's concern that people have water and food.

Notice that the people grumble. They ask, "What shall we drink?" (Ex 15:24) and charge Moses, "If only we had died by the hand of the Lord in the land of Egypt, when we sat by the fleshpots and ate our fill of bread; for you have brought us out into this wilderness to kill this whole assembly with hunger" (Ex 16:3).

This grumbling doesn't sound like it should be coming from the people who saw God's mighty saving acts at the Reed Sea. The people seem almost like Pharaoh in their constant turning away from God. Yet as the traditions are now combined, God's response to this grumbling is not punishment but provision. "Then the Lord said to Moses, 'I am going to rain bread from heaven for you . . .' " (Ex 16:4). The J tradition seems to be the tradition that tells the story so as to emphasize God's providence.

The P tradition, on the other hand, continues its constant interest in the Sabbath observance. You may remember that the P tradition made Sabbath observance central in its creation story, the creation of the world in six days, by saying that even God rested on the Sabbath (Gen 1:1–2:4).

It is the P editor who says that the manna spoiled when gathered in quantity during the week but did not spoil when gathered in quantity before the Sabbath (Ex 16:24). In P's account the "bread from heaven" fell on other days, but it did not fall on the sabbath. "Moses said, 'Eat it today, for today is a sabbath to the Lord; today you will not find it in the field. Six days you shall gather it; but on the seventh day, which is a sabbath, there will be none' " (Ex 16:25–26). In other words, the P editor pictures even God as resting on the sabbath as a way of teaching the importance of sabbath observance.

Still a third emphasis has appeared in these first stories of trials in the desert. Rather than emphasizing God's gracious care or the importance of ritual, this source emphasizes the importance of

## TIMELINE

| | | |
|---|---|---|
| | 1850 B.C. — | Abraham experiences God's call<br>Isaac<br>Jacob<br>Joseph |
| | | Slavery in Egypt |
| | 1250 B.C. — | Moses and the exodus |
| Time of J<br>Editing<br>Tradition | 1000 B.C. — | Period of the Judges<br>Saul<br>David<br>Solomon |
| | 922 B.C. — | Kingdom divides |
| Time of E<br>Editing<br>Tradition | | Prophets call the people to<br>fidelity |
| Time of D<br>Editing<br>Tradition | 721 B.C. — | Northern kingdom falls to<br>Assyrians |
| | 630 B.C. — | Josiah's reform |
| | 587 B.C. — | Southern kingdom falls.<br>Beginning of Babylonian exile |
| Time of P<br>Editing<br>Tradition | 537 B.C. — | Cyrus, a Persian, conquers the<br>Babylonians and lets the<br>Israelites return to the holy land |
| | 450 B.C. — | Time of reinterpretations in the<br>light of events |

obedience. "He (the Lord) said, 'If you will listen carefully to the voice of the Lord your God, and do what is right in his sight, and give heed to his commandments and keep all his statutes, I will not bring upon you any of the diseases that I brought upon the Egyptians, for I am the Lord who heals you' " (Ex 15:26).

The point of view expressed in this verse perfectly represents the point of view of a tradition which we have not yet mentioned but which will become increasingly important as we read I and II Samuel. This view is attributed to the "Deuteronomic" historian who taught that obedience to God's law is rewarded with victory and prosperity, while disobedience is punished by failure and suffering. We will have much to say about this tradition in articles to come.

In our present account, though, the traditions of J and P are still predominant, and their emphases on God's provident care and on the importance of ritual dominate the accounts of these first desert trials.

## Review Questions

1. How did the Israelites avoid starvation while in the desert?
2. What is manna? How is it provided daily?
3. What is the emphasis in the J tradition's recounting of the experience?
4. How does God respond to the people's grumbling?
5. What interest is emphasized in the P tradition?
6. What third point of view appears in Exodus 15:26? What tradition consistently maintains this point of view?

## Discussion Questions

1. Are you aware of relying on God's daily care? Explain.
2. Do you think some life-styles make a person more aware of our dependence on God than do others? For instance: farmers as compared to office workers? Explain.
3. When you pray, "Give us this day our daily bread," what do you mean?

# ARTICLE 15

# God's Power Present in Moses

**Question: "What theological purpose lies behind the description of Moses having to keep his hands up in order for the Israelites to defeat Amalek?" (Ex 17:8–13; Ex 17:1–7; 18:21–22 also discussed)**

This is a good question. Notice that the questioner understands the literary form. Otherwise she would have asked, "Why was it necessary for Moses to keep his hands up in order for the Israelites to defeat Amalek?" The questioner is not assuming that the intent of the author is to teach history. Rather the assumption is that the intent of the author is to teach something about God.

What about God is being taught? As you may have guessed, the account of the battle against Amalek belongs to the J tradition. As you may remember, it was the J tradition which introduced the staff as a mighty sign of God's presence. In J the staff was to be used to persuade the Israelites that God was with Moses. Here the staff is used to show that God is still with Moses, and through Moses God is with the Israelites.

You may also remember that it is the J editor who tells the story of the Israelites' time in the desert in such a way that it emphasizes God's constant providential care. We see this emphasis maintained in this incident as it was in the scene which immediately preceded the battle with Amalek.

In this previous scene (Ex 17:1–7) the people are murmuring against Moses, and therefore against God. God does not punish the people but responds by fulfilling their need for water. The incident is told not as a test of the people but as a test of God's nurturing presence. As the J tradition says, ". . . the Israelites quarreled and tested the Lord, saying, 'Is the Lord among us or not?' " (Ex 17:7).

In addition to emphasizing God's saving power the story of the battle with Amalek pictures Moses as a chosen person who cannot do the job alone. Moses' arms grow so tired that he is unable to continue to hold them up by himself. "But Moses' hands grew weary; so they took a stone and put it under him, and he sat on it. Aaron and Hur held up his hands, one to one side, and the other on the other side; so his hands were steady until the sun set" (Ex 17:12). Moses is God's chosen instrument, but Moses needs help.

The fact that Moses needs help is central to the story which we read next in which Jethro, Moses' father-in-law, comes to Moses with Moses' wife and two sons. The day after their arrival Jethro offers Moses some advice. Seeing Moses involved in judging disputes from morning until night Jethro says, ". . . you should also look for able men among all the people, men who fear God, are trustworthy, and hate dishonest gain; set such men over them as officers over thousands, hundreds, fifties and tens. Let them sit as judges for the people at all times; let them bring every important case to you, but decide every minor case themselves. So it will be easier for you, and they will bear the burden with you" (Ex 18:21–22).

Scholars believe that this episode from the E tradition pictures a division of authority that occurred long after Moses but was later attributed to Moses. We will see that attribution of later laws and distributions of authority to Moses is common as we continue to read Exodus.

By attributing later developments to Moses the same theological purpose is served as by describing the battle with Amalek as progressing only when Moses' arms are raised. Both the attribution and the description of raised arms are narrative techniques used to tie the action to God. God defeats Amalek and God's authority is present in the division of authority among the judges. As Moses says, ". . . the people come to me to inquire of God. . . . I make known to them the statutes and instructions of God" (Ex 18: 15, 16b).

In the person of Moses God's power and presence are experienced, just as they were at the Reed Sea and in the manna, quail and water. Through God's servant, Moses, God's provident care remains with God's people.

## Review Questions

1. What theological purpose is behind the account of Moses and his staff?
2. Who is being tested in the story of the people needing water in Exodus 17:7? Explain.
3. What is signified by the fact that Moses' arms got so tired?
4. What suggestion does Jethro give Moses?
5. Why are later developments attributed to Moses?

## Discussion Questions

1. Have you ever wanted to "test" God? Why might someone want to test God? Explain.
2. In your experience have you observed that even God's chosen instruments are dependent on others for help? Explain. Do you think this dependence is a good thing or not? Explain.
3. Do you think it is "honest" to attribute later developments to Moses? Explain.

# ARTICLE 16

# A Chosen People

**Question: "What does God mean when God says, '. . . You (the Israelites) shall be my treasured possession out of all the peoples. Indeed the whole earth is mine, but you shall be for me a priestly kingdom and a holy nation' (Ex 19:5b–6). It sounds as though God loves Israel more than other nations."**

First let us reword this question to take into account what we have learned about literary form. We know we aren't reading exact quotations from God. So the question becomes, "What does the biblical author/editor mean when he pictures God as saying . . .?"

Scripture scholars do not assign these beautiful verses (Ex 19:3b–6) to P, J, or E, but to an independent source. The words are a poetic reflection on the theological meaning of the experience of the Israelites at Sinai, an experience which we will be reading about throughout the rest of the book of Exodus.

You may remember that Moses experienced his call to become God's chosen instrument at Sinai (Ex 3). Now we begin to read how the people as a whole received a similar call. The Israelites are chosen to perform a particular role in God's plan for the human race.

In this theological reflection on the meaning of the call, the biblical author uses the image of a covenant, an image which we discussed at length in Article 13 of the Genesis articles when we read that God entered into a covenant with Abraham.

We see once more that the covenant involves mutual obligations. God is pictured as saying that Israel will be God's treasured possession, "if you obey my voice and keep my covenant" (Ex 19:5a). If the Israelites agree to the covenant they will be "a priestly

168

kingdom and a holy nation." In other words, they will have the function among nations that priests have within the nation. They will become a worshipping people through whom God's will is made manifest.

This theological reflection is used to introduce the J and E traditions regarding the "theophany," that is, regarding God's self-manifestation to the Israelites at Sinai. This experience is the absolute core of the Israelites' self-understanding. Everything which occurred before Sinai and everything that will occur in the future will be seen in the light of this experience.

Structurally, the account of this experience is the core of the Pentateuch (the first five books of the Old Testament). Israel will remain camped at Sinai from Exodus 19:1 to Numbers 10:10.

As we read the two traditions of God's self-revelation we will see that the holiness of God is emphasized in every detail. First, the people must be "consecrated." In preparation they must wash all their clothes and abstain from sexual relationships.

The people must not get too close to the mountain, otherwise they must die. This reflects a tradition seen often in the Old Testament that God is so holy that no one can actually see God and live through the experience.

God's holiness is also emphasized by the imagery selected by both the J and E traditions to represent God's presence on the mountain. The J tradition uses fire, smoke, and the whole mountain shaking, imagery that reminds us of a volcano. The E tradition uses the images of storm and thunder.

Still another detail which emphasizes God's holiness is the fact that neither the people nor the priests are to come up the mountain, only Moses with Aaron as his assistant (see Ex 19:24).

These details and images are chosen in order to describe the awesomeness of the original experience as well as to emphasize God's total power, transcendence and holiness. They are in sharp contrast to the image with which this chapter began in which God is pictured as saying, "I bore you on eagles' wings and brought you to myself" (Ex 19:4b).

The fearsome images and the gentle images are both "true." They both represent the Israelites' understanding of Yahweh as

## YAHWIST EDITING TRADITION

*Cumulative Chart*

Dates to time of monarchy (1000 B.C.).

Refers to God as Yahweh throughout narrative.

Called J rather than Y because German scholars identified source and German word for Yahweh in *Jahve.*

Pictures God anthropomorphically.

Emphasizes growth in sinfulness of human race but offers hope.

Moses' objection: Suppose they don't believe me? Rod turns to snake . . . Aaron.

Appropriates and reinterprets folklore (i.e., Moses and Zipporah).

Israel is a chosen nation (Egypt is not).

Wind and tide at exodus experience.

God nurtures his people by providing water and food in desert. Emphasis is on God's providence.

God's presence on Sinai represented by fire, smoke, whole mountain shaking.

---

**ELOHIST EDITING TRADITION**

*Cumulative Chart*

Developed in north after division of kingdom (922 B.C.).

Calls God "Elohim" until time of Sinai revelation so referred to as E.

Appears most often in doublets.

Exhibits moral sensitivity.

God's presence is mediated by angels, dreams, etc.

Deemphasizes kings in favor of prophets.

Describes characters as having "fear of God."

Big emphasis on scene in which God reveals self as "I Am."

Attributes division of authority that came later to Moses.

At Sinai God's presence represented by storm and thunder.

---

they came to know Yahweh, not only in their experience of being chosen at Sinai but also in their reflection on the experience in the following centuries.

**Review Questions**

1. What is a covenant?
2. What obligation rests on covenant people?
3. For what function has Israel been chosen?

4. What does "theophany" mean?
5. What is the Pentateuch?
6. What was the core experience of the Israelite people?
7. What must the people do in preparation for the theophany? Why?
8. What images are used by the J and E traditions to represent God's presence? What do these images signify?


## Discussion Questions

1. Do you feel chosen? Explain.
2. Do you more often think of God as powerful and transcendent or as gentle and immanent? Explain.
3. Are we a priestly people? Explain. Do we act as though we are? Explain.
4. Have you had a "core" experience that defines who you understand yourself to be? Explain.

# ARTICLE 17

# Law: The Social Expression of Covenant Love

**Question: "Some of these laws seem completely out of place. Why would God be giving the people laws about their fields and vineyards (Ex 22:5–6) while they are still in the desert?" (Ex 20:1–17; 20:22–23:19; 24:1–11 also discussed)**

You may remember that in Article 15 we read about a division of authority (Ex 18:13–27) that scholars think occurred long after Moses, but which is later attributed to Moses. The purpose of the attribution was a theological one: Moses represented God's authority. To attribute the action to Moses was to express the belief that the action reflected God's will.

The laws which we now read in the setting of the Sinai theophany are not in this setting as an historical claim that all the laws received were received in 1200 B.C. Rather, the laws which developed after the people reached Canaan, and up to the beginning of the kingdom, are included as a way of expressing the belief that the laws are the social expression of covenant love. To obey the law is to be faithful to the covenant relationship between God and God's people.

Two sets of laws appear in this Sinai setting. The first set consists of the ten commandments (Ex 20:1–17). The form of the ten commandments represents a kind of law called apodictic law. In apodictic law a command is imposed on a person, directing that person to do or to refrain from doing a specified action.

Although the command which is stated in apodictic law could be expressed in the third person or in the second person, the ten commandments are expressed in the second person. God is pictured as

173

---

**KINDS OF LAW**

**Apodictic Law:** Command imposed on a person to do or not do a specified action.

**Case Law:** Command imposed on a judge to render a certain punishment for a given action.

---

addressing each individual Israelite directly: "You shall," or "You shall not." In other words, the law is based on the personal relationship between Yahweh and his people. Not only the way one treats Yahweh but the way one treats other people is an expression of covenant love.

Notice that this "direct address" is present not only in the "second person" formula but in the narrative itself. Despite the fact that God's holiness demands that the people cannot see God, the ten commandments are presented as having been spoken by God to all the people. The people's reaction is fear. They say to Moses, "You speak to us and we will listen; but do not let God speak to us; or we will die" (Ex 20:19). The people are then pictured as standing at a distance while only Moses hears the other laws.

This second collection of laws is called the Covenant Code or the book of the Covenant (Ex 20:22–23:19). While one part of the Covenant Code is apodictic in form, most of the Covenant Code is an example of case law. Instead of obliging each individual to behave in a certain way, case law obliges a judge to render a certain punishment for a given action. Case law says, "If such and such occurs, then this is what should happen." As our questioner noted, this law dates to the time when Israel had left the desert and had settled in the land.

The Covenant Code includes laws regarding slaves, offenses which will result in the death penalty, directions as to the proper punishment for bodily injury and property damage, social laws and religious laws. The fact that all of these laws are seen in the context of covenant love is perfectly evident.

## Steps in the Interpretation of the Image Covenant

| | Mutual Responsibilities | | (Abstract beliefs become embodied and take on material, concrete expression in rituals, institutions, people, etc.) |
|---|---|---|---|
| *Experience* Abraham experiences God's call | *God* Will give protection, land, and descendants | *The People* Will have faith and obey | *Signs* ■ Rite of cut animals ■ Circumcision ■ Isaac |
| *Experience* | *Mutual Responsibilities* | | *Signs* |
| God leads Moses and his people through the exodus experience | *God* Will give protection, a nation—the sense of na tion, an extension of land and descendants, grew through the exodus experience | *The People* Will have faith, and obey the commandments | ■ Circumcision ■ Passover meal— to remember that the lamb's blood had given life ■ Covenant ceremonies—the sacred meal and the animal sacrifice ■ Ark of the covenant |

Notice, for example, that if someone has been trusted with another's property during the time when that property is stolen, the person entrusted with the property must be brought "before God" (Ex 22:8) to determine whether or not that person has stolen the property himself. No matter what human judge is involved, the real judge is God.

Notice, too, that God is pictured as being on the side of those who are most vulnerable in society. Abuse to a widow or orphan is a particular offense against God (Ex 22:21–24).

Covenant love even affects the way one must treat an enemy. Should an enemy's ox or donkey be found, it must be returned (see Ex 23:4–5).

The account of all the laws in the book of the Covenant is followed by two covenant rituals. In one, representatives of the people ritualize the covenant through a sacred meal (Ex 24:1–2, 9–11). In the second the people themselves participate in a ritual involving animal sacrifice (Ex 24:3–8). While in the first account no mention is made that the covenant demands the peoples' obedience, the necessity for obedience is directly stated in the second account. "Moses came and told the people all the words of the Lord and all the ordinances and all the people answered with one voice, and said, "All the words that the Lord has spoken we will do" (Ex 24:3).

Moses then takes the blood of the sacrificed animals and dabs half of it on the altar and half on the people, an action which symbolizes the shared life between God and the Israelites. Moses then says, "See the blood of the covenant that the Lord has made with you in accordance with all these words" (Ex 24:8). The "Words," the laws, are integral to the covenant relationship. One cannot be in right relationship with Yahweh and not be in right relationship with one's neighbor.

### Review Questions

1. What belief is expressed by picturing laws that developed later as revealed at Sinai?
2. What is apodictic law? Give an example.

3. What belief is reflected by the fact that the ten commandments are in the second person?
4. Who is pictured as receiving the ten commandments?
5. What is the second collection of laws called?
6. What is case law? Give an example.
7. Who is bound by case law?
8. Give some examples that show that the laws are understood to be in the context of covenant love.
9. How do the two covenant rituals differ?

### Discussion Questions

1. Do you regard church law as an expression of God's will? State law? Any law? Explain.
2. Do you believe that the way you treat every other person affects your relationship with God? Explain.
3. Do you believe that God is on the side of the most vulnerable? If so, why do you believe this?
4. What is our covenant renewal ceremony? Does it have anything in common with the two ceremonies described in Exodus 24:1–11?

# ARTICLE 18

# God Dwells Among God's People

**Question: "Why are all these minute directions given about every-
thing? (Ex 25–30) Do you think God really cares?"**

The minute directions are given by the P tradition. First we need
to see why they are important to that tradition. Once we understand the reason for their importance in that context we can better
take a stab at the second question, "Do you think God really cares?"

You may remember that we previously had reason to note that
the P tradition sees God's chosen people as a worshipping people.
We noticed this when we saw that the P tradition incorporated
rituals that developed later into the accounts of the Passover events.
The liturgical celebrations which developed later were placed in the
Sinai setting as a way of demonstrating their connectedness to the
redeeming acts of Yahweh.

In these chapters (Ex 25–30) we once again see the P tradition
link the cultic practices of the Israelites to the Sinai setting, not as a
claim that they all originated there, but as a way of emphasizing
their underlying importance. Just as Yahweh was present on
Mount Sinai, so is Yahweh present in the cultic practices of the
worshipping people. Yahweh is a God who dwells in the midst of
the people.

The P tradition explains this underlying purpose in the introduction to the instructions. Before Moses is pictured as receiving any of
these instructions he goes up to the mountain. "The glory of the
Lord settled on Mount Sinai and the cloud covered it for six
days . . ." (Ex 24:16).

It is in order to house, celebrate and worship this presence of the

178

living God, that all the instructions about the furnishings for the dwelling, the dwelling itself, its priests, their functions, the choice of the craftsmen, and the observance of the sabbath are given.

The tent, or dwelling of the Lord, is described as a portable structure within which are curtains which separate various sections, one from another: the Holy of Holies, the Holy, and the court outside. The tent does not sound very portable to us, partially because its design is influenced by later sanctuaries. This desert dwelling is described as one-half the size of Solomon's temple.

However, it would be a mistake to think that P's description of the dwelling has nothing in common with the actual desert sanctuary. In fact, scholars think P's description is partially based on descriptions of the tent in which the Canaanite god, El, was said to dwell. To some extent P is picturing the Israelites as adapting and reinterpreting the religious customs of the contemporary Canaanite culture.

The ark of the covenant was most probably housed in the tent. It was a wooden box which contained the stone tablets on which were written the ten commandments. The propitiatory was a gold plate on the top of the ark. The ark and propitiatory were God's dwelling place. "There I will meet you and there, from above the propitiatory, between the two cherubim on the ark of the commandments, I will tell you all the commands that I wish you to give the Israelites" (Ex 25:22).

The P tradition goes on to describe the investiture of priests and the sacrifices which the priests will offer. Once again, some of what is described is a later development, but by describing these later developments as having occurred at Sinai the P tradition is teaching that the "glory of God" continues to dwell with God's people through these ceremonies.

The theological intent of the P tradition is clearly stated. "I will meet with the Israelites there (at the tent), and it shall be sanctified by my glory; I will consecrate the tent of meeting and the altar; Aaron also and his sons I will consecrate, to serve me as priests. I will dwell among the Israelites, and I will be their God. And they shall know that I am the Lord their God, who brought them out of the land of Egypt that I might dwell among them; I am the Lord their God" (Ex 30:43–46).

## PRIESTLY EDITING TRADITION

### *Cumulative Chart*

Dates to time after Babylonian exile (587–537 B.C.).

Called P after priests who did editing.

Uses genealogies as a structural device.

Responsible for "creation in six days" story.

Emphasizes that human beings are made in God's image, creation is good, God's blessing is coming to realization.

Uses repetitive formulas.

Emphasizes importance of circumcision.

Interest in God's promise of land, in God's justice as it relates to innocent people, and in the role of wisdom.

Adopts J's mighty signs to be used to persuade Pharaoh.

Interested in the tribe of Levi and the role of priests.

Interest in rubrics. Inserts Passover instructions.

Sees Israel as a worshipping people. Israel must, through liturgical celebrations, give witness to God's saving power.

Moses performs marvelous works at exodus.

Interest in sabbath appears in story of manna.

Includes all the instructions about the "dwelling," priests, etc. Emphasis on God choosing to dwell with God's people.

For the P tradition, the great significance of the Sinai event is not the Sinai covenant, a tradition which comes from the J and E sources. Rather, it is the personal relationship which God initiates with God's people (see Ex 6:3), and the fact that God chooses to "tent," to "tabernacle," to "dwell" with God's people.

Yahweh's presence with the community is ritualized through the institutions which are part and parcel of religion. Thus the specific instructions as to dimensions, garments, ceremonies, etc., all serve a single purpose, to enable the chosen people to understand themselves as a holy people who exist to give witness and worship to God.

"Does God really care?" our questioner asks. Once one understands the purpose of the details one can certainly affirm that God does care, if not about exact measurements at least about the P tradition's purpose in passing on such specific details. The P tradition reemphasizes this purpose as it once more teaches the importance of the sabbath. "You shall keep my sabbath, for this is a sign between me and you throughout your generations, given in order that you may know that I, the Lord, sanctify you" (Ex 31:13). God certainly cares that the people know that God has made them and that God has made them holy.

### Review Questions

1. Which tradition gives us all this detail about ritual?
2. How does this tradition see God's people?
3. Why are cultic practices that originated later placed in the Sinai setting?
4. What is the tent?
5. What is the ark of the covenant?
6. For the P tradition what is the great significance of the Sinai event?
7. What is the purpose of the sabbath observance?

### Discussion Questions

1. Do you believe that God dwells in our midst? Just how involved in minute details do you think God is?

2. Do you like ritual? If so, why? What do you see as the purpose of ritual?
3. Do you observe the sabbath in any way other than attending church? How? Do you regard this day of "rest" as a gift in any way? Do you think God wants it to be a gift?

# ARTICLE 19

# God Dwells with a Sinful People

**Question: "This story about the molten calf, Moses making the people drink it, and all the killing is awful. (Ex 32) Why is this story in the Bible?" (Ex 33–34:35 also discussed)**

This story is in the Bible because it illustrates and teaches a core truth in the Israelites' self-understanding as a people: We have already seen that the Israelites view themselves as a covenant people. We have seen that the law is the social expression of covenant love. We have seen that Yahweh dwells with his people. Now we see that Israel is a sinful people who, nevertheless, remain in covenant relationship with Yahweh who dwells in their midst.

The part of the story which has upset our questioner is the part that deals with punishment. To understand this part we must put it in the larger context of chapters 32–34:35, in which we read of sin, punishment, atonement, and covenant renewal.

As we read these chapters we will not discuss some questions which will undoubtedly come to mind since it is hoped that what we have already learned will help the student reach answers to these questions. For instance, "How could the golden calf take shape all by itself?" (Remember what we have learned about legends.) "Was the tent of meeting inside or outside the camp?" (Remember what we have learned about the effects of combining various traditions into a single narrative.)

Armed with this knowledge we should now be able to read this arrangement of inherited legends with our eyes focused steadily on the core message.

First, the sin. While Moses is on the mountain for forty days getting instructions on "the dwelling" (i.e., on God's way of being present with

God's people), the people become impatient and decide to choose their own leader (Aaron) and their own method for God's being present in their midst. "When the people saw that Moses delayed to come down from the mountain, the people gathered around Aaron, and said to him, 'Come, make gods for us, who shall go before us . . . ' " (Ex 32:1). They then proclaimed that the gods which they had made themselves had brought them out of Egypt (see Ex 32:4).

The people thus broke the law which is at the core of covenant love. "I am the Lord your God, who brought you out of the land of Egypt, out of the house of slavery; you shall have no other gods before me" (Ex 32:19).

Scholars think the details of Moses' destruction of the golden calf, in which the calf is burned, ground and the remains drunk by the people, are an adaptation of details from a Canaanite story about the destruction of Mot, the god of death, who is also burned, ground up, and consumed, although in Mot's case the ashes are eaten by birds. It is interesting to note, however, that to consume what is forbidden has now twice been a symbol for sin. (Remember the forbidden fruit in Genesis.) Eating or drinking what has been forbidden is a good symbol for sin and its effects because sin, like eating, involves individual choice and results in the person being changed. That which is eaten or drunk becomes a part of the person.

A second ramification or "punishment" for sin is death. This ramification was also present in Genesis as the man and woman no longer had access to the tree of life. Here death appears as the Levites kill those who had worshipped the golden calf (Ex 32:25–29). Scholars think this detail comments on a situation which occurred under Jeroboam I (931–910 B.C.) who was king of the northern kingdom at the time the kingdom split. Jeroboam established cultic practices in the north which involved a bull image, and he selected priests who were not Levites. This episode, in which the Levites are formally dedicated to God, may be influenced by a desire to teach against the cultic actions of Jeroboam I.

The atonement which follows sin is accomplished because Moses intercedes for the sinful Israelites. Moses puts his own life on the line. "But now if you will only forgive their sin—but if not, blot me out of the book that you have written" (Ex 33:32). While God does not pretend that sin has no negative effects, neither does God forget God's promise. God tells Moses, "Go leave this place, you and the people whom you have brought up out of the land of Egypt, and go to the land of which I swore to Abraham, Isaac, and Jacob, saying, 'To your descendants I will give it' " (Ex 33:1).

Although Moses has to argue with God, God finally agrees to go with the people. "God said, 'My presence will go with you, and I will give you rest' " (Ex 33:14).

To symbolize the renewal of the broken covenant Moses is told to cut two tablets so that God can write "the words which were on the former tablets which you broke" (Ex 34:1).

Through the story of the golden calf, then, an important element of the self-concept of Israel is dramatically presented. Israel is a chosen nation but a sinful people. Because Israel sins Israel is constantly involved in covenant renewal. Despite sin, God still dwells with God's people.

### Review Questions

1. What sins did the Israelites commit?
2. What action of Moses symbolizes the fact that the people have sinned?
3. Why is eating or drinking what has been forbidden a good symbol for sin and its effects?
4. What message might be behind the passage in which the Levites are formally dedicated to God?
5. How is atonement accomplished?
6. What element of Israel's self-concept is taught through the story of the golden calf?

### Discussion Questions

1. Do we have rituals that symbolize our realization that we are a sinful people? What are they?
2. Do we have rituals to bring about atonement? What are they?
3. What do you regard as the effects of sin? Can these effects be undone? Explain.
4. Are we constantly involved in covenant renewal? How? Why?

# ARTICLE 20

# Worship as Re-creation

**Question: "Why does the author keep repeating that Moses is doing as the Lord commanded (Ex 40:16, 19, 21, 23, 25, 27, 29, 32) when Moses erects the dwelling? We already know that he is following instructions because we have read the instructions twice already." (Ex 24:12–31:18; 35–39; Gen. 1:1–2:4 also discussed)**

The author keeps repeating that Moses is doing exactly as the Lord commanded because the author is drawing a parallel between the construction of God's dwelling and the story of the creation of the world. So, first we will point out how the P tradition parallels the two stories. We will then discuss the theological and pastoral reasons for making such a comparison.

You may remember that in the story of creation there is a certain structure to each day's creation. Each day starts with God's saying what should be done. "Then God said, 'Let there be light . . . ' " (Gen 1:3a). Each creation comes into existence in direct response to God's command. ". . . and there was light" (Gen 1:3b). With each day God sees what has been created and judges the workmanship. "And God saw that the light was good" (Gen 1:4). After finishing all the work God blesses the seventh day. "So God blessed the seventh day and hallowed it, because on it God rested from all the work that he had done in creation" (Gen 2:3).

As we read the instructions for the building of the dwelling place (Ex 24–31), the account of its construction (Ex 35–39), and the account of its erection by Moses (Ex 40), we are constantly reminded of the Genesis creation story.

The comparison is explicit in the instructions to observe the sabbath. Yahweh is pictured as saying, "It (the sabbath) is a sign forever between me and the people of Israel, that in six days the Lord made heaven and earth, and on the seventh day he rested, and was refreshed" (Ex 31:17).

The comparison is less explicit but still present as we read about the selection of the craftsmen. "See, I have called by name Bezalel son of Uri son of Hur, of the tribe of Judah: and I have filled him with divine spirit, with ability, intelligence, and knowledge in every kind of craft . . ." (Ex 31:3). God's spirit had also hovered over the waters before creation. ". . . and God's spirit hovered over the water" (Gen 1:2; Jer. Bible translation).

As we move from the instructions to the carrying out of those instructions we find the pattern which our questioner has noted. Each instruction is carried out "as the Lord had commanded by Moses to be done" (Ex 35:29; 36:1, 5; 39:1, 5, 7, 21, 26, 29, 30).

P concludes the account of the work much as he concluded the account of God's work at creation, with a statement that the work was done and with a blessing. "The Israelites had done all the work just as the Lord had commanded Moses. When Moses saw that they had done all the work just as the Lord had commanded, he blessed them" (Ex 39:42–43).

As we move on to the erection of the dwelling it is once more a "first day" (Ex 40:2), as it was when God created light (see Gen 1:5). The narrative structure remains the same—each thing is done "as the Lord commanded Moses." Again the statement that the work is finished precedes a blessing, but this time the blessing is of an extraordinary and permanent nature. "So Moses finished the work. And the cloud covered the tent of meeting and the glory of the Lord filled the tabernacle" (Ex 33b–34). This cloud represents God's presence as it did earlier when the cloud covered Mount Sinai. "Then Moses went up on the mountain, and the cloud covered the mountain. The glory of the Lord settled on Mount Sinai, and the cloud covered it for six days . . ." (Ex 24:15–16).

Why is the P editor comparing the institution of cultic practices to God's creation of the world, and why does this P tradition establish so clearly that God's presence remains with his people through these same cultic practices?

One need only remember the needs of P's audience to respond to these questions. P's audience has suffered the horrible shock of losing the temple and the land, and of living in exile in Babylon. A "re-creation" is just what they need. Now, as the priests try to help the people resettle in the holy land, rebuild the temple, reinterpret their understanding of covenant, and recommit themselves to fidelity to Yahweh the P tradition assures them of two things. Their cultic practices are not merely customs made by humans. Rather, worship is in response to God's own command and is integral to covenant love. Second, Yahweh still dwells with Yahweh's people. Just as surely as the glory of God filled the dwelling at Sinai, and just as surely as God continued to dwell with his people after their sin and led them to the holy land, so will God forgive, dwell with, and guide God's people now.

As the P tradition promises God's presence and guidance to those who experienced the Babylonian exile, so does this tradition promise God's presence and guidance to each succeeding generation. God journeys with each generation to "the promised land," God forgives and re-creates each generation into a worshipping people, and God finds it very good.

## Review Questions

1. Why does P keep repeating that Moses is doing exactly what God commanded?
2. In what ways does the story about the tabernacle resemble the story of creation?
3. What is the cultural setting of P's audience? What do they need?
4. Of what two things does the P tradition assure the audience?

## Discussion Questions

1. Have you ever had an experience which you would describe as a re-creation? What was it?
2. To what degree do you regard the church as made by human beings? To what degree do you regard it as made by God? Explain.
3. Where is "the glory of God" dwelling with God's people most evident to you? Why?

# Summation and Transition
# from Exodus to 1, 2 Samuel

When we left the Israelites in the desert at the end of the book of Exodus we noted that the promise of land, made to Abraham, had yet to be fulfilled. As we start to read 1, 2 Samuel, which were originally one book, we are reading about a people who had reached the promised land two hundred years earlier and who are now in the process of changing their form of "government." They are moving from a loose confederacy of tribes to a nation with a king. So, from the point of view of plot, we have skipped some two hundred years.

From the point of view of literature we have also made a big jump. In reading Exodus we were reading the second of five books in a literary unit called the "Pentateuch" or "the Law." In reading 1 Samuel we are reading the third of six books in a literary unit called the "Deuteronomistic History," or the "Former Prophets."

So before we move on to 1 Samuel we should fill in the missing pieces. We should know a little something about each of these literary units as well as something about the last three books of the Pentateuch and the first two books of the Deuteronomistic History.

The word "Pentateuch" means "five scrolls." The books of the Pentateuch are Genesis, Exodus, Leviticus, Numbers, and Deuteronomy.

The five books of the Pentateuch form a literary unit because the events that are described in them and the beliefs that are expressed in them form the foundation of all that will follow in both the Old and New Testaments. The Pentateuch contains the source and the inspiration for all the rest of salvation history.

---

**THE PENTATEUCH**

Genesis—All stories

Exodus—Mixture of stories and laws

Leviticus—All laws

Numbers—Mixture of stories and laws

Deuteronomy—All laws

---

Since you have already read Genesis and Exodus you know that Genesis was made up of a number of stories. Exodus also included a number of stories, but in addition it included a number of laws.

The remaining three books contain these same elements. Leviticus is made up entirely of law, Numbers is made up of laws and stories, and Deuteronomy is again made up entirely of laws.

So it is the book of Numbers which moves the plot forward. In Numbers 10–36 we read of the people leaving Mount Sinai and proceeding to the border of the promised land.

Deuteronomy then pictures the people, poised on the border, listening to Moses as he not only reiterates the law but applies it to the Israelites' future life in the promised land.

The way in which the law pertains both to the past and the future gives us an illustration of why it is true to say that the events described in the Pentateuch and the beliefs expressed form the foundation of all that will follow in the rest of the Bible.

You may remember from reading Exodus that we pointed out that the laws were not all contemporary with Moses. Laws that developed after the people had settled in Canaan are found on Moses' lips. Laws, as they developed, were understood to be the social expression of covenant love. This understanding did not die in the desert. As new laws developed to address new situations these laws, too, were attributed to Moses. This attribution was a way of professing the belief that obedience to the law was an expression of covenant love. So we see that all that follows is understood in the

---

**DEUTERONOMISTIC HISTORY**

Joshua—People enter Canaan

Judges—People settle in Canaan (200 year period)

1, 2 Samuel—Israel becomes a nation with a king

1, 2 Kings—Israel has kings until the Babylonian exile

---

context of those foundational experiences which we read about in the Pentateuch.

As you may have guessed from its name, the book of Deuteronomy sets the stage for the second literary unit, the Deuteronomistic History. In fact, over the years, there has been some discussion as to which of these literary units, the Pentateuch or the Deuteronomistic History, the book of Deuteronomy actually belongs.

In the book of Deuteronomy the people are warned that if they obey the law things will go well for them, but if they disobey they will meet with disaster. The Deuteronomistic History assesses Israel's history according to this criterion set forth in the book of Deuteronomy, and it is this characteristic that identifies it as a literary unit.

The Deuteronomistic History consists of Joshua, Judges, 1, 2 Samuel, and 1, 2 Kings. In the book of Joshua the people enter and claim the land. The book of Judges tells of the two hundred years from 1200–1020 B.C., known as the period of the Judges. During this time the people were organized into a loose tribal confederacy. When threatened by a political enemy, a "judge," a charismatic political leader, would mobilize the people to repel the enemy. When the threat was over all returned to their individual tribes.

As you will soon discover, 1 Samuel covers the period of time when the Israelites moved from a tribal confederacy to a nation with a king. The rest of the Deuteronomistic History tells us of life in the land under the kings. In its present form, the Deuteronomistic History follows the Israelites up to the time of the Babylonian exile.

As was true when we were reading the Pentateuch, when reading the Deuteronomistic History we are reading a collection of edited writings that reached its present form after the Babylonian exile (587–537 B.C.).

The particular point of view of the Deuteronomist, though, probably dates to the time of Josiah who, as you know, was king of Judah at a time of great reform (d. 609 B.C.).

As was true in the Pentateuch, the Deuteronomistic History reflects all the characteristics of an edited text. Sometimes the sources used by the Deuteronomist contain divergent, even incompatible points of view. Nevertheless, the Deuteronomist uses a variety of sources to tell Israel's history in such a way that it illustrates the rewards of fidelity and the punishments of infidelity.

We will learn more about the particular concerns of the Deuteronomist as we read 1, 2 Samuel. As before, read the biblical text before you read the following articles. As you read, remember what you have learned about the effects of multiple editings on a text. This knowledge alone will help you understand some puzzling aspects of the text. Write down any questions which come to mind. Many of your questions will be discussed in the following articles.

# ■ THE BOOK OF 1 SAMUEL ■

# ARTICLE 1

# Samuel's Birth Narrative

**Question: "This prayer of Hannah's sounds a lot like Mary's prayer after she conceived Jesus. (1 Sam 2:1–10; Luke 1:46–55) Why is this?" (1 Sam 1:11; Num 6:2–8 also discussed)**

Hannah's prayer does remind a Christian of Mary's prayer at the time she visited Elizabeth (see Luke 1:46–55). In both instances the prayer is placed on the lips of the new mother to say something about the destiny of the child.

You may remember that we have already talked about the function of a birth narrative. When discussing the story of Moses' birth we said that the story is told, not to give specific historical details, but to foreshadow the role of a person who is known, in hindsight, to have become a great leader.

Of course, the original readers of this story would not have associated it with the story of Jesus' birth since that still lay in their future. Rather, the original readers would have been reminded of the story of Isaac's birth to Sarah and of Joseph's birth to Rachel. Remember, in each of these stories, too, a woman who was unable to bear a child was taunted by a woman who could bear children—Sarah by Hagar, and Rachel by Leah. After years of barrenness and suffering, the woman bore a child who was to have a profound effect on the destiny of the chosen people.

Samuel was such a person. Samuel will become a great prophet of Israel, one through whom God's word will be made known. As the author tells the story of Samuel's birth, every detail foreshadows his greatness.

First, Samuel's conception is an answer to prayer. Because of

195

Hannah's barrenness the reader is left in no doubt that the child is a gift from God. In fact, the name Samuel means, "he who is from God." As events unfold we will see that Samuel is a gift not only to Hannah, who longed to be a mother, but to the nation, Israel, which longed to be in right relationship with the God of the covenant.

Hannah, because she realizes that she will conceive only if God intervenes, promises to dedicate the child to God. "O Lord of hosts, if only you will look on the misery of your servant, and remember me, and not forget your servant, but will give to your servant a male child, then I will set him before you as a nazirite until the day of his death. He shall drink neither wine nor intoxicants, and no razor shall touch his head" (1 Sam 1:11).

The passage itself illustrates what a nazirite is: one who has been set apart by vow. Had we read either the book of Numbers or the book of Judges we would already be familiar with nazirites. In the book of Numbers (see Num 6:2–8) we read that nazirites are not to drink wine and intoxicants, they are not to cut their hair, and they are not to become ritually unclean by coming in contact with a corpse. In the book of Judges we read about Samson, the nazirite, whose strength was in his hair (i.e., his strength was in his right relationship with God as a nazirite).

A person could become a nazirite by taking a vow himself, and the vow could be for a specified length of time. So Samuel's total dedication to God is emphasized by the facts that he is set apart by vow even before his conception, and the vow is for life. Samuel belongs completely to God and will become an instrument of God's will.

It is obvious that Hannah's prayer of praise and thanksgiving (1 Sam 2:1–10) is one that has been placed on her lips by the editor of inherited materials, because in the prayer Hannah says:

> The Lord will judge the ends of the earth
> he will give strength to his king
> and exalt the praises of his anointed (1 Sam 10b).

Since Hannah lived and bore Samuel before Israel had a king it is obvious that this prayer is not contemporaneous with the setting in which it appears.

Nevertheless, the prayer emphasizes the theme which the Deuteronomist will emphasize. God is in control of events. Both good fortune and bad are in God's hands. If one wants to have good fortune one must obey.

> He will guard the feet of his faithful ones,
> but the wicked shall be cut off in darkness;
> for not by might does one prevail (1 Sam 2:9).

One prevails by being open to the Lord, as was Hannah, and by listening to God's word, a word that will be made known through the great prophet Samuel.

For a Christian reader, Hannah does foreshadow Mary and her prayer of praise, for in Hannah's child, too, although in a lesser way, God's word will take flesh and dwell among God's people.


## Review Questions

1. What is the function of an infancy narrative?
2. What does the story of Samuel's conception have in common with other biblical birth narratives?
3. How does the story foreshadow Samuel's greatness?
4. What is a nazirite?
5. Why is it obvious that Hannah's song developed later than the time of Hannah?
6. What in the song reflects the point of view of the Deuteronomist?


## Discussion Questions

1. Do you agree with the point of view of the Deuteronomist? Why or why not?
2. Have you ever longed for something for a long time and finally had your hopes and prayers fulfilled? Explain.
3. Samuel means, "He who is from God." Is there someone in your life whom you view as a gift from God? Explain.

# ARTICLE 2

# Families in Contrast: Samuel's and Eli's

**Question: "Why does God treat Eli's family so harshly? For instance, why does God 'decide on the death of Eli's sons'?" (1 Sam 2:15; 1 Sam 2:11–36; 3:13; 3:19; Lev 7:29–36 also discussed)**

The person who asked this question is having trouble remembering the effect that a narrator's methods and point of view have on a text. We encountered a similar question when we read in Exodus that God had "hardened Pharaoh's heart."

It is obvious even from the structure of 1 Samuel 2:12–36 that the editor has arranged his materials so that a good example, Samuel and his family, is contrasted with a bad example, Eli and his family.

We have just finished reading Hannah's song, in which she praises the God who judges, when we are introduced to the sins of Eli's sons. Eli and his sons are priests at Shiloh, the central sanctuary of the tribal confederacy and the place where the ark of the covenant now resides. While the child Samuel remains at the sanctuary in the service of the Lord (see 1 Sam 2:11), Eli's sons mistreat both the people and God by abusing the ritual sacrifices. As priests they should have a portion of the sacrificial animal, but certainly not before the customary rituals have been completed. Literally and figuratively, Eli's sons put themselves and their own desires before God and God's will as expressed in the law (see Lev 7:29–36).

Before we read of the rebuke which Eli gives his sons, the contrast to Samuel and his family is made once more (see 1 Sam 2:18–21). The God who judges rewards Hannah by letting her conceive five more children.

---

**INTERWEAVING OF SAMUEL AND ELI MATERIAL**

1 Sam 2:12–17 Eli material

1 Sam 2:18–21 Samuel material

1 Sam 2:22–36 Eli material

1 Sam 3 ff. Eli and Samuel materials joined

---

The sins of Eli's sons multiply. In addition to their ritual sins they "lay with the women who served at the entrance to the tent of meeting" (1 Sam 2:22b). Eli tells his sons that sins against other people can be forgiven but not sins directly against God. It is at this point that the narrator remarks, "But they would not listen to the voice of their father; for it was the will of the Lord to kill them" (1 Sam 2:25b). This is simply the narrator's way of saying that no fate but doom could await such sinners since God is a just judge and those who sin will inevitably meet with destruction.

Once again, working through contrast, the editor holds up young Samuel who continues "to grow both in stature and in favor with the Lord and with the people" (1 Sam 2:26).

We move now from the naming of the sins of Eli's family and the warning of the ramifications of such sins to the pronouncement of God's just judgment. Eli himself is now implicated as he, too, benefited from the portions wrongfully taken. Eli's whole family will be punished. God says, ". . . for those who honor me I will honor, and those who despise me shall be treated with contempt" (1 Sam 2:30b). Again we recognize the theme of the Deuteronomist.

The contrast continues as God says that God will "raise up for myself a faithful priest, who will do according to what is in my heart and in my mind. I will build him a sure house, and he shall go in and out before my anointed one forever" (1 Sam 2:35).

Although many of the future leaders of Israel might be understood to have been referred to in this statement, the most obvious and immediate reference is to Samuel.

In fact, the final judgment against Eli's family reaches Eli's ears through Samuel himself, thus uniting the juxtaposed Samuel and Eli passages into a single narrative.

While the braided and then united materials seem very neatly organized in this final edited version, the editor used a variety of sources which were not always in agreement with each other. For instance, when God appears to Samuel and tells him that Eli's family will be destroyed, God is pictured as saying, "For I have told him (i.e., Eli) that I am about to punish his house forever, for the iniquity that he knew, because his sons were blaspheming God, and he did not restrain them" (1 Sam 3:13). The editor includes this charge despite the fact that it is contradicted by the earlier account in which Eli did correct his sons.

Now that Samuel has assumed his role of prophet, the people's longing for a faithful servant of the Lord is fulfilled, just as Hannah's longing for a son has been fulfilled. While Eli's sons abused both God and the people, Samuel faithfully served both. "As Samuel grew up, the Lord was with him and let none of his words fall to the ground. And all Israel from Dan to Beersheba knew that Samuel was a trustworthy prophet of the Lord" (1 Sam 3:19).

The dismal fate of Eli's sons, as well as the rise of Samuel, both serve to illustrate the point which the Deuteronomist is constantly making. Those who sin meet with utter destruction, while those who obey meet with constant blessing.

## Review Questions

1. Who are Eli and his sons?
2. Why is Shiloh important?
3. How do Eli's sons sin?
4. What does the narrator mean when he says that it was the will of the Lord to kill Eli's sons?
5. How is the contrast between the two families emphasized in structure?
6. Do the traditions always agree? Explain.
7. How do the stories of Eli's and Samuel's families illustrate the Deuteronomist's theme?

**Discussion Questions**

1. Do you know anyone who, like Samuel, seemed destined for greatness from childhood and fulfilled that destiny? What characteristics did this person have when he or she was a youth?
2. Do you agree with Samuel's distinction between sins against other people and sins against God? Why or why not?
3. What do you think is meant by, "the Lord let none of Samuel's words fall to the ground"?

# ARTICLE 3

# The Ark of the Covenant

**Question: "Why did the Israelites think that the ark would be a help in battle? (1 Sam 4:3) You'd think it would be in the way." (1 Sam 4:1–7:1 also discussed)**

As you may remember from reading Exodus, the ark of the covenant had become a symbol of God's presence dwelling with God's people. The ark contained the Law and functioned as God's throne. Where the ark was, there was God.

The ark had recently been kept at Shiloh, the central shrine where Eli's sons failed to worship God properly. The text tells us why the Israelites brought the ark into battle. Israel had been defeated in battle by the Philistines. When the defeated troops returned to camp, "the elders of Israel said, 'Why has the Lord put us to rout today before the Philistines? Let us bring the ark of the covenant of the Lord here from Shiloh, so that he may come among us and save us from the power of our enemies" (1 Sam 4:3).

Notice that the elders presume that the Lord had been in charge of the losing battle because they ask, "Why has *the Lord* put us to rout?" Still, they would expect the Lord to choose victory for them, not defeat. Something was definitely wrong. By bringing the ark into the battle they express symbolically what they had said they believed all along. The Lord is present in the battle.

However, the Lord's will in battle does not change by the Lord's presence in the ark. The Israelites are still defeated. So the Israelites are left with the questions: "Has God lost power, or has God chosen to withdraw his glory and his power from his chosen people? Why would God let Israel suffer defeat?"

A hint of an answer appears in a detail of the story. "So the people sent to Shiloh and brought from there the ark of the covenant of the Lord of hosts, who is enthroned on the cherubim. The two sons of Eli, Hophni and Phinehas, were there with the ark of the covenant of God" (1 Sam 4:4). We already know that God has withdrawn his favor from Eli and his sons, so the fact that the two sons are accompanying the ark is an ominous sign. The sons, as well as Eli, will die on the same day that the ark is lost.

As the narrative continues the narrator leaves no doubt in anyone's mind that, while the Israelites lose both the battle and the ark, it is not because the ark is no longer God's dwelling place nor is it because God has lost power. Wherever the ark goes, the Philistines are defeated without the Israelites even being a part of the action.

First, the god of the Philistines, Dagon, appears to worship the God of Israel enthroned on the ark, and then is destroyed in the presence of the ark. Next, successive Philistine cities, Ashdod, Gath, and Ekron all suffer from the presence of the ark and long to be rid of it. After all, the Philistines say, look what happened to the Egyptians when they resisted this same God! This is the God who sends plagues on Israel's enemies.

In order to confirm this theory the Philistines decide to let the ark find its own home, accompanied by "guilt offerings," symbols of the plagues from which they hope to be delivered. The Philistines' theory is confirmed as the cows, which lead the ark, fail to return to their calves but instead set out for Bethshemesh of Israel, the dwelling place of the Lord after all.

However, when the ark returns to Israel, it is accompanied, not by blessings, but by suffering. Seventy men die in Bethshemesh because they do not join in the celebration at the ark's return. So the ark moves on to Kiriathjearim where it will remain for many years. We will not read of the ark again until we get to 2 Samuel 6 when David takes the ark to Jerusalem.

What does all this mean? At the very least it means that a period of great change is underway for Israel. With the departure of the ark Eli and his sons die, and the newborn child of Eli's line is named Ichabod, which means "the glory has departed from Israel" (see 1 Sam 4:21). The "glory" returns to Israel, for Israel is where the glory of God truly does dwell, but God's glory returns to a place of no distinction. "God's glory" is no longer the center of Israel's life and worship.

The elders were right. The defeat of the Israelites at the hands of the Philistines had, after all, been God's work. The question remains, "Why has God let Israel be defeated? What will God, still dwelling with Israel, bring about through this defeat?"

## Review Questions

1. What is the significance of the ark of the covenant?
2. Why do the Israelites bring the ark into the battle?
3. What questions do events force the Israelites to ask?
4. What ominous detail appears in the story? Why is this an ominous detail?
5. What happens when the ark is with the Philistines?
6. How do the Philistines test out their theory that their being in possession of the ark is causing the plagues?
7. What is the significance of the fact that the ark resides in a place of no distinction?

## Discussion Questions

1. Do you think that God is more with you in victory or in defeat? Explain.
2. Do you have any objects that concretize God's presence for you? Do you think God is more present when you have that object with you? Explain.
3. Have you ever tried desperately to accomplish something, finally left it in God's hands, only to find that God accomplishes it without your involvement? Explain.

# ARTICLE 4

# Samuel: Prophet, Judge, Priest

**Question: "What does it mean to say that Samuel 'judged' Israel?"**
**(1 Sam 7:6, 17; 1 Sam 7:3; 7:5; 7:8–9; 8:3; 8:5 also discussed)**

Samuel, in addition to being a prophet, was also both judge and priest for Israel. Each of these roles was distinct. Only Samuel, of all Old Testament figures, functioned in all three roles.

We have already spoken of Samuel as a prophet, as one called to bring God's word to God's people. We see Samuel function in that role at the beginning of chapter 7 when he is pictured as saying to the house of Israel, "If you are returning to the Lord with all your heart, then put away the foreign gods and the Astartes from among you. Direct your heart to the Lord, and serve him only, and he will deliver you out of the land of the Philistines" (1 Sam 7:3). As a true prophet, Samuel calls the people to worship the one true God.

Samuel called the people to gather at Mizpah for prayer (see 1 Sam 7:5). It is at Mizpah that our narrator comments, "And Samuel judged the people at Mizpah" (1 Sam 7:6b).

As we mentioned earlier, a judge was a charismatic leader who rallied the tribes so that they could offer a united front when opposing a political enemy. When they first lived in Canaan the twelve tribes really had no structural unity. They did have a common devotion to Yahweh. In the name of their covenant God they shared legal and religious responsibilities. Under the leadership of the judges they acted as one to defeat their enemies. But after the threat was over, no unifying structure remained.

As you will see, Samuel is the last of the judges and the facilitator

---

**CHANGING MODELS OF LEADERSHIP**

| *Before Samuel* | *Samuel* | *After Samuel* |
|---|---|---|
| Judges ⟶ | Judge ⟶ | Kings |
| Priests ⟶ | Priest ⟶ | Priests |
| | Prophet ⟶ | Prophets |

---

of the transition from a tribal confederacy to a united nation with a king. Samuel functions as a judge at Mizpah as he leads his people to temporarily defeat the Philistines. "So the Philistines were subdued and did not again enter the territory of Israel; the hand of the Lord was against the Philistines all the days of Samuel" (1 Sam 7:13).

In addition to being prophet and judge, Samuel also functioned as a priest. "The people of Israel said to Samuel, 'Do not cease to cry out to the Lord our God for us and pray that he may save us from the hand of the Philistines.' So Samuel took a suckling lamb and offered it as a whole burnt offering to the Lord; Samuel cried out to the Lord for Israel, and the Lord answered him" (1 Sam 7:8–9).

The phenomenon of a single person being prophet, judge and priest will never again occur. The role of judge will disappear completely. Although Samuel names his sons as judges over Israel they are not good judges. They "took bribes and perverted justice" (see 1 Sam 8:3). So the elders of Israel ask Samuel to appoint them "a king to govern us like other nations" (see 1 Sam 8:5). With the birth of the monarchy the role of the judge disappears.

While the role of the prophet grows and becomes all-important during the time of the monarchy, this role will not be combined with the role of priest. The two functions will become distinct.

So Samuel is a transitional figure not only because he ushers in the monarchy but also because he, in his person, accomplishes the transition from the age of the judges to the age of the prophets. From now on, prophets will indeed "judge" Israel, but not in the sense of offering charismatic political and military leadership.

Rather, prophets will "judge" Israel by confronting Israel with the question, "Who really is king of Israel?"

## Review Questions

1. In what three roles did Samuel function?
2. What is the function of a prophet?
3. What is a judge?
4. How did Samuel serve as a priest?
5. In what two ways was Samuel a transitional person?

## Discussion Questions

1. What do you think is more necessary, priests or prophets? Why? Do we have both in our society? Are the roles distinct? Explain.
2. Samuel lived at a time of great transition when old forms were dying and new forms were being born. Do you think the same is true today? Explain.

# ARTICLE 5

# "Give Us a King!"

**Question: "Why does God tell Samuel to grant the people a king if it is tantamount to idolatry?" (1 Sam 8:8; 1 Sam 8; Judges 7–8 also discussed)**

As the text appears in this final arrangement it seems that God told Samuel to grant the people a king simply because the people kept asking for one. However, scripture scholars surmise that we are reading the combination of at least two traditions, one much more negative about kingship than the other.

For the Israelites the question of whether or not to have a king was not simply a political question. It was also a theological question. The reason many people wanted a king was that the loose tribal confederacy no longer seemed an adequate structure to respond to the continued threat of the Philistines. Samuel's sons, who had been appointed judges, did not have the moral authority to fulfill their roles. They were a far cry from the charismatic leaders of the past. Another alternative, a government through an inherited priesthood, was also impossible, as we know from having read about Eli and his sons.

To many, the idea of a united kingdom with a king seemed the only reasonable alternative. So the elders are pictured as asking Samuel to appoint a king to govern them like other nations.

However, Israel is not "like other nations." Israel already has a king, and that king is God. Would having an earthly king blind Israel to the fact that God is king? Would a king become so powerful that the king himself would forget that he was just as accountable to God as anyone else?

The elders' request for a king was not the first such request in the

208

---

### AMBIVALENCE ABOUT KINGS

*Ambivalence contemporary with the birth of the monarchy:* If Israel has a king like other nations will Israel forget that God is king?

*Ambivalence in hindsight:* Look what happened with the kings! Since it didn't work out all that well, was it God who gave us kings or not?

---

history of Israel. Had we read the book of Judges we would have read that a previous judge, Gideon, had turned down a request to be crowned king (see Judges 8). The people had said to Gideon, "Rule over us, you and your son and your grandson also . . ." (Judges 8:22). But Gideon refused, saying, "I will not rule over you, and my son will not rule over you; the Lord will rule over you" (Judges 8:23).

However, Gideon had a son by a woman who lived in Shechem, and this son, named Abimelech, had ambitions to be king (see Judges 9). The story is told that Abimelech killed seventy brothers in order to destroy his rivals and then had himself crowned king. After three years a revolt occurred which Abimelech put down by destroying the city of Shechem. Abimelech eventually died while attempting to quiet another rebellion. So an initial experience of kingship had been an extremely negative one.

Also, we must remember that our accounts are all edited in hindsight, so another problem arises. In addition to the ambivalence about kings which would have been contemporary with the establishment of the nation, there is the ambivalence about kings that comes from having lived under them. When Samuel is pictured as describing the negative aspects of having a king (see 1 Sam 8:11–17), he describes a much more developed kingdom than existed at the time Samuel lived. The abuses that kings committed later, which were now known, are included in Samuel's warning about kings.

Since, in hindsight, kings are understood to have been a mixed blessing, one is left with the question, "Did God establish the nation with a king or was this a human initiative?" Central to the concept of "king" was the idea that God had chosen the king. But if God chose the king, how could having a king be a mixed blessing? This hindsight ambivalence is wonderfully expressed in the passage at hand. God does, through Samuel, appoint the king, but God, too, is ambivalent about it. God is pictured as interpreting the request for a king as a rejection of the fact that God is king. Nevertheless, God accedes to the request, since that is what the people want.

## Review Questions

1. From a political point of view, why did some want a king?
2. Why is the question of having a king a theological question as well as a political one?
3. Was this the first time some Israelites had requested a king? Explain. How did this work out?
4. How does the fact that our accounts have the advantage of hindsight affect their discussion of whether or not Israel should have a king?
5. How is "hindsight ambivalence" about kings expressed in this narrative?

## Discussion Questions

1. Have you ever prayed for something, received it, and then realized you didn't want it? Explain.
2. Do you think God is behind political structures and those in authority? Explain.
3. Is there any form of government about which people would not be ambivalent? Explain. Are you ambivalent about democracy? Why or why not?

# ARTICLE 6

# A Prophet: More Than a Seer

**Question: "What is this distinction between a prophet and a seer?"**
**(1 Sam 9:11; 1 Sam 9:6; 9:9; 9:15–16; 10:5; 19:20 also discussed)**

The story we read at the beginning of chapter 9, in which we first meet Saul, is obviously a different strand of tradition than we have just finished reading, in which the people have demanded a king. Here God takes the initiative to appoint a king. Also, Samuel is described differently: He is described as "a man of God . . . whatever he says comes true" (1 Sam 9:6a), and later as a "seer." We do not at first know that Samuel is the person being described. In fact, the story may not have originally involved Samuel, but may have been incorporated into its present context at a later date. At any rate, the narrator finds it necessary to say, "for the one who is now called a prophet was formerly called a seer" (1 Sam 9:9b). Samuel was a prophet, not just a seer. The distinction is an important one.

The role of the prophet in Israel is born in Samuel and so the understanding of that role is gradual. One might not immediately recognize the difference between a prophet and a seer, but the difference would become apparent over time. Many countries had seers. Prophets, in the full sense of the word, were unique to Israel.

A seer could also be called a "diviner." In the Mesopotamian world such a person was thought to have superhuman knowledge and so might be consulted in just such a case as Saul consults Samuel. Saul is looking for some lost animals and hopes that the seer might know where they are.

A prophet, on the other hand, is one who speaks for God. While a seer and a prophet might both speak in the form of an oracle, the

211

---

**ORACLES: PROPHETIC UTTERANCES**

*Form:* Use a formula which attributes the insight to God. "Yahweh says this."

*Function:* Often denounce people for their sins. Warn of ramifications if people do not change their ways.

---

---

**PROPHETS AND SEERS**

*Prophet:* One who speaks for God.

*Seer:* One who has "supernatural" knowledge.

---

resemblance between them is only in form. The unique role of the prophet is that by a special gift from God, the prophet is enabled to know God's will and speak God's will to his contemporary audience.

As we read 1 Samuel we are seeing the birth of the role of the prophet in Israel. True, earlier biblical characters, such as Abraham and Moses, have been referred to as prophets, but this is a retrojection. A concept which developed later has been applied to earlier characters. While no one could deny that Moses spoke for God, his contemporaries would not have called Moses a prophet. The concept of the function of a prophet developed as the monarchy developed.

You will notice in chapter 10, that Samuel tells Saul he will "meet a band of prophets coming down from the shrine with harp, tambourine, flute and lyre playing in front of them; they will be in a prophetic frenzy" (1 Sam 10:5). Although this group is called "a band of prophets," scripture scholars do not think that these "prophets" fulfilled the function of prophecy which Samuel will fulfill. Rather they participated in worship in song and dance. In chapter 19 we will read that Samuel presided over such a group (see 1 Sam 19:20). They were part of Samuel's entourage. Nevertheless, it is Samuel, not the "band of prophets" who has the unique inspiration, the understanding, and the compelling duty to make God's will known to God's people.

The quality which makes Samuel a prophet rather than a seer is described narratively by having God speak directly to Samuel. "Now the day before Saul came, the Lord had revealed to Samuel: 'Tomorrow about this time I will send to you a man from the land of Benjamin, and you shall anoint him to be ruler over my people Israel. He shall save my people from the hand of the Philistines; for I have seen the suffering of my people, because their outcry has come to me' " (1 Sam 9:15–16).

Because Samuel is the person who perceives and speaks God's will to God's people, Samuel is more than a seer; Samuel is a true prophet.

## Review Questions

1. What is the difference between a prophet and a seer?
2. What is the unique role of a prophet?
3. What does "retrojection" mean? Why is it retrojection to call Moses a prophet?
4. What narrative technique is used to make the special gift which a prophet receives evident?

## Discussion Questions

1. In what ways do you think God speaks?
2. Have you ever felt compelled to speak up and say something you believed to be true? Why do you think you felt this way?
3. If something is supernatural does that mean it is from God? Explain.
4. Why is it dangerous to get involved with the occult?

# ARTICLE 7

# The Monarchy: From God or from Men?

**Question: "Why does Samuel anoint Saul secretly? (1 Sam 9:27–10:1) You'd think everything should be public." (1 Sam 8–12 also discussed)**

In chapters 8 through 12 we are reading braided traditions, as we already know from the ambivalent, even contradictory, attitudes toward kingship. The secret anointing of Saul belongs to the tradition which wants and approves of a king. The choosing of Saul publicly by lot (see 1 Sam 10:17–24) belongs to the tradition which sees the request for a king as a rejection of Yahweh as king. It will be helpful to separate the traditions so that each is seen individually. Then we will be able to understand the effect of the unified text, which illustrates the point of view of the Deuteronomist.

The tradition in which Samuel secretly anoints Saul is a continuation of the passage we have just read in which Samuel is described as a seer/prophet who has been told by God to anoint Saul as ruler over Israel (see 1 Sam 9:16). Obviously there is no negative attitude toward the idea of kingship here. The idea is God's. The initiative is God's. God has heard the outcry of God's people and is responding by establishing the monarchy.

While Samuel follows God's directions and anoints Saul, he anoints him in secret because Saul does not grow into the role nor do the people recognize Saul in the role until after Saul has defeated the Ammonites (see 1 Sam 11:1–11). After this victory the people want Saul to be king. So Samuel gathers everyone in Gilgal where Saul is publicly proclaimed king.

Another tradition, which is interwound with this one, pictures

---

**SAUL TRADITIONS**

| | |
|---|---|
| 1. Samuel a judge | 1. Samuel a seer/prophet |
| 2. Samuel appoints his sons as judges. They are no good. | 2. God chooses Saul and Samuel anoints him secretly. |
| 3. People want a king. This is seen as a rejection of Yahweh. | 3. Saul defeats the Ammonites. |
| 4. Saul is chosen by lot at Mizpah. | 4. People proclaim Saul king at Gilgal. |
| 5. Samuel's farewell address | |

---

Samuel not as the seer/prophet but as the judge. We were reading this tradition when we read that Samuel tried to provide the people with leadership by appointing his own sons as judges. However, the people did not accept Samuel's sons in the role and asked for a king. It is in this tradition that Samuel regards the request for a king as a rejection of God as king (see 1 Sam 8).

This tradition continues with the begrudging selection of Saul as king by lot (see 1 Sam 10:17–27). Samuel calls the people together at Mizpah. The people are reminded of God's saving acts on their behalf in the past and are accused of having rejected God by having asked for a king. Nevertheless, Samuel chooses first the tribe of Benjamin, then the family of Matrites, and finally Saul himself, all by lot. The people shout, "Long live the king"—but not all the people. "But some worthless fellows said, 'How can the man save us?' They despised him and brought him no present" (1 Sam 10:27).

This second tradition continues in chapter 12 as Samuel gives his farewell address as a judge. Samuel continues to be pictured as disapproving of the monarchy. However, there is one possible way in which this new institution might work, and Samuel states clearly what it is. "If you will fear the Lord and serve him and heed his voice and not rebel against the commandment of the Lord, and if both you and the king who reigns over you will follow the Lord your God, it will be well; but if you will not heed the voice of the Lord, but rebel against the commandment of the Lord, then the hand of the Lord will be against you and your king" (1 Sam 12:14–15).

The combined traditions reveal very clearly the dilemma of trying to balance two apparently contradictory truths. On the one hand, God did establish the monarchy. On the other hand, the monarchy, especially as embodied in Saul, did not work out well. How can both of these statements be true? The editing of the Deuteronomist gives us a clue. God established the monarchy but the monarchy will succeed only if the king is obedient to God's word. With this truth clearly stated we move on to the story of Israel's first king, Saul, who is a sad example of the truth of the Deuteronomist's point of view.

## Review Questions

1. What are the story elements in the tradition in which there are no negative attitudes toward kingship?
2. In this tradition, why is Saul anointed in secret?
3. What are the story elements in the tradition in which there is a negative attitude toward kingship?
4. What is the one possible way in which kingship might succeed?
5. What are two apparently contradictory facts which seem to be true? How does the Deuteronomist make these truths compatible?

## Discussion Questions

1. Do you think the editor would have done better to have used one or the other tradition involving Saul's selection by Samuel? Why or why not?
2. Have you ever made a decision by lot? If so, did you regard the result as random or as providential? Explain.

# ARTICLE 8

# Saul's Fatal Flaw

**Question: "How did Saul break the Lord's command by offering the holocaust and peace offering?" (1 Sam 13:10–14; 1 Sam 9:12–13; 10:8; 13, 15 also discussed)**

Saul's sin is disobedience, but the fact that Saul disobeyed in this particular way reveals a fatal spiritual flaw: Saul has more faith in the externals of performing rituals than in the Lord. He performs rituals in disobedience rather than in obedience. This flaw is the basis for two stories in which Saul is rejected as king, the first here in chapter 13, and the second in chapter 15.

In chapter 13 Saul is pictured as sinning by offering the holocaust and peace offering himself rather than waiting for Samuel. Two previous passages have prepared us to understand that Saul must wait for Samuel. The first was when Saul was looking for the seer and asked directions from some girls who had come to draw water. In describing Samuel's role to Saul they say, "Hurry; he has come just now to the town, because the people have a sacrifice today at the shrine. As soon as you enter the town, you will find him, before he goes up to the shrine to eat. For the people will not eat until he comes, since he must bless the sacrifice; afterward those eat who are invited" (1 Sam 9:12–13). So Saul knows from the beginning that the sacrifice cannot start without Samuel.

The second passage which prepares us to understand the nature of Saul's disobedience appears when Samuel is giving Saul instructions after having anointed him. Samuel says, "And you shall go down to Gilgal ahead of me; then I will come down to you to present burnt offerings and offer sacrifices of well-being. Seven

217

days you shall wait, until I come to you and show you what you shall do" (1 Sam 10:8).

As we read in chapter 13, Saul does wait the prescribed seven days (see 1 Sam 13:8), but Samuel is late. Saul sees his troops starting to become discouraged and slip away. He decides not to wait for the prophet, the one through whom God's will would be made known. Instead he just usurps Samuel's role and offers the holocaust and peace offering himself. In other words, Saul puts his trust in the external ritual rather than in the Lord. He thinks his ritual actions will "do the trick" rather than his internal submission of mind and heart, his true trust in the Lord.

When Samuel learns what Saul has done, Samuel tells Saul that he will lose his kingdom. ". . . The Lord has sought out a man after his own heart . . ." (see 1 Sam 13:14a), who will be given the kingdom.

While the second rejection story in chapter 15 has a completely different story line, it nevertheless focuses on the same core fault in Saul and pictures the same tragic result: Saul will lose the kingdom.

In this story Saul disobeys by not putting everyone and everything under "the ban" when he defeats the Amalekites. The concept of "the ban," under which all living things—women, children, and animals—in a conquered town are killed as a way of giving all to God and thus acknowledging that the victory is totally God's, is abhorrent to us. We do not think a loving God would want us to do such a thing, but in 1050 B.C. the people believed that they were praising God and bringing about God's will on earth by completely destroying the enemy. This belief was expressed in law.

So Saul disobeyed God when Saul decided not to destroy what he saw had value (see 1 Sam 15:19). Instead, he spared the best of the sheep and cattle. When Samuel confronted Saul, Saul claimed that he had saved these animals in order to sacrifice them to the Lord. Samuel rebukes Saul, pointing out the same spiritual flaw which we noted earlier. Samuel says:

> Has the Lord as great delight in burnt offerings and
>   sacrifices
> as in obeying the voice of the Lord?
> Surely, to obey is better than sacrifice,
> and to heed than the fat of rams (1 Sam 15:22).

Once more Saul has revealed, through his behavior, that he trusts external ritual more than he trusts the Lord. Instead of obeying the Lord, Saul hopes to enlist the Lord's favor through ritual.

Again Samuel tells Saul that he will lose the kingdom. Samuel says, "The Lord has torn the kingdom of Israel from you this very day, and has given it to a neighbor of yours, who is better than you" (1 Sam 15:28).

In both stories Saul's fault is the same. Saul does not obey the word of the Lord as it is known to him through the Lord's prophet and through the law. Saul has not passed the test which the Deuteronomist has told us will determine whether or not a king will survive. If a king does not obey the Lord, that king will not remain king but will meet with utter destruction.

### Review Questions

1. Where does Saul put his faith?
2. What sin of disobedience is Saul described as committing in chapter 13? Why was this wrong?
3. What sin of disobedience is Saul described as committing in chapter 15?
4. What was "the ban"? What was the purpose of the ban?
5. According to Saul, why did he not kill all the animals? What is Samuel's response to this claim?
6. What will be the result of Saul's disobedience?

### Discussion Questions

1. Why might the Israelites have thought that "the ban" was a good idea? Have you encountered similar thinking in our country? What do you think Jesus would have said about the ban?
2. Do you think we trust ritual rather than God? What behavior on our part might reveal this flaw?

# ARTICLE 9

## Discovering God's Will by Drawing Lots

**Question: "What is all this about God responding with Urim and Thummim? (1 Sam 14:41) How did Urim and Thummim designate Jonathan as the one who disobeyed his father's ban on eating?" (1 Sam 2:18; 14:3; 14:19–20; 14:41; 22:18; 23:9–10; 30:8; Ex 28:2–14 also discussed)**

Urim and Thummim were evidently objects used to draw lots. In the days before and up to the time of the monarchy they were used by the priests to discern God's will.

We first read of Urim and Thummim when we read the book of Exodus (see Ex 28:30). There Urim and Thummim are described as having been worn in the breastplate of the high priest.

Also described in Exodus 28:2–14 is a garment worn by the high priest called an "ephod." During the time of Samuel and Saul it appears that the Urim and Thummim were carried in a pocket of the ephod, but it is not clear whether the ephod is a garment worn by a priest, a cultic image, or a garment placed on a cultic image.

You may have noticed that Samuel, as a child, was described as wearing an ephod while ministering before the Lord in Shiloh (see 1 Sam 2:18). However, here in chapter 14, the priest, Ahijah, is said to be carrying an ephod (see 1 Sam 14:3). Nevertheless, in chapter 23 you will see that the priests are once again described as wearing the linen ephod (see 1 Sam 22:18). No matter what the ephod was, exactly, it is associated with the Urim and Thummim, and the person wearing or carrying it is to be consulted when one is determining God's will.

We do not know exactly what these objects looked like, but by drawing them at random people believed they received a direct response from God to a question posed so that the answer would be one of two alternatives.

In this passage where Saul is trying to determine who disobeyed his ban on eating he is clearly using the Urim and Thummim as lots. After placing all the people on one side and his son Jonathan with himself on the other side Saul said, "O Lord God of Israel, why have you not answered your servant today? If this guilt is in me or in my son Jonathan, O Lord, God of Israel, give Urim; but if this guilt is in your people Israel, give Thummim. And Jonathan and Saul were indicated by the lot" (1 Sam 14:41). We will see David consult the Lord in exactly the same way when he wants to know whether or not he should enter a battle. Again, the question must be posed so that there are only two alternatives, in this instance "yes" or "no." David had heard that Saul was plotting evil against him, so "he said to the priest Abiathar, 'Bring the ephod here.' David said, 'O Lord, the God of Israel, your servant has heard that Saul seeks to come to Keilah to destroy the city on my account. And now, will Saul come down as your servant has heard? O Lord, the God of Israel, I beseech you, tell your servant.' The Lord said, 'He will come down' " (1 Sam 23:9–10). The Lord's answer came in the drawing of either the Urim or the Thummim. As you will see, David will use the same method to determine God's will when he has to decide whether or not to pursue the Amalekites (see 1 Sam 30:8).

Sometimes the reference to Urim and Thummim is quite specific. Other times one is led to believe that Urim and Thummim are being used even though they are not specifically named. As you already know, one tradition pictures Samuel as selecting Saul to be king by drawing lots. Another example is here in chapter 14, when Saul is talking to a priest while the tumult in the camp of the Philistines grows. The narrator merely says, ". . . and Saul said to the priest, 'Withdraw your hand.' Then Saul and all the people who were with him rallied and went into the battle . . ." (1 Sam 14:19b–20a). Undoubtedly the "hand" held either Urim or Thummim, assuring Saul that he would win the battle.

References to Urim and Thummim do not appear in the Bible after the earliest days of the monarchy. The method is similar to divinization, a practice which became outlawed. As the role of the prophet grew, methods of consulting Yahweh which were similar to the occult practices of other nations died out. We have already noticed the distinction between a seer and a true prophet of Yahweh. We will soon read that Saul had banished "mediums" and "wizards" from the land (see 1 Sam 28:3). With the growth of true prophets, such primitive methods of consulting Yahweh were no longer used.

## Review Questions

1. What were Urim and Thummim?
2. What might the word "ephod" mean?
3. When using Urim and Thummim how must the question to God be posed? Why?
4. When do references to Urim and Thummim disappear? Why?

## Discussion Questions

1. How do you "consult" God?
2. Have you ever believed that God wanted you to do something? How did you arrive at this conclusion?
3. Do you think "God's will" need be consulted routinely in life? Why or why not?

# ARTICLE 10

# Saul: A Tragic Hero

**Question: "Why would the Lord send an evil spirit to torment Saul?" (1 Sam 16:14; 1 Sam 14:28–30; 14:45; 18:8; 22:11–19; 28:6 also discussed)**

The intent of the statement that "an evil spirit from the Lord" tormented Saul will be better understood if we look at the verse as a whole. Our narrator says, "Now the spirit of the Lord departed from Saul, and an evil spirit of the Lord tormented him" (1 Sam 16:14). What does the narrator mean by this statement?

In order to understand the intent behind the statement we must remember the point of view from which the traditions about Saul have been preserved. The traditions about the monarchy were preserved in the circles around Jerusalem. David, who will succeed Saul, was from a southern tribe and established Jerusalem, a southern city, as the center of the kingdom. Saul was from a northern tribe. The traditions we have are defending David's rise to power by showing that it was the result of God's will and action rather than the result of David's cleverly usurping the role of a duly anointed king. It is very important to the narrator that the reader understand that God chose David over Saul, and that is why David's star rose while Saul's declined.

God, of course, reveals God's will through events. Saul, when he was the recognized and undisputed king of Israel, was a charismatic leader. As the first king, he had none of the monarchical structures in place which would develop over time. Rather, Saul had much in common with the charismatic judges.

Remember that Saul was first recognized as king because "the spirit had rushed on him" (see 1 Sam 10:10–11), and because he had successfully saved the people from the Ammonites (see 1 Sam 11:6–7). His was a charismatic leadership, confirmed by Samuel.

However, as events unfolded, the spirit appeared to leave Saul. His leadership was not recognized as charismatic by the people. This will become more and more evident as we continue to read 1 Samuel, but we have seen evidence of it already. In addition to Saul's acts of disobedience which we have already discussed, Saul seems to lack sound judgment. Jonathan openly disagrees with Saul's ban against letting the people eat when they need the energy from food in order to fight (see 1 Sam 14:28–30). All the people openly disagree with Saul's judgment that Jonathan should die after eating the honey (see 1 Sam 14:45).

As Saul's story continues we seem to be reading about a man who has lost his mental stability. In a prepsychological age such a condition would be described as having an evil spirit. And, since all is within the bounds of Yahweh's power, such an "evil spirit" would be described as having been sent by the Lord.

Indeed, Saul does seem to be psychologically disturbed. He is pictured as being insanely jealous of David's success, even though David's success is Saul's success. His jealousy leads him to want David dead. Since both Saul's son, Jonathan, and Saul's daughter, Michal, love David, Saul's hatred of David has the effect of separating him from his own family. Finally Saul's hatred of David leads him to order the slaughter of the priests of Nob (see 1 Sam 22:11–19). This was such a terrible deed that Saul's own henchmen refused to carry it out.

Even worse than Saul's estrangement from his people, from his immediate family and from his immediate entourage is the estrangement Saul felt from God.

Saul is pictured as interpreting events as meaning that David, not he, was destined by God to become king. Early on, after the defeat of Goliath, when the people say, "Saul has killed his thousands, and David his ten thousands," Saul was very angry. "He said, 'They have ascribed to David ten thousands, and to me they have ascribed thousands; what more can he have but the kingdom?'" (1 Sam 18:8). So Saul felt that he was no longer God's chosen leader.

With the denunciation from Samuel, and finally Samuel's death, Saul felt that he had no way to be in touch with God. When threatened by the Philistines, Saul was afraid. "When Saul inquired of the Lord, the Lord did not answer him, not by dreams, or by Urim, or by prophets" (1 Sam 28:6). Saul will finally disobey his own law by consulting a medium, hear his worst fears confirmed by Samuel, called up from the dead, suffer defeat at the hands of the Philistines, whom he had been anointed to conquer, and end his own life.

Saul is truly a tragic hero. As the first king of Israel he was a recognized charismatic leader who did succeed in protecting his people for some time. However, Saul did not understand what trust in God rather than trust in religious ritual meant, and his fear and insecurity led him to actions which left him separated from family, countrymen, and God. Our narrator vividly describes this condition as being "tormented by an evil spirit from the Lord."

## Review Questions

1. From what point of view have the traditions about Saul been preserved?
2. What did Saul have in common with the judges?
3. What events seemed to signify that the spirit had left Saul?
4. In a prepsychological age how might mental illness be described? Why?
5. How did Saul become estranged from his people? His family? His entourage? His God?
6. Why does Saul resort to consulting a medium? What does he hear?

## Discussion Questions

1. Why do you think jealousy is called "the green eyed monster." Do you think this is a better or worse description than "an evil spirit sent by the Lord"? Why?
2. Have you ever felt separated from God? Why? What did you do about it? What could one do about it?
3. As you read these accounts do you see any virtue in Saul? Do you see any fault in David? Do you agree that the traditions "defend" David as opposed to "defending" Saul? Why or why not?

# ARTICLE 11

# David and Goliath: A Legend

**Question: "Was David a grown man or a little boy when he defeated Goliath? If he could wear Saul's clothes he couldn't have been small since Saul stood head and shoulders above the others." (1 Sam 17:1–54; 1 Sam 10:23; 2 Sam 21:19 also discussed)**

The inconsistencies in the story of David and Goliath which this reader has noted are due, as you by now probably realize, to the melding of various traditions, not all of which are compatible with each other. The chapters in which we read of David's introduction to Saul's court are confusing for this very reason. We will compare various traditions in our next article, but first we will look at that tradition which includes what can accurately be described as the legend of David and Goliath.

You may remember that a legend is an imaginative story with an historical core. In fact, the historical core of this story will come into question when we read 2 Samuel. There we will read that Elhanan of Bethlehem defeated Goliath (see 2 Sam 21:19). However, the question of the accuracy of the specific historical core of the legend is irrelevant to the point of the legend, because the real point of the story is not that David slew Goliath but that David was God's chosen instrument. In fact, the story is told in such a way that we realize that it is the Lord who slew Goliath.

In this legend as it probably existed independently of its present context, David was a youth unknown to Saul. Unlike his brother, David was not yet one of Saul's soldiers. He still lived at home and watched over his father's sheep. The story makes a point of David's youth, just as it makes a point of Goliath's size and experience, in order to contrast the two.

Young David learns of Goliath's threat when he is sent by his father to bring food to his brothers and their commander. While there David hears not only Goliath's threat but the fact that the king would greatly reward the person who conquered Goliath. The king would give that person his daughter's hand in marriage (see 1 Sam 17:25).

Much to his older brother's annoyance, David is extremely interested in this opportunity. "David said to the men who stood by him, 'What shall be done for the man who kills this Philistine and takes away the reproach from Israel?' " (1 Sam 17:26a). When we read David's brother's petty and jealous accusations we are reminded of Cinderella's sisters. Who is David to be asking such questions? But David keeps asking (see 1 Sam 17:28–30).

David's interest in the matter is brought to the attention of Saul. Saul has already been described as cowering in fear in the face of Goliath's challenge (see 1 Sam 17:11). He sees no possibility that young David could be of any help. "Saul said to David, 'You are not able to go against the Philistine to fight with him; for you are just a boy, and he has been a warrior from his youth' " (1 Sam 17:33).

David argues with Saul not just on the basis of his own skill but on the basis of his belief that the living God will win the battle for him. "David said, 'The Lord, who saved me from the power of the lion and the paw of the bear will save me from the hand of the Philistine.' So Saul said to David, 'Go, and may the Lord be with you!' " (1 Sam 17:37).

As the story proceeds, David's youth and his total dependence on God continue to be emphasized. When Goliath sees David, "he disdained him, for he was only a youth, ruddy and handsome in appearance" (1 Sam 17:42b). David does not fear Goliath. He says, "You came to me with sword and spear and javelin, but I come to you in the name of the Lord of hosts, the God of the armies of Israel, whom you have defied. . . . The Lord does not save by sword and spear; for the battle is the Lord's and he will give you into our hand' " (1 Sam 17:45, 47).

So, as the legend goes, young David slew the mighty Goliath and married the king's daughter. David is a folk hero. However, as is true in other biblical legends, the story of the folk hero is not told just to make a hero of David, but to make a hero of God. David is not a hero because of his own courage and ability. David is a hero because he is God's chosen instrument. The legend is told to illustrate the fact that God has chosen one "after God's own heart," and that chosen one is David.

## Review Questions

1. What is a legend?
2. What is the point of the story of David and Goliath?
3. What does David hear that grabs his attention?
4. What is Saul's reaction to Goliath's challenge?
5. Why does Saul doubt David's ability to help?
6. On what basis does David argue with Saul?
7. Who are the two heroes in the story of David and Goliath?
8. Why is David a hero?

## Discussion Questions

1. What is the point of the legend of George Washington and the cherry tree? If it turned out that George's parents had no tree would the point be lost? Why or why not?
2. Have you ever been sure that it was God's help and not your ability that resulted in your success? Why?
3. Do elements of this legend remind you of any fairy tale motifs? Explain.

# David: From Court Favorite to Outcast

**Question: "How did Saul first meet David? I'm all confused." (1 Sam 16:14–17; 16:18–22; 17:12–30; 17:55–58; 18–20; 23:17 discussed)**

There are a number of incompatible traditions about how Saul first met David. If one has not realized this by the time one is reading the end of chapter 17, one certainly realizes it then. As David defeats Goliath, Saul is pictured as asking, "Whose son is this?" (see 1 Sam 17:55). Neither Saul nor his commander seem to have any prior knowledge of the boy.

We will not be able to completely separate and identify traditions, but we can find several strains. One strain is that Saul met David because David was brought to the court in order to play for Saul and soothe Saul's melancholy spirit (see 1 Sam 16:14–17).

Another strain, perhaps compatible with the first and perhaps not, is that David was a stalwart soldier whom Saul recognized as someone who would be very helpful in the battle against the Philistines. In this tradition Saul asks Jesse to send David so that David can enter Saul's service, and Saul makes David his armor-bearer (see 1 Sam 16:18–22). In our present account these two traditions are interwound.

An additional tradition is the one we identified in the legend of David and Goliath in which David comes to Saul's attention precisely because he volunteers to meet Goliath's challenge (see 1 Sam 17:12–30, 55–58).

No matter how Saul first met David, once David had experienced success against the Philistines he was, for a short time, part of Saul's court. The series of stories in chapters 18–20, while they, too, undoubtedly come from several sources, serve to explain that it was Saul's fault and not David's that David became a guerilla soldier rather than a person who fought side by side with his king.

At first David is welcomed into Saul's entourage by everyone, including Saul. However, it does not take long for Saul to have a change of heart. As we have already mentioned, Saul was filled with jealousy as he heard the women chant: "Saul has killed his thousands, and David his ten thousands" (1 Sam 18:7b).

Jonathan had just as much reason to be jealous and fearful of David as did Saul, since Jonathan would be Saul's natural successor. Jonathan, however, is presented in sharp contrast to Saul.

Jonathan loved David from their first acquaintance until the day of his death. "Jonathan made a covenant with David, because he loved him as his own soul" (1 Sam 18:3). When Jonathan has to chose between his father, Saul, who was absorbed in jealous rage, and his friend, David, who is presented as completely undeserving of Saul's jealousy, Jonathan chooses David. As Jonathan helps David he prays, "May the Lord be with you, as he has been with my father" (1 Sam 20:13b). This is a most unusual prayer. It could be interpreted to mean that Jonathan preferred David as heir to the throne to himself. Later Jonathan will tell David that David will be the next king (see 1 Sam 23:17).

In addition to the story in which Jonathan seems to promote David's succession to the throne, the story of David's marriage to Saul's daughter suggests that David should be the next king.

As you may remember, in the legend of David and Goliath, David was presented as having been interested in slaying Goliath in order to be rewarded with the king's daughter for his bride. When Saul suggests to David that he might become the king's son-in-law, it is not to reward David but to endanger his life. Despite Saul's best laid plans, David is not killed in his encounters with the Philistines as he tries to win Merab's hand, nor is he killed in his endeavor to get one hundred Philistine foreskins as he subsequently tries to win Michal's hand. (The folklore tone of impossible obstacles has certainly reappeared. See 1 Sam 18:17–29.) So David wins his bride and Saul is confronted with one more reason to fear David. Like Jonathan, Michal puts David's interests before her father's and helps David escape from Saul's jealous rage (see 1 Sam 19:8–17).

---

**CHAPTERS 18–20: IN DEFENSE OF DAVID**

- Jonathan loves David.
- David carries out successfully every mission on which Saul sends him.
- Saul becomes terribly jealous.
- Saul offers daughters as war prize hoping David will be killed.
- Saul plots to kill David himself.
- God protects David from Saul, with Samuel's help.
- Jonathan helps David escape Saul.

---

Finally, even Samuel prefers David to Saul. It seems that the "prophetic frenzy" of Samuel's group of prophets could be used to protect David, for first Saul's messengers and then Saul himself fall into a prophetic frenzy which prevents them from capturing David (see 1 Sam 19:18–24).

The stories that have been preserved about the contention between Saul and David all agree. It was Saul's fault and not David's that David had to leave Saul's entourage and become a soldier in exile from his king rather than a soldier fighting with his king.

**Review Questions**

1. Describe three traditions of how David met Saul.
2. What is the point of the stories in chapters 18–20?
3. What was Jonathan's reaction to David? Why is Jonathan's reaction extremely important?
4. What is Saul's motive in suggesting that David become his son-in-law?
5. What is Michal's attitude toward David?
6. Whose fault is it that David leaves Saul's entourage?

**Discussion Questions**

1. Do you know of any two people who seem to be permanently estranged? Does it seem to you to be all one person's fault or not? Explain.

2. Have you ever completely changed your mind about someone from good to bad or from bad to good? Why do you think first impressions can be completely reversed?
3. Do you think David had any choice other than to flee? Why or why not?

# ARTICLE 13

# David's Political Savvy

**Question: "Why does David pretend to be insane when he meets Achish?" (1 Sam 21:13; 1 Sam 21:2; 22:2; 22:20–23; 23:6; 25:6–8; 30:24–26 also discussed)**

When David pretends to be insane he reveals one of the many uncannily clever methods he used to survive as an outcast, feared and pursued by the king. As David builds a power base for himself he exhibits all the political savvy of an undercover agent.

David's first strategy is to lie. When he meets the priest, Ahimelech, he does not tell him of the rift between himself and Saul, but instead claims to be on a secret mission for the king (see 1 Sam 21:2). Ahimelech believes David and gives him food and Goliath's sword. Ahimelech will pay dearly for this when Saul hears of it.

When David meets Achish he pretends to be mad, thus putting himself among the untouchables and removing himself as a perceived threat to Achish. No one need bother about a poor, drooling madman.

Next, David gathers around himself others who, like him, are on the fringes of society. "Everyone who was in distress, and everyone who was in debt, and everyone who was discontented gathered to him; and he became captain over them" (1 Sam 22:2a).

As Saul makes additional enemies through his irrational actions, David's followers increase. Because Saul ordered that the priests of Nob be killed, one of the priests, Abiathar, who was able to escape with the ephod, joins David (see 1 Sam 22:20–23; 23:6). Now David is able to consult God and choose his actions accordingly.

David also increases his numbers by a kind of "good neighbor" policy. When Nabal, a wealthy sheep owner, has a shearing festival,

233

---

**WHO'S WHO**

**Ahimelech:** A priest who helped David by giving him holy bread and Goliath's sword.

**Achish:** King of Gath who let David alone because David appeared to be mad.

**Priests of Nob:** The priests who were slaughtered at Saul's orders because Ahimelech had helped David.

**Nabal:** The wealthy sheep owner who failed to help David and died.

**Abigail:** Nabal's wife who later married David.

---

David sends representatives to remind Nabal of the good treatment his shepherds had received at David's hands (see 1 Sam 25:6–8). While Nabal himself is unimpressed, Nabal's wife, Abigail, is not. Abigael makes sure that David and his men are treated well, and, after the death of her husband, she marries David.

Still another politically astute move made by David is his insistence that the spoils of war be divided in such a way that many are indebted to him. Some of David's soldiers were left behind when David raided the Amalekites. Those who had fought the battle thought they should receive more of the booty than those who did not. David objected to this. "But David said, 'You shall not do so, my brothers, with what the Lord has given us. He has preserved us and handed over to us the raiding party that attacked us. Who would listen to you in this matter? For the share of the one who goes down into the battle shall be the same as the share of the one who stays by the baggage; they shall share alike.' From that day forward he made it a statute and an ordinance for Israel; it continues to the present day" (1 Sam 30:24–25).

Not only does David ingratiate himself with his troops by his division of the spoils, but David uses the spoils to win favor with the elders of Judah. He gives the elders of each town a gift, saying, "Here is a present for you from the spoil of the enemies of the Lord . . ." (1 Sam 30:26b).

Although David proves himself to be a master of political intrigue, he does not use that ability to destroy Saul. In fact, as we shall see, David does not believe that God wants him to destroy Saul, so he refrains from doing it. It is not David, but God, who is behind Saul's defeat.

**Review Questions**

1. How does David persuade Ahimelech to help him?
2. Why does David pretend to be mad?
3. Who gathered around David?
4. Why does Abiathar join David? What does he bring with him? Why is this important?
5. How does David benefit from his "good neighbor" policy?
6. How does David divide the spoils of war? Why is this smart?
7. How does David win favor with the elders of Judah?
8. Who is behind Saul's defeat?

**Discussion Questions**

1. Do you disapprove of any of David's strategies for survival? Why or why not? Have you ever had occasion to use any of them yourself? Explain.
2. Do you know of instances in modern times in which "malcontents" have banded together for political purposes? Explain.
3. What do you think a person should do if confronted with duly constituted but completely unreasonable authority?

# ARTICLE 14

# God's Anointed One

**Question: "Wasn't David finally a traitor? He was willing to fight against Saul with the Philistines." (1 Sam 24, 26–27, 29)**

David is certainly never presented as a traitor, either to Saul personally or to Israel. In fact, the traditions which we are reading bend over backwards to affirm David's loyalty. David becomes king not because he ruthlessly seeks to usurp Saul, but because God chooses David over Saul.

David's personal loyalty to Saul, despite Saul's pathological fear and hatred of David, is made perfectly clear in the two stories in which Saul is delivered into David's hands, but David refrains from hurting Saul (see 1 Sam 24, 26). In the first episode David cuts off a piece of Saul's cloak and then regrets his action. "He (David) said to his men, 'The Lord forbid that I should do this thing to my lord, the Lord's anointed, to raise my hand against him; for he is the Lord's anointed' " (1 Sam 24:6).

In the second instance David takes Saul's spear and water jar, but does not harm him. Abishai wanted David to kill Saul while he had the chance but David said, "Do not destroy him; for who can raise his hand against the Lord's anointed, and be guiltless? . . . As the Lord lives, the Lord will strike him down; or his day will come to die, or he will go down into battle and perish. The Lord forbid that I should raise my hand against the Lord's anointed, but now take the spear that is at this head and the water jar, and let us go" (1 Sam 26:10–11).

It is true that David takes refuge with the Philistines, but the text

236

---

**WHO'S WHO**

**Abishai:** David's companion who wanted David to kill Saul while he had the chance.

**Achish:** The Philistine leader with whom David fought for some time.

---

does not support the suggestion that David would have fought for the Philistines in the battle against Saul.

David's motivation in going to the land of the Philistines was to flee Saul, not to conquer Saul militarily (see 1 Sam 27:1). It is true that David leads a number of raids on enemies of the Philistines, raids which please Achish, the leader of the Philistines. However, the conquered people were also enemies of the Israelites (see 1 Sam 27:8–12).

The real test would have come had David faced Saul in battle, fighting with the Philistines. However, events unfold in such a way that David is not put in this position, and God, of course, is behind events.

It does appear, at least to Achish, that David would have fought with the Philistines against Saul. However, we have noticed David's cagey double agent skills, so his words appear to us to be purposefully ambiguous. When Achish tells David about the upcoming confrontation with Saul, Achish says, " 'You know, of course, that you and your men are to go out with me in the army.' David said to Achish, 'Very well, then you shall know what your servant can do' " (1 Sam 28:1b–2). The reader knows that David could turn on Achish as well as fight with him if he believed that God would have him do that.

The other Philistine leaders are well aware that David might fight against them rather than with them once the battle begins. They insist that Achish tell David that he may not join them in battle, which Achish does. "David said to Achish, 'But what have I done? What have you found in your servant from the day I entered your service until now, that I should not go and fight against the enemies of my lord, the King?' " (1 Sam 29:8). Which "Lord and King" does David have in mind? Achish presumes that David is referring to him, but the reader is well aware that David may be referring to the Lord's anointed lord, Saul.

Since David is rejected by the Philistine leaders he is not present for the battle in which Saul is soundly defeated. David's dearest friend, Jonathan, who had recognized that David would be the next king, is killed, along with his brothers. Knowing that the battle is over and not wanting to be killed by the Philistines, Saul falls on his own sword. The Philistines abuse Saul's body. On hearing of this, some of Saul's fellow countrymen retrieve his body, cremate him, and bury his bones in Jabesh. It is ironic that Saul should be buried in Jabesh, because Jabesh had been the site of Saul's first victory against the Philistines after having been anointed king.

David was not a traitor to Saul. In fact, David remained loyal to Saul under extremely adverse conditions. Saul was finally defeated because Saul, after his disobedience, was no longer God's choice. God had chosen another, and that other, though secretly anointed by Samuel, did not challenge Saul's right to be king as long as Saul was alive. However, as an outcast, he conducted himself in such a way that by the time Saul died, David had a power base from which to operate. 1 Samuel ends with Saul dead and David poised to bring to fulfillment through events the anointing which he had received from Samuel. One after the Lord's own heart would soon be acclaimed king of Israel.

### Review Questions

1. Why does David regret cutting Saul's cloak?
2. Why won't David kill Saul?
3. Why does David go to the land of the Philistines?
4. Why does David not face Saul in battle, fighting with the Philistines?
5. What double meaning can be understood in David's two comments to Achish?
6. How does Saul die?
7. Was David a traitor to Saul? Explain.
8. How does 1 Samuel end?

**Discussion Questions**

1. Have you ever been called upon to "turn the other cheek," and to "love your enemy"? Explain. Do you think David did this? Why or why not?
2. Do you agree that David's words to Achish are purposefully ambiguous? Why or why not?
3. Do you agree that "all is fair in love and war"? Why or why not?
4. Would you consider Saul's death a suicide or a defeat in battle? Explain.

# THE BOOK OF 2 SAMUEL

# ARTICLE 1

# Saul's Death: A National and Personal Grief

**Question: "Did David kill the messenger who told him of Saul's death? Why?" (2 Sam 1:15; 2 Sam 1; 4:8–10; Ex 15:21 also discussed)**

David did order the death of the Amalekite who told him of Saul's death. However, the Amalekite did a good deal more than inform David of Saul's death. The Amalekite told David that he himself had killed Saul, albeit at Saul's request, and he also offered David Saul's crown. One can only conclude that the Amalekite misjudged David, thinking that David would be pleased to have Saul out of the way so that he could have the crown, even when offered to him by a non-Israelite.

We already know, however, that David would never raise his hand against the Lord's anointed. We have already read two accounts in which David could easily have killed Saul but did not. We also know that the editor is interested in showing that David did not usurp Saul's power. David became king, not because he grabbed the crown when it was offered to him by a non-Israelite, but because God had chosen David to be king. Events resulted in David's becoming king, and God is the author of events.

So the news of Saul's death is an occasion for both national and personal grief, not an occasion for rejoicing. This grief is expressed both in David's actions and in David's beautiful lament.

First, David expresses the national grief in his actions. "Then David took hold of his clothes and tore them; and all the men who were with him did the same. They mourned and wept, and fasted until evening for Saul and for his son Jonathan, and for the army of the Lord and for the house of Israel, because they had fallen by the sword" (2 Sam 1:11–12).

Next David confronts the Amalekite who actually killed Saul. He believes the man deserves death because he raised his hand against the Lord's anointed (see 2 Sam 1:16). The same fate will await the two who kill Saul's son, Ishbaal. They, too, presume that they will please David and curry favor by their actions (see 2 Sam 4:8). But David is furious. David says, "As the Lord lives, who has redeemed my life out of every adversity, when the one who told me, 'See, Saul is dead,' thought he was bringing good news, I seized him and killed him at Ziklag—this was the reward I gave him for his news" (2 Sam 4:9b–10). David kills these men, too, because they have unjustly killed another and because he does not want to be partners with anyone who disobeys God. David will not disobey God to win the throne, but will win the throne because he obeys God.

After killing the Amalekite who brings the bad news, David is pictured as expressing both the national and personal grief brought on by the defeat in one of the most beautiful laments ever written. Our editor tells us that this poem was written in the book of Jashar, a written source available to the editor but no longer extant. (In addition to being quoted here, it is quoted in Joshua 10:13 and in 1 Kings 8:13.) The poem begins with the grief of the nation:

> Your glory, O Israel, lies slain upon your high places!
> How the mighty have fallen! (2 Sam 1:19)

Next there is a warning not to let the news reach the daughters of the Philistines who would rejoice on hearing it. Here the author uses "synonymous parallelism," a common poetic technique in Hebrew poetry. That is, the author says the same thing in adjacent lines but in different words:

> Tell it not in Gath,
>     proclaim it not in the streets of Ashkelon;
> or the daughters of the Philistines will rejoice,
>     the daughters of the uncircumcised will exult. (2 Sam 1:20)

The center of the poem praises both Saul and Jonathan for their bravery. Both were "swifter than eagles" and "stronger than lions" (see 2 Sam 1:23b).

---

**GROWTH PROCESS BEHIND SCRIPTURE**

*Events:* Jonathan and Saul die in battle.

*Oral Tradition:* The refrain and the song take form in oral tradition.

*Written Tradition:* The poem is written in the book of Jashar.

*Edited Tradition:* The Deuteronomist includes the poem in his Deuteronomistic History.

---

Next, with perfect structural balance, the daughters of Israel are addressed. Unlike the daughters of the Philistines, the daughters of Israel will weep over Saul who had provided them with many good things.

Finally, personal grief overcomes all other considerations as David mourns Jonathan whom he loved:

> I am distressed for you, my brother Jonathan;
> greatly beloved were you to me.
> Your love to me was wonderful,
> passing the love of women (2 Sam 1:26).

The poem ends with a refrain which has not merely been repeated but which has moved the poem progressively forward through the battle to defeat: From "How the mighty have fallen," to "How the mighty have fallen in the midst of battle," to "How the mighty have fallen, and the weapons of war perished" (see 2 Sam 1:19b, 25a, 27).

Scholars think that this refrain, like Miriam's refrain at the defeat of the Egyptians which we read in Exodus 15:21, is very old and finds its roots in the actual event. We are indebted to the Deuteronomist for including this poem in his arrangement of inherited materials even though it exalts Saul and doesn't even mention God. The grief which it expresses comes straight from the heart.

Although David does not accept Saul's crown and armlet from the Amalekite, with the death of Saul and Jonathan, David is the person to whom the people turn for leadership. David will not grasp the leadership but the leadership will come to him.

## Review Questions

1. What did the Amalekite do in addition to informing David of Saul's death?
2. How does the Amalekite misjudge David?
3. How does David express his grief?
4. What does David do to the Amalekite?
5. What is synonymous parallelism?
6. Where was the lament previously recorded?
7. What about this beautiful lament makes it "less useful" than the Deuteronomist might have wanted?

## Discussion Questions

1. Have you ever had someone bring you news which he or she considered good but you considered bad? Explain.
2. Have you ever had someone completely misjudge your motives and reactions? Explain.
3. Why do you think this lament never mentions God or hope?
4. Do you agree that this refrain has the flavor of the actual grief of the moment? Why or why not?

# ARTICLE 2

# King of Judah and Israel

**Question: "What does 'King of the Judahites' mean? (2 Sam 2:4; 2:11) What is the relationship between the Judahites and Israel?" (2 Sam 2:1–5:5; Gen 49:10 also discussed)**

The word "Judahites" refers to those from the tribe of Judah, the tribe which we noted at the conclusion of Genesis because, in Jacob's deathbed blessing, it is said that Judah will be the ruler of his brothers (see Gen 49:10).

The tribe of Judah settled in the southern part of Canaan and was an obscure tribe up until the time of the monarchy. David is from the tribe of Judah.

"Israel" refers to a number of northern tribes, all of whom recognized Saul as their king. The tribes which were called Israel are never specifically named, so, suffice it to say, that Israel, at this time, refers simply to the northern tribes which were united under Saul.

At the time of Saul's death David was a recognized leader of a fringe group who had fought both with Saul and with the Philistines. After consulting God David left the Philistines and returned to Judah, specifically to Hebron. It is there that the men of Judah anointed David "King of the Judahites."

The next several chapters of 2 Samuel, chapters 2:1–5:5, describe how David became king, not only of the Judahites, but of all Israel as well.

After Saul's death God does not choose a king for the northern tribes, for "Israel." Abner does. Abner was the commander of Saul's army and he, evidently on his own authority, made Saul's son, Ishbaal, king (see 2 Sam 2:8).

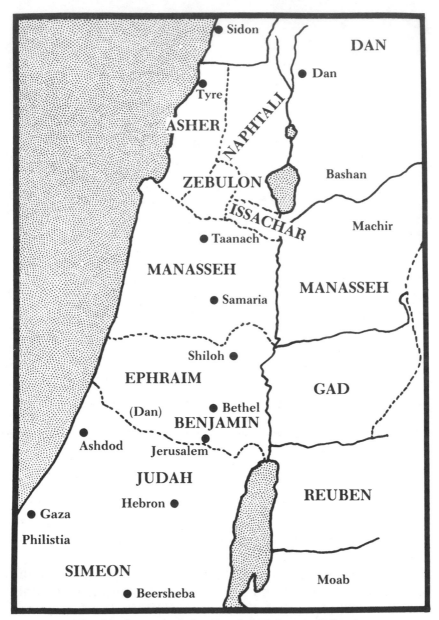

**The Settlement of the Twelve Tribes in Palestine**

---

**WHO'S WHO**

**Joab:** David's commander.

**Ishbaal:** Saul's son who succeeded him.

**Abner.** Ishbaal's commander who is eventually killed by Joab.

**Asahel:** Joab's brother who is killed by Abner.

---

Trouble between the Judahites and the Israelites is constant. First we read of a confrontation between David's men under his commander, Joab, and Ishbaal's men under his commander, Abner. The conflict begins with a duel between twelve men from each side. Since all twenty-four are killed this duel settles nothing and escalates into a confrontation which, while it causes each side damage, harms David's side less than it harms Ishbaal's side.

The confrontation between Judah and Israel deteriorates into a confrontation between Joab's brothers and Abner. Although Abner does not want to kill Joab's brother, Asahel, he does because Asahel will not stop pursuing Abner (see 2 Sam 2:18–23). By killing Asahel, Abner makes himself subject to blood revenge.

At Abner's call for a truce, Joab temporarily backs down. Again, there are losses on both sides but the losses on David's side are much less than the losses suffered by the Israelites.

It is God and not David or Joab who is responsible for the Israelites turning to David for leadership.

First Ishbaal angers his commander, Abner, by accusing him of sleeping with one of Saul's concubines, so Abner deserts Ishbaal. "Abner sent messengers to David at Hebron, saying, 'To whom does the land belong? Make your covenant with me, and I will give you my support to bring all Israel over to you'" (2 Sam 3:12). David replies that a condition of this covenant would be that Saul's daughter, Michal, be returned to David as David's wife. This was a shrewd political move because, as Saul's son-in-law, David would have a more credible claim to the throne of Israel.

While David is willing to make peace with Abner, Joab is not. Joab has not forgotten that Abner killed his brother, and so he disobeys David and kills Abner. David goes to great pains to make it clear to everyone that he had no part in Abner's death.

Neither does David have anything to do with the death of Ishbaal. As we already noted, two men thought they would be pleasing David by murdering Ishbaal and bringing David his head, but they were wrong. David commanded that these murderers be killed.

With no leadership remaining in Israel, David is sought out. "So all the elders of Israel came to the king at Hebron; and King David made a covenant with them at Hebron before the Lord, and they anointed David king over Israel" (2 Sam 5:3).

David will remain king for forty years. The Israelites will never have a greater king. However, even as David establishes his kingdom he plants the seeds which will lead to dissension, for David will not only be a great king, a great soldier, and a great political strategist, but he will also be a great sinner. Both the glory and the downfall of Israel are foreshadowed in the life of David, the first king of both Judah and Israel.

## Review Questions

1. To whom does the word "Judahites" refer?
2. Where did we read of Judah before?
3. What claim to fame does the tribe have?
4. To whom does "Israel" refer?
5. Where was David first anointed king of Judah?
6. Who is Abner? What does he do?
7. Who succeeded Saul in Israel?
8. Who is Joab?
9. How does Abner make himself subject to blood revenge?
10. Why does Abner desert Ishbaal?
11. How does Abner die?
12. How does Ishbaal die?

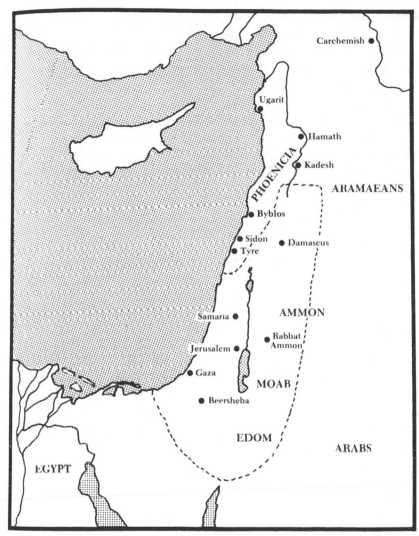

**The Empire of Israel under David and Solomon
(1000–930 B.C.)**

## Discussion Questions

1. What is your reaction to the idea of "blood revenge"? In a society that has no police or court system, do you think this is a good idea? Why or why not?
2. Do you have any reaction to Michal's treatment? What is it?
3. Do you think it was all right for Joab to kill Abner? Why or why not?

# ARTICLE 3

# Life's Central Question

**Question: "This story about Michal being passed back and forth for political reasons is very sad. (2 Sam 3:13–16) 1, 2 Samuel seem to reflect the idea that life is about being victorious in battle rather than about being loving and faithful in relationships. Why is this book considered inspired?" (2 Sam 6:23; Ex 20:17 also discussed)**

While it may seem on the surface that the editor of 1, 2 Samuel thinks life is about victory in battle rather than about love and fidelity in relationships, on closer look one can see that this charge is not true. While the editor of the book has some presumptions which we don't share, his attitude toward women among them, nevertheless 1, 2 Samuel, at the core, are about love and fidelity in relationships. They are about love and fidelity in people's relationships with God. In order to defend this thesis we will first name some of those presumptions which the editor of 1, 2 Samuel shared with his audience, but not with us. Then we will see how the core of the book is about fidelity to God rather than about victory in battle.

In the culture about which we are reading, and in the culture of the Deuteronomist, women are property. Because women are property they are treated as property. The fact that women are property is perfectly evident in the book of Exodus. Remember, one of the commandments was, "You shall not covet your neighbor's house. You shall not covet your neighbor's wife, or his servant, man or woman, or his ox, or his donkey, or anything that is his" (Ex 20:17).

Michal, as the daughter of a king, is valuable property in that marriage to her gives one some claim to the throne. Concubines,

---

**A CONTEXTUALIST**

*Reads scripture passages in context.*

- What is the literary form?
- What is the social context within which the author is addressing the audience?
- How does this writing fit into the process of revelation which we find in the Bible?

---

too, are property. So while the treatment which women receive in this culture is abhorrent to us, we make a mistake if we take our value system and insist that it be shared by a culture which preceded us by some 3000 years.

A second concept, not as foreign to our culture as one might hope, is the idea of a holy war. The Israelites felt they were doing God's work when they conquered other Canaanite peoples. They felt they were acknowledging that the victory actually belonged to Yahweh by putting all living things under the ban. So, again, we cannot bring our attitudes toward war to our reading of 1, 2 Samuel and expect Saul, David, Abner, or Joab to share our value system. They simply did not.

Still a third belief held by David's contemporaries, as well as by the Deuteronomist, is that all suffering is due to sin. While our culture might accept the fact that sin always causes suffering, we would not agree that all suffering is due to sin. The idea that not all suffering is due to sin is not proposed in scripture until after the Babylonian exile, when the book of Job was written. In the eyes of the Deuteronomist, if a person suffers, then that person must have sinned because sin is the cause of suffering. It is this belief that is behind the editor's interpretation of the fact that Michal remained childless all her life (see 2 Sam 6:23). Michal's suffering must have been due to sin.

Why, then, if the Deuteronomist considers women property, war holy, and all suffering due to sin, is the Deuteronomist's work considered inspired? What can we learn from the Deuteronomist that is true?

The core insight which the Deuteronomist holds before us is this: The most important question in life is, "Am I in right relationship with my God?" If the answer to this question is "yes," all will ultimately be well. If the answer is "no," all will ultimately not be well. While our culture would certainly not always agree with the Deuteronomist on what "in right relationship" would mean in terms of beliefs and behavior, the central importance of the question remains firm. Life's order and meaning come from one's answer to the question, "Am I in right relationship with my God?"

Saul lost favor with God because he did not make his relationship with God the core of his life. David does make his relationship with God the core of his life. In the Deuteronomist's eyes, that is the difference between them.

That is not to say that David does not sin. As we shall soon see, he sins grievously. However, David, unlike Saul, does not defend himself in sin as Saul did when he failed to enforce the ban. Nor does David confess fault but fail to repent as Saul did when he tried to kill David. David is pictured as accepting the Deuteronomist's premise. The moral order is established by God. Human beings must obey God and this moral order or they will suffer the consequences.

So, 1, 2 Samuel are not really about victory or defeat in battle. Rather, victory and defeat in battle depend on something which is much more important than the outcome of the battle itself. 1, 2 Samuel are about love and fidelity in one's relationship with God. The state of that relationship determines everything else, not only the fate of individuals but the fate of nations as well.


**Review Questions**

1. At the core, what are 1, 2 Samuel about?
2. What attitude toward women do 1, 2 Samuel reflect?
3. What attitude toward war do 1, 2 Samuel reflect?
4. What belief about the cause of suffering is reflected in 1, 2 Samuel?

5. To the Deuteronomist, what is the core question in life?
6. In the Deuteronomist's eyes, what is the main difference between Saul and David?
7. For the Deuteronomist, on what does success in battle depend?

## Discussion Questions

1. Do you think people still hold the concept of a holy war today? Are there circumstances which might make war holy? Discuss?
2. Do you think sin always causes suffering? Does it matter whether or not one is "caught"? Explain.
3. Do you agree that all order in life flows from one's right relationship with God? Explain.

# God "Tabernacles" in Jerusalem

**Question: "Why was Uzzah struck dead for stabilizing the ark?" (2 Sam 6:17; 1 Sam 6:19; 1 Chron 13–15 also discussed)**

The story as it is told in 2 Samuel does not tell us why Uzzah "inflamed God's anger." Another account of these same episodes appears in 1 Chronicles 13–15. In this account David draws the conclusion that God had been angered because the priests had not been given a proper role in moving the ark. David says to the priests, "It was because you were not there the first time that Yahweh our God broke out against us, because we did not approach him in the right way" (1 Chron 15:13).

As you know from reading the stories of the ark in 1 Samuel, the ark narratives picture the ark as wreaking havoc wherever the ark went, be it in Philistine or Hebrew territory. That is why the ark ended up in a backwater in the first place.

Just as the withdrawal of the ark from the center of the Israelites' life and worship signaled the beginning of a time of great change, so does the retrieval of the ark signal a significant change in the life of the people.

Now that David was king of both Judah and Israel he needed to consolidate his lands and power. So David shrewdly picked a capital which belonged to neither the Judaizers nor the Israelites. Jerusalem lay on the border of the tribes of Judah and Benjamin. David wrested Jerusalem from the hands of the Jebusites and built himself a palace. The fact that David had time to build reflects the fact that he was less threatened by invading parties than he had been in the past. That he selected a site that belonged to neither the

---

**I CHRONICLES 10:1–29:30**

1. Written after Babylonian exile.

2. Used Deuteronomistic History as a source.

3. Traces his own worshipping community primarily back to the worshipping community which God established through David.

4. Idealizes David so does not mention David's sin nor revolts described by the Deuteronomist.

5. Emphasizes the role of priests.

---

northern or southern tribes shows that he wanted to rise above factional disputes and unite the tribes into a single nation.

Having secured Jerusalem David decided to make Jerusalem the cultic center as well as the political center of the nation. So he went to Baala of Judah (another name for Kirithjearim where the ark was left in 1 Samuel 7) to retrieve the ark.

As the people celebrated and made merry before the ark, Uzzah, after steadying the ark, dropped dead. In our culture such an event would be considered a sudden death, not a sudden punishment. In the Israelite's culture the death was interpreted as a punishment. David himself interpreted the death as a sign of God's anger and so feared to bring the ark to Jerusalem. Perhaps he would fare no better than had the Philistines and the seventy men of Bethshemesh who had not joined in the celebration of the ark's return to Israel (see 1 Sam 6:19). So David diverted the ark to the house of Obededom.

Contrary to David's fears, the ark did not wreak havoc but was accompanied by blessing. This encouraged David to complete his plan to bring the ark to Jerusalem. "The ark of the Lord was brought in and set in its place within the tent David had pitched for it" (2 Sam 6:17a).

With the ark of the covenant once more in a tent in the midst of the people, David was able to bring the traditions of the Sinai covenant to bear on the establishment of the monarchy. As God had "tabernacled" with God's people in the desert, so did God now tabernacle with his people in Jerusalem. By moving the ark to Jerusalem David was able to clearly express his understanding that the establishment of the monarchy was not a denial of the kingship of God. Rather, the Mosaic tradition, that the people belonged to God and were in covenant relationship with God, remained. As part of God's covenant love for the people God had chosen David to shepherd his people. David was now clearly established in the eyes of all as God's anointed, king of a united nation.

## Review Questions

1. Why was Jerusalem a shrewd choice for the capital?
2. What happened to Uzzah?
3. How did the people interpret Uzzah's sudden death?
4. What significance did bringing the ark to Jerusalem have?

## Discussion Questions

1. Do you know people who interpret natural phenomena as punishments from God? Do you agree with them? Why or why not?
2. Why is Washington, D.C. not in any state? What does this question have to do with 2 Samuel?
3. Do you believe that God "tabernacles" with us? Do we have concrete signs of this belief? What are they?

# ARTICLE 5

# The Kingdom of God

**Question: "Is Nathan a false prophet? The promise which he said God made to David didn't come true, since David's kingdom and David's line weren't secure forever." (2 Sam 7:3–17; 2 Sam 12 also discussed)**

Nathan was not a false prophet. In fact, Nathan's role here and when he accuses David of sin (see 2 Sam 12) illustrates both how the role of the prophet grew under the monarchy and just how important that role actually became. Nathan was a very great prophet whose words had a profound effect on both the Jewish and Christian concepts of our covenant relationship with God.

However, the passage to which the questioner refers does need an explanation, for Nathan tells David, "Your house and your kingdom shall be made sure forever before me; your throne shall be established forever" (2 Sam 7:16). It is true that the kingdom eventually divided, and that both the northern kingdom, Israel, and the southern kingdom, Judah, were eventually defeated. So how can we still think of Nathan as a great prophet?

In order to answer this question we will first look at the passage in its present context in the text. Next we will discuss how the passage reflects a new understanding and so a new "imaging" of covenant love. Finally we will see how, from the point of view of Christians, the passage played a role in forming expectations which Christians believe have been fulfilled.

As you already know, David has brought the ark of the covenant to Jerusalem and has placed it in a tent so that God can be seen to be "tabernacling" with God's people. However, David thinks that it is not right that he should be living in a palace while God is still living in a tent. When he expresses his concern to Nathan, Nathan initially says, "Go, do all that you have in mind; for the Lord is with you" (2 Sam 7:3b).

However, that night the Lord speaks to Nathan and tells him to tell David that he does not want David to build him a house (i.e., a temple). Rather, the Lord will build David a house (i.e., a dynasty), a house that will be secure forever.

Scripture scholars believe that Nathan's change of mind about David's building a temple reflects the accommodation made to those who were still negative toward the idea of a king. The dwelling tent, along with the ark, was a central cultic object for the Israelites. Perhaps David was acting too quickly to replace it.

Nevertheless, the prophecy supports a belief which was to become central to the Israelites' understanding of covenant love. That belief was that just as Yahweh had acted dramatically and decisively in the lives of the people when he had saved them from the Egyptians and established the Sinai covenant, so has God acted dramatically and decisively in their lives now in establishing the monarchy, and in choosing David and David's line to shepherd the people, Israel. God has entered into a covenant relationship with David, and through David with the nation. This covenant is now understood to be expressed in the person of the king and in the kingdom itself. In only one more generation it will also be expressed in the existence of the temple, which would be built by David's son, Solomon.

With new experience and understanding of God's covenant love come new images to describe and celebrate that love. The images surrounding covenant begin to change from images connected to the Passover experience and the Sinai covenant experience to images connected to the experience of living in a kingdom, God's kingdom, which was ruled by God's chosen king.

It is true that the kingdom was eventually defeated, the temple destroyed, and the king taken into exile. During this traumatic time the people remembered Nathan's words to David. Based on their understanding of covenant love the people hoped and expected that God would send his "anointed one" (i.e., a "messiah"), a "king" to establish his "kingdom" forever.

## Steps in the Interpretation of the Image Covenant

| | Mutual Responsibilities | | (Abstract beliefs become embodied and take on material, concrete expression in rituals, institutions, people, etc.) |
|---|---|---|---|
| *Experience* Abraham experiences God's call | *God* Will give protection, land, and descendants | *The People* Will have faith and obey | *Signs* ■ Rite of cut animals ■ Circumcision ■ Isaac |
| *Experience* | *Mutual Responsibilities* | | *Signs* |
| God leads Moses and his people through the exodus experience | *God* Will give protection, a nation— the sense of nation, an extension of land and descendants, grew through the exodus experience | *The People* Will have faith, and obey the commandments | ■ Circumcision ■ Passover meal— to remember that the lamb's blood had given life ■ Covenant ceremonies—the sacred meal and the animal sacrifice ■ Ark of the covenant |
| *Experience* | *Mutual Responsibilities* | | *Signs* |
| Israel has a king like other nations | *God* Will give protection, a kingdom, a king of David's line; God will never withdraw his favor | *The People* Will have faith and obey the commandments | ■ The king ■ The kingdom ■ The temple (the ark of the covenant was taken to the temple) ■ Circumcision |

Jesus used Nathan's covenant image of kingdom when he came preaching, "The kingdom of God is at hand." So the images of king and kingdom became central to a Christian's understanding of our covenant relationship with God, too. Although for Christians the kingdom is a spiritual reality rather than a geopolitical one, and the king is God who became man, not a man chosen by God, Christians still claim that Nathan's words to David have been fulfilled. The kingdom and the king of David's line are secure forever.

## Review Questions

1. What important prophecy does Nathan deliver to David?
2. What does David tell Nathan he wants to do for God?
3. What is Nathan's original response?
4. What is Nathan's response the next day?
5. What new understanding of covenant is reflected in Nathan's words?
6. How is this new understanding of covenant expressed?
7. Based on this understanding of covenant what hopes and expectations developed after the kingdom was destroyed?
8. What image did Jesus use that grew out of this way of understanding covenant love?
9. How have the meanings behind the images "king" and "kingdom" changed since Nathan's time?

## Discussion Questions

1. How do you ritualize your relationship with God? If this way of ritualizing were denied you, would you feel "out of touch" with God? Why or why not?
2. What does the phrase "kingdom of God" mean to you?
3. Do you think Nathan's words have been fulfilled? Why or why not?

# ARTICLE 6

# The Court History: An Insider's View

**Question: "Why would David ask if there was anyone left from the house of Saul? (2 Sam 9:1) You'd think he would keep aware of Saul's sons since they might cause trouble." (2 Sam 9:1–13; 9–20; 16:3–4; 19:28; 21:7; 21:10 also discussed)**

We have already seen both the love and the pain involved in David's relationship with the house of Saul. David had loved Jonathan and felt obligated to Jonathan's descendants. David's own wife, Saul's daughter Michal, bore no children, a fact which David threw up to her in anger. Our questioner is right in suspecting that other descendants of Saul might well be a political threat to David. As we will see, this most difficult relationship between the house of David and the house of Saul continues to plague David.

This present scene, in which Meribbaal (Mephibosheth in some translations), Jonathan's son, is taken into Saul's home (see 2 Sam 9:1–13) is better understood if seen in the context of some passages which come later.

One such passage, which is appended to 2 Samuel rather than woven into the narrative, tells us that seven of Saul's descendants were turned over by David to the Gibeonites as a guilt offering. Because there was famine in the land, and suffering was seen as the result of sin, the famine was thought to be punishment for sin. It was attributed to the fact that Saul had sinned against the Gibeonites. The Gibeonites ask that seven of Saul's sons be turned over to them to be killed, and David agrees to these terms. "But the king spared Meribbaal, the son of Saul's son Jonathan, because of the oath of the Lord that was between them, between David and Jonathan son of Saul" (2 Sam 21:7). As the story goes, this guilt offer-

264

---

### WHO'S WHO

**Meribbaal:** Also called Mephibosheth; Jonathan's son whom David brought to his own table.

**Ziba:** Meribbaal's servant who told David that Meribbaal had turned traitor.

---

ing does reverse the famine, for the mother of two of those killed is described as guarding the bodies "from the beginning of the harvest until rain fell on them" (2 Sam 21:10).

Since this story is not in historical sequence there is no way of telling at what point Saul's sons died. However, the incident does cast light on David's question, "Is there still anyone left of the house of Saul to whom I may show kindness for Jonathan's sake?" (2 Sam 9:1).

Scholars debate whether Meribbaal was really a guest at David's table or whether he was under house arrest. That David did not entirely trust Meribbaal is evident later in the story when Meribbaal's servant, Ziba, accuses Meribbaal of treason (see 2 Sam 16:3). David evidently believes the servant without investigating his charge. "Then the king said to Ziba, 'All that belonged to Meribbaal is now yours!' " (2 Sam 16:4a).

Later Meribbaal tries to win back favor with David. He claims that his servant falsely accused him. "He (i.e., Ziba) has slandered your servant to my lord the King. But my lord the King is like the angel of God; do therefore what seems good to you. For all my father's house were doomed to death before my lord the King; but you set your servant among those who eat at your table. What further right have I, then, to appeal to the King?" (2 Sam 19:28).

David evidently does not know who is telling the truth. Nor does he seem to have any burning desire to find out. He tells Meribbaal that he and Ziba should divide the land. However, Meribbaal wants the king's protection more than he wants the land and so he does not press the point.

All of this puts a slightly different slant on David's "kindness" to

Meribbaal. However, the narrator seems to undercut any suspicion that Meribbaal might be a threat to David's throne, because he keeps mentioning that Meribbaal is crippled. A crippled descendant could be no real threat.

The story of Meribbaal's and David's relationship, full of personal details, appearing and reappearing throughout the text, is typical of the kind of "inside story" we will be reading as we read 2 Samuel 9–20. These chapters, along with 1 Kings 1–2, form a remarkable literary unit called the "Court History" or the "Succession Narrative." These chapters are so vivid in their details that scholars think the original source must have been someone inside the court. Unlike later materials which emphasize David's good points and idealize him as a legendary hero, the Court History shows David in all his vulnerability. We get a view of David that only a member of the family would have.

The picture we get of David's ambivalent feelings in regard to Saul's family, crystallized in his difficult relationship with Meribbaal, is a case in point. The Court History allows us to see David as we might see a family member with a mixture of contradictory motivations and feelings, struggling through relationships over time. But we can be sure that David was always well aware of any threat that might continue to come from the house of Saul. To stay aware was probably one of David's motivations for having Meribbaal at his table in the first place.

### Review Questions

1. Why were Saul's sons sacrificed?
2. Why was Meribbaal spared?
3. Name two possibilities that would explain Meribbaal's presence in David's house.
4. Did David trust Meribbaal? How do you know?
5. What is the "Court History"? What is another name for the same work?
6. From what point of view is the Court History written?

**Discussion Questions**

1. When it comes to biblical characters, do you like knowing their faults as well as their virtues or would you prefer an idealized picture? Why?
2. Do you agree with the expression, "blood is thicker than water"? What does this question have to do with this article?
3. Have you ever not trusted someone with whom you had daily contact? Explain. What does lack of trust do to a relationship?

# ARTICLE 7

# David's Sin

**Question: "Why did David so roundly condemn the rich man who took the poor man's lamb? Didn't David know the story was really about him?" (2 Sam 12:5–6; 2 Sam 11–12:14, 16:7–8; 1 Sam 21:6 also discussed)**

David did not know the story was really about him. The fact that the person to whom such a story is directed does not realize that the story is about him or her is the reason such stories, called parables, are so effective. Jesus taught in this same tradition of telling parables, specifically because telling parables enables the teacher to get around people's defense systems and forces them to see things about themselves that they don't want to see. Nathan's parable to David is a perfect example.

It seems that the fears which some had about the way a king might conduct himself had started to be realized in David. David has become so powerful that when there is a battle he can send other men to endanger their lives to save the nation (see 2 Sam 11:1). David can remain in the city, napping and walking.

In fact, David has become so powerful that he has forgotten that he is accountable to God. When David sees Bathsheba and is filled with lust, the news that she is the wife of one of his own soldiers does not deter him. He simply sends for her and she comes. David sleeps with Bathsheba and she conceives a child.

David's moral depravity is emphasized by the contrast between his behavior and Uriah's moral integrity. David, in an attempt to hide the fact that he, rather than Uriah, has fathered Bathsheba's child, tries to make it possible for Uriah to sleep with Bathsheba.

---

**HOW TO INTERPRET A PARABLE**

Look for one basic comparison between an element in the story and the audience listening to the story. The lesson comes from this comparison. Ask yourself—

- To whom is Nathan speaking?
- With whom in the story does the audience compare?
- What is the lesson?

- Nathan is speaking to David.
- David compares to the wealthy man who took the poor man's sheep.
- Like that man, David has sinned.

---

You may remember from a passage in 1 Samuel (see 1 Sam 21:6), that men who were involved in battle refrained from sexual intercourse. When David and his men wanted to eat the holy bread, the priest inquired if they had abstained from women. David replied, "We have indeed been segregated from women as on previous occasions. Whenever I go on a journey, all the young men are consecrated—even for a secular journey. All the more so today, when they are consecrated at arms!" (1 Sam 21:6). Uriah, who was "consecrated at arms," did not sleep with his wife.

David's next plan is to have Uriah killed. To do this he must enlist the help of Joab. In leaving Uriah vulnerable, Joab must leave others vulnerable, too, so additional officers of David's army are killed (see 2 Sam 11:17). David's sins are definitely infecting the community.

The role of a prophet was to speak for God. The prophet's role grew as the monarchy grew specifically because someone had to make it clear to everyone, including the king, that God was still king of Israel. David showed that he had forgotten that God was king by disobeying God's word. It was Nathan's role to confront David with his sin.

---

**WHO'S WHO**

**Bathsheba:** The woman with whom David committed adultery.

**Uriah:** Bathsheba's husband whom David has killed.

**Joab:** David's commander who cooperates in the plot against Uriah.

**Nathan:** God's prophet who confronts David with his sin.

**Shimei:** A Benjamite who curses David and calls David a sinner as David leaves Jerusalem.

---

So Nathan tells David the parable of the man who, despite the fact that he had many flocks, insisted on taking the one beloved ewe lamb from his poor neighbor in order to provide a meal for his visitor. David's anger flares out. " 'As the Lord lives, the man who has done this deserves to die; he shall restore the lamb fourfold, because he did this thing, and because he had no pity.' Nathan said to David, 'You are the man!' " (2 Sam 12:5–7a).

Only at this point does David realize that Nathan is confronting him about his sins, about his lust and murder. While David will not die, the fruits of lust and murder will remain in the kingdom.

Nathan's description of the ramifications of David's sins has, of course, been written in hindsight. The editor allows the reader to see clearly that sin causes tremendous suffering by spelling out in the succeeding chapters specific sufferings endured by David. As Nathan says, because David had Uriah killed with a sword, the sword will not depart from David's house. Because David acted in lust, the sins of lust will continue to plague David's house. As David brought death to others, so shall he be in grief as death comes to his loved ones. Sin causes suffering and David has sinned grievously.

David's defenses are conquered by Nathan and his parable. David realizes that he has sinned and he repents.

A sense of having sinned seems to have stayed with David. In chapter 16 you will read that a man named Shimei curses David and says, "Out!, Out! Murderer! Scoundrel! . . . See, disaster has overtaken you, for you are a man of blood" (2 Sam 16:7b,8b). David's companion wants to kill Shimei but David says, "If he is cursing because the Lord has said to him, 'Curse David,' who then shall say, 'Why have you done so?' " (2 Sam 16:10b).

David knew, in his heart, that the man's words were true. Nathan had succeeded in reminding the king that even he must remember, only God is the real king of Israel.

## Review Questions

1. Why is telling parables a good teaching technique?
2. What fears about kings have been realized in David?
3. How does David sin?
4. How do David's sins infect others?
5. How does Nathan confront David with his sin?
6. What does Nathan say will be the ramifications of this sin?
7. What does Shimei say to David? What is David's response?

## Discussion Questions

1. Have you ever had the experience of being corrected by a parable? Explain.
2. Why do you think the role of the prophet grew with the rise of the monarchy?
3. Do you think there is such a thing as "private sin" or does sin always affect the larger community?
4. Do you think the experience of having sinned and then truly repented makes people less defensive? Why or why not?

# ARTICLE 8

# Absalom's Plot to Kill Amnon

**Question: "Were Absalom and Jonadab in cahoots to kill Amnon? It seems they were since Jonadab tells David that Absalom had not killed all the princes, but had killed only Amnon in revenge for Tamar's rape." (2 Sam 13)**

Jonadab was certainly in Absalom's confidence when Absalom killed Amnon. Otherwise Jonadab would not have been able to defend Absalom's action to King David by claiming that Absalom's motive was justifiable revenge for the rape of his sister. After all, in killing Amnon, Absalom was also killing the son who was in line for the throne, thereby making himself next in line. Absalom's motives were suspect.

The real question is, "Was Jonadab in cahoots with Absalom to kill Amnon when Jonadab helped Amnon rape Tamar? After all, it was Jonadab who initiated the conversation with Amnon and who thought of a way for Amnon to be alone with Tamar (see 2 Sam 13:3–5). The reader, immersed in the "inside story" by the court historian, is inclined to ask, "Did Absalom have a role in Tamar's rape? After all, Absalom is slowly revealed to be a vicious opportunist, who plans to seize the throne from his father, David.

In order to answer this question let us first back up and follow the plot. Then we will be able to see how the court historian seems to subtly foreshadow Absalom's wickedness.

Notice how the story begins. "David's son Absalom had a beautiful sister whose name was Tamar; and David's son Amnon fell in love with her" (2 Sam 13:1). Absalom is given center stage right from the beginning, suggesting that he is a major actor right from the start.

---

**WHO'S WHO**

**Absalom:** David's son who kills his brother Amnon.

**Amnon:** David's son who rapes Tamar.

**Tamar:** David's daughter who is raped by Amnon.

**Jonadab:** Absalom's confidant who helps Amnon trap Tamar before Tamar is raped.

---

Next we are told that Amnon "loves" Tamar so much that he is sick because he cannot have her. The author then says, "But Amnon had a friend whose name was Jonadab . . . and Jonadab was a very crafty man" (2 Sam 13:3). The author has given us fair warning: Absalom is central to the story and Jonadab is a very crafty man.

Jonadab suggests a way in which Amnon might get Tamar into his bedroom so that he can rape her. The plan works. Once Tamar is alone with Amnon in his room "he took hold of her, and said to her, 'Come lie with me, my sister' " (2 Sam 13:11b). Tamar's plea is not simply based on her personal safety and on her personal desires. She appeals to the law which is the expression of covenant love. "She answered him, 'No, my brother, do not force me: for such a thing is not done in Israel; do not do anything so vile!' " (2 Sam 13:12). Tamar does not want to be shamed, nor does she want Amnon to be discredited. She even suggests that Amnon try to get the king's permission to have her. Despite her pleas, Tamar is raped and shamed.

Absalom's response to his sister's debasement is strange. Absalom merely says, "Has Amnon your brother been with you? Be quiet for now, my sister; he is your brother; do not take this to heart" (2 Sam 13:20). David also knows what has happened to Tamar, but he neglects to punish Amnon (see 2 Sam 13:21).

It is not until two years later that Absalom kills Amnon at the shearing festival. The plot to get Amnon to the festival seems similar to the plot to get Tamar to the bedroom, in that David is unwittingly persuaded to send the victim to the scene of the crime. Was Absalom, with the help of Jonadab, the mastermind behind both crimes?

There is no question that Absalom has taken the crafty Jonadab into his confidence in his plot against Amnon. Otherwise, as our questioner has pointed out, Jonadab would have no way of knowing that the report that all the princes had been killed was not true.

Another suspicious note is that the reader is puzzled by the fact that David immediately believes the report that Absalom has killed all the princes. This must mean that David was already aware of Absalom's desires to put himself on the throne.

By leaving Jonadab with David, Absalom has left a defender who will provide a legitimate excuse for his having killed his brother. At the same time Absalom lessens David's authority in the court, for one would have expected David to have punished Amnon for the rape of Tamar. David had left this responsibility unfulfilled, thus paving the way for Absalom to take things into his own hands and to kill the brother who stood between him and the throne.

The court historian tells the story with all the skill of a modern mystery writer. One is not immediately aware of the degree of wickedness which the plot casts on Absalom. But as the story progresses, as Jonadab reappears in Absalom's confidence, and as Absalom himself openly fights for the throne, the reader suspects Absalom in hindsight.

Jonadab was certainly Absalom's confidant in the murder of Amnon, and perhaps his confidant in the rape of Tamar as well.


## Review Questions

1. Who is Absalom? Amnon? Tamar? Jonadab?
2. What two motivations might Absalom have had for killing Amnon?
3. Who helped Amnon arrange for Tamar's rape?
4. On what does Tamar base her plea not to be raped?
5. What is Absalom's immediate response to Tamar's rape?

6. Is there any evidence that Absalom plotted with Jonadab to help Amnon rape Tamar?
7. Does David trust Absalom? How do you know?

## Discussion Questions

1. Do you agree that the author casts suspicion on Absalom in the story of the rape of Tamar? Why or why not?
2. Are you surprised to be reading about this kind of mystery and intrigue in the Bible? Why or why not?
3. Do you think the "court historian" should have reported all this? Explain.

# ARTICLE 9

# Absalom's Return to David's Court

**Question: "What does the widow from Tekoa mean when she tells David that the guilt for forgiving her son should be on her and her family, not on David?" (2 Sam 14:9; 2 Sam 14:7, 14, 33; Ex 21:23–25 also discussed)**

The woman from Tekoa is trying to persuade David that mitigating circumstances should save her "son" (evidently a fictitious son) from paying the price which the law would demand because he had killed his brother. Of course, the woman is really trying to persuade David to forgive Absalom, and to let him return from his place of exile, but David does not initially realize this.

The guilt which the woman says should come to her and her family rather than to David is the guilt involved in not fulfilling one's responsibility to avenge the death of a family member.

When the Israelites were a nomadic people they developed laws which were designed to protect the family unit. Remember, there were no police to call in the case of crime. If a family member was killed it became the responsibility of the nearest relative to "avenge" the death. In the Hebrew's law, the "vengeance" had to be what today is called "a proportioned response." In the name of justice you could not inflict worse than you received.

You may remember that when we read Exodus we read an example of this kind of justice. "If any harm follows then you shall give life for life, eye for eye, tooth for tooth, hand for hand, foot for foot, burn for burn, wound for wound, stripe for stripe" (Ex 21:23–25).

The problem which the woman from Tekoa presents, however, is extremely complicated because the crime has been committed

276

within the family. Since the purpose of the vengeance is to protect the family unit, the whole system is called into question when, in order to carry out the vengeance, one destroys rather than protects the family unit.

This was the case with the woman from Tekoa. She presented herself to David as a widow with two sons. One son had killed the other. Were vengeance executed she would lose her only son and her husband would lose his progeny (see 2 Sam 14:7). In such a case, the law is self-defeating. To exact vengeance would be to destroy the family unit rather than to protect it.

David seems to have no difficulty at all in passing judgment in this case. The murderer should be received back into the family. He should not be killed.

However, if the murderer is not punished to whom belongs the guilt for not fulfilling the obligation of the law to avenge the killing? The woman says that the guilt should be on her and on her family, not on David.

After David has spared the life of the killer, the woman points out to David that he has a similar situation in his own family. He, too, has a son who killed a son. That murderer, Absalom, is in exile. However, since Amnon is dead, Absalom is heir to the throne. Should not David consider doing for his own son what he was willing to do for the son of the woman? Should David not forgive Absalom and let him return? The woman points out to David that God himself seeks ways of retrieving the lost. She says, "But God will not take away a life, he will devise plans so as not to keep an outcast banished forever from his presence" (2 Sam 14:14).

With this argument, David recognizes the hand of Joab in the woman's performance. Nevertheless, he is persuaded. David agrees to let Absalom return to the city, but not to the court.

Absalom reveals his wicked character in the way he treats Joab, his intercessor. When Joab does not immediately respond to Absalom's summons, Absalom sets Joab's fields on fire. When Joab does come to Absalom, Absalom sends Joab to David to ask that Absalom be readmitted to the court. David again agrees. "So he (Absalom) came to the king and prostrated himself with his face to the ground before the king; and the king kissed Absalom" (2 Sam 14:33b).

Remember we are reading the court history which is full of intimate details, which pictures David in all his sin and weakness. Yet all we read about this reunion, after four years of separation, is that David kissed Absalom. There is no account of words exchanged in repentance and forgiveness, no account of tearful gratitude. David kissed Absalom. Perhaps even as he kissed Absalom, David realized that this son would continue to bring him nothing but suffering. The guilt for not avenging Amnon's death would be on David, along with the guilt of David's own sins. Nathan had been right: lust and the sword would continue to wreak havoc in David's court.

## Review Questions

1. Why did the law of "blood revenge" exist?
2. What does "a proportioned response" mean?
3. What is the purpose of vengeance?
4. Why does a crime inside the family subvert the purpose of "vengeance"?
5. What "case" did the woman from Tekoa present to David?
6. How does David decide this case?
7. What problem does this decision leave unresolved?
8. How does all this relate to David's own situation?
9. What does David do in his own case?

## Discussion Questions

1. Is the motivation behind "blood revenge" revenge? Explain.
2. What do you think should be a parent's response when one child mistreats another?
3. Do you think the woman from Tekoa was right in her plea? Explain.
4. Have you ever had something dreadful to forgive? Do you think there are any exceptions to Jesus' teaching that we must forgive one another from our heart? Why or why not?

# ARTICLE 10

# David: The Brokenhearted Father

**Question: "Why did David and his followers flee Jerusalem rather than fight Absalom?" (2 Sam 15:13–14; 2 Sam 15; 18:3–4; 18:33 also discussed)**

David and his followers fled Jerusalem because Absalom had gathered so many followers around himself that they feared defeat. In addition, it seems that David had a divided heart about this battle. To fight an enemy is one thing, but to fight a rebellion led by your own son, whom you have loved and forgiven, is quite another. David's fatherly grief seems to be as strong or stronger than his military instincts. We see both at work as David flees.

David could not have been unaware of the way in which Absalom was undercutting David's authority. Of course, it started with Absalom's revenge of Tamar's rape, a revenge that should have been David's responsibility. In addition, after Absalom's return from exile, he spent four years ingratiating himself to the people by telling them that were he king their claims of injustices would have a better hearing. Absalom would say, " 'Your claims are good and right; but there is no one deputed by the king to hear you.' Absalom said moreover, 'If only I were judge in the land! Then all who had a suit or cause might come to me, and I would give them justice' " (2 Sam 15:4).

Nor could David have failed to suspect a motive in addition to a desire to fulfill his vow to worship when Absalom said he was going to Hebron. After all, Hebron is the place where the people were willing to crown David king while Saul was still king of Israel. However, David did not prevent Absalom from going. He merely sent him off in peace. Where David's own children were concerned

---

**WHO'S WHO**

**Absalom:** David's son who tries to seize the throne.

**Ittai:** The foreigner whom David says does not owe him loyalty.

**Hushai:** An advisor who is loyal to David and is told to return to Jerusalem and act as a double agent.

**Ahithophel:** A trusted advisor of David's who joins Absalom in his revolt.

---

his ability to enforce the law or to act with military astuteness simply fell by the way.

David seems to be a defeated and disillusioned leader as he flees Jerusalem. First, he questions why anyone would be loyal to him, telling Ittai the Gittite to return to the "king" (Absalom) since he does not owe David loyalty (see 2 Sam 15:19–22). Next he declines to take the ark with him. David says, "If I find favor in the eyes of the Lord, he will bring me back and let me see both it and the place where it stays. But if he says, 'I take no pleasure in you,' here I am, let him do to me what seems good to him" (2 Sam 15:25–26).

In fact, the procession from Jerusalem to the Mount of Olives and then to the Jordan has the air of a funeral procession. "David went up the ascent of the Mount of Olives, weeping as he went, with his head covered and walking barefoot; and all the people who were with him covered their heads and went up weeping as they went" (2 Sam 15:30).

However, despite his disillusionment and grief, the military man is still alive in David. When David sends the priests back with the ark he advises them that he will need them as spies (2 Sam 15:28). In addition, David sends Hushai, an advisor, back as a "double agent" to counteract the effect of the traitor, Ahithophel's, advice. As we shall see, it is these strategic moves that contribute to the fact that David's men will eventually defeat Absalom's.

David's men realized that David's love for his traitorous son would make him ineffective on the battlefield. They persuade David to stay out of the battle, saying that his life is too valuable to risk (see 2 Sam 18:3–4). David agrees, sending the troops off with a warning to "deal gently" with Absalom.

And, in fact, when the battle is won and Absalom is killed, it is David the grieving father and not David the victorious king who responds to the news. David, overcome with grief, says, "O my son Absalom, my son, my son Absalom! Would I had died instead of you, O Absalom, my son, my son!" (2 Sam 18:33).

David's grief is so great that he neglects to thank or congratulate his men on their victory. It is only at Joab's insistence that David leaves his chambers and goes to the gate to meet the victorious troops. Yahweh has given David the victory, but for David the victory is empty because David has a broken heart.

## Review Questions

1. Why did David flee Jerusalem?
2. What actions on Absalom's part should have made David suspicious?
3. What was David's mood as he fled Jerusalem? How do you know?
4. What two militarily astute moves did David make as he fled Jerusalem?
5. What role does David play in the battle? Why?
6. How does David greet the news of victory? Why?

## Discussion Questions

1. Have you ever noticed (or experienced) that parents apparently love the "black sheep" in the family the most? Why do you think this is? Do you think God is the same way? Explain.
2. Do you think Joab was right to correct David? Why or why not?
3. Do you think David's behavior is understandable? Why or why not?

# ARTICLE 11

# David Remains God's Choice

**Question: "Why did Ahithophel hang himself before he knew how the battle turned out? After all, Absalom's side might have won." (2 Sam 17:23; 2 Sam 12:11–12; 15:12; 15:31; 16:16–18; 16:22–23; 17:14; 18:8; 20:3 also discussed)**

Ahithophel hung himself because he was in despair. Ahithophel had made a terrible mistake when he had chosen Absalom over David, and by the time Ahithophel killed himself he had realized this.

Ahithophel made his choice early, before David was informed that there was a conspiracy underway. In fact, the reader knows of Ahithophel's treachery before David does (see 2 Sam 15:12). David, when he hears the news at the Mount of Olives, prays, "O Lord, I pray you, turn the counsel of Ahithophel into foolishness" (2 Sam 15:31b). As we will see, the Lord doesn't turn Ahithophel's advice into foolishness, but he does prevent Absalom and his men from recognizing good advice when they hear it.

After David flees Jerusalem and Absalom enters the city, Ahithophel's foil, Hushai, arrives in Absalom's camp to serve as David's double agent. Hushai exhibits the same talent for purposeful ambiguity which David had exhibited when he offered to fight with the Philistines against Saul. Hushai says, "Long live the king! Long live the king . . . The one whom the Lord and this people and all the Israelites have chosen, his I will be, and with him I will remain" (2 Sam 16:16b, 18). Absalom presumes that he is the "king" to whom Hushai pledges allegiance, but the reader knows that it is to David that Hushai refers.

Next Absalom asks Ahithophel's advice, presumably about how

to make it clear that he is in charge in Jerusalem. Ahithophel suggests a strategy which is totally repugnant to us, that Absalom make it clear to all that he has replaced his father by having relations with his father's concubines in the view of all. "So they pitched a tent for Absalom upon the roof; and Absalom went in to his father's concubines in the sight of all Israel" (2 Sam 16:22).

As we read this passage we cannot but remember David on that same roof, lusting after Bathsheba, and Nathan's words to David about the ramifications of David's sin: "Thus says the Lord: I will raise up trouble against you from within your own house; and I will take your wives before your eyes, and give them to your neighbor, and he shall lie with your wives in the sight of this very sun. For you did it secretly; but I will do this thing before all Israel, and before the sun" (2 Sam 12:11–12). As we will see, when David returns to the court after Absalom's defeat he provides for these women but no longer has relations with them. From that point on they will live as "widows" (see 2 Sam 20:3).

Next Ahithophel advises Absalom on how David might be defeated without a great battle, without unnecessary bloodshed, and without Absalom being part of the action. Ahithophel and some men will pursue David immediately while David is exhausted, kill only him, and bring the others back to proclaim Absalom king.

Although up until now Ahithophel's counsel had been held in such high esteem it was as though one had consulted "the oracle of God" (see 2 Sam 16:23), nevertheless Absalom turns to Hushai, the double agent, and asks his advice. Hushai reminds Absalom that David is a great warrior. He suggests a tremendous battle in which Absalom would be the great leader and in which not only David but all of those with him would be killed.

Such a plan could only be preferred by a person of great pride who was wicked enough to enjoy a slaughter. Absalom was such a person. "Absalom and all the men of Israel said, 'The counsel of Hushai the Archite is better than the counsel of Ahithophel.' For the Lord had ordained to defeat the good counsel of Ahithophel, so that the Lord might bring ruin on Absalom" (2 Sam 17:14).

When Ahithophel saw that his counsel was not followed he killed himself (see 2 Sam 17:23). Ahithophel also undoubtedly saw that he had bet on the wrong man. He knew Hushai's advice was wrong, he knew Absalom had yielded to an absurd plan out of pride, he knew he could not return to David, so he killed himself.

Ahithophel was a good counselor even as a traitor. Absalom was foolish to receive Hushai into his inner circle and to accept his advice, for Hushai immediately reported all to David who was able to plan accordingly.

Once more, however, we see that the Lord rather than kings or advisors is responsible for the outcome of battle. The battle was fought in the forest, and while David's side won, "The forest claimed more victims that day than the sword" (2 Sam 18:8b). Ahithophel should never have bet on Absalom. There really wasn't a chance that Absalom would win because God had not chosen Absalom. God, despite everything, was still choosing David.

## Review Questions

1. Who is Ahithophel?
2. When does Ahithophel desert David?
3. Who is Hushai?
4. How are Hushai's words purposefully ambiguous?
5. How does Absalom demonstrate that he is in charge in Jerusalem?
6. How does Ahithophel think Absalom should defeat David?
7. How does Hushai advise Absalom to defeat David?
8. From the narrator's point of view, why was Hushai's advice accepted over Ahithophel's?
9. Why did Ahithophel kill himself?
10. How was the battle won?

## Discussion Questions

1. Do you think it is acceptable for a person to be a double agent and lie? Why or why not?
2. Do you think pride very often gets in the way of making good decisions? Have you seen this in others? In yourself? Explain.
3. Do you think it is ever permissible to commit suicide? Why or why not? What were Ahithophel's other options?

# Joab: A Dangerous Man

**Question: "Why does David make Amasa the commander of his army in place of Joab? (2 Sam 19:13) He seems to be rewarding treason rather than loyalty." (2 Sam 8:16; 18:14; 19:6–8; 19:14; 19:41–43; 20:9; 20:23; 1 Kings 2:6; 2:28–35 also discussed)**

David had at least two motives for demoting Joab and giving his job to Amasa. One was that David held Joab responsible for the death of Absalom. Another was that David wanted to reach out to his former enemies and unite the people once more.

First, David's relationship with Joab was very painful. Remember that it was Joab who was responsible for persuading David to let Absalom return, first to the kingdom and finally to the court. However, when Absalom turned out to be a traitor, Joab fought for David against Absalom. Despite David's orders not to kill Absalom, Joab did just that (see 2 Sam 18:14). Then, when the king was overcome with grief, Joab took it on himself to scold the king for not greeting the victorious soldiers on their return (see 2 Sam 19:6–8). David showed his anger and resentment by demoting Joab.

However, David also wanted to reach out to his former enemies. It is in the process of reaching out to Absalom's soldiers that David replaces Joab with Amasa. His ploy is helpful in reuniting the people for "Amasa swayed the hearts of all the people of Judah as one, and they sent word to the king, 'Return both you and all your servants' " (2 Sam 19:14). However, Joab viciously retrieves his power, as we shall soon see.

As David crosses the Jordan and returns to Jerusalem he reconciles with exactly the same people with whom he had been at odds

---

**WHO'S WHO**

**Joab:** David's commander.

**Amasa:** Absalom's commander.

**Shimei:** Man who cursed David and then apologized.

**Meribbaal:** Jonathan's son who denies having been a traitor.

**Solomon:** David's son who will eventually succeed David on the throne.

**Jeroboam:** King of Israel when the kingdom splits.

**Sheba:** The Benjamite who led a rebellion.

**Abishai:** Joab's brother whom Joab followed as Joab went to kill Amasa.

---

on his way out of Jerusalem. First he meets Shimei, the Benjamite who had cursed David and called him a murderer. Shimei begs pardon, and David forgives him.

Next David meets Jonathan's son Meribbaal who, as we have already discussed, denies having been a traitor to David. David offers Meribbaal the return of half his land although Meribbaal does not accept the offer.

Despite David's attempts at unity, the Judaites and the Israelites continue to be at odds (see 2 Sam 19:41–43). This division will continue throughout David's reign, and Solomon's, until the kingdom splits under King Jeroboam.

Another revolt breaks out, led by Sheba the Benjamite. It is this revolt that enables Joab to come back to power. After David returns to Jerusalem he tells Amasa to gather the men of Judah together in order to fight Sheba. However, Amasa delays and so David turns to Abishai, Joab's brother, instead. For reasons that are not explained, Joab and his men go out with Abishai. When Joab encounters Amasa he greets him warmly and pretends to kiss him (see 2 Sam 20:9). However, Joab has a hidden sword and kills Amasa, just as he had earlier killed Abner, the commander of Saul's army.

With this action Joab seems to have reestablished himself in power. He is now the obvious leader of the troops as they continue to pursue Sheba. When Sheba hides in a town, thus endangering its residents, it is Joab who negotiates with a townswoman to spare the town in exchange for Sheba's head.

So, as 2 Samuel ends, Joab is still listed as the man in charge of the whole army (see 2 Sam 20:23), just as he was when David first established the monarchy in Jerusalem (see 2 Sam 8:16).

We will not read of Joab's fate because it is not described until 1 Kings. David, before his death, tells Solomon that Joab deserves to die for killing Abner and Amasa. When Joab supports a challenger to Solomon's throne rather than supporting Solomon he chooses the wrong man. Joab takes asylum at the altar in the tent of the Lord where Solomon has him killed in accordance with David's wishes (see 1 Kings 2:28–35).

In the end David did not consider Joab loyal. David considered Joab a murderer. Not only did he "retaliate in peacetime for blood that had been shed in war" (see 1 Kings 2:6), thus killing unjustly, but he disobeyed David's order and killed Absalom. David considered Joab a dangerous and disloyal man.

## Review Questions

1. Who is Amasa? Joab?
2. What are two motives which David had in giving Joab's job to Amasa?
3. Why was David's relationship with Joab so painful?
4. Did Amasa help David reunite the fractured kingdom? How?
5. Who does David meet on his return to Jerusalem? How does David treat these people?
6. Who is Sheba? What does he do?
7. How does Joab retrieve his power?

8. In the end, what does David think of Joab?
9. What finally happens to Joab?

## Discussion Questions

1. What do you think the leader of a nation should do with a vicious but personally loyal associate? Can you think of any modern examples? What are they?
2. Do you think it is wrong to settle war debts in peacetime as Joab did? Why or why not?
3. Do you think David was right in demoting Joab in order to build an alliance with Absalom's followers? Why or why not? Can you think of any modern parallels? What are they?

# Theological Themes in 1, 2 Samuel

**Question: "Are these last chapters just random additions? They don't seem to have any organization at all." (2 Sam 21–24; 1 Sam 8:11–12 also discussed)**

With chapter 20 we have concluded the section of the Court History which is included in 2 Samuel. The Court History ends in 1 Kings 2. 2 Samuel 21–24 might be called "random additions" if one were thinking in terms of historical chronology. From that point of view they fit only because they are all about David's reign. However, these additions do move the story forward in the sense that they further theological themes. They help establish and reinforce the ideas that God has promised David that his house will be secure forever, that God will not withdraw his favor from David even should David sin, and that Jerusalem is to become the holy city, the center of worship.

The story of the massacre of Saul's sons (see 2 Sam 21:1–14) shows clearly that David's house has replaced Saul's house. David is not merely a member of Saul's house, as Saul's son-in-law. Rather, Saul's house is destroyed and David's house has replaced it.

The stories of the Philistine warriors who are conquered (2 Sam 21:15–22) and David's warriors who are honored (2 Sam 23:8–39) are evidence of God's promise that David's house will be secure. God will cause David's men to triumph over their enemies.

The story of the census and the plague illustrates God's promise that even if David and his descendants offend God, God will not withdraw God's favor from them. The reason it was offensive for David to take the census is that the census was the means through which kings recruited their troops. You may remember that when

---

### CONTENTS OF 2 SAMUEL 21–24

Saul's sons are turned over to the Gibeonites

Philistine warriors are defeated

David's song of thanksgiving

David's last words

David's warriors

Census and punishment

Purchase of the threshing floor

---

Nathan first warned the people against having a king he described what a king's way would be. "These will be the ways of the king who will reign over you; he will take your sons and appoint them to his chariots and to be his horsemen, and to run before his chariots; and he will appoint for himself commanders of thousands and commanders of fifties . . ." (1 Sam 8:11b–12a). Notice, it is Joab and the commanders of the army who take the census. For a king to do such things, said Nathan, would be a rejection of God as king. This sin, too, is one from which David repents. God does not withdraw his favor from David but lets David choose a way to be reconciled. David trusts God's mercy more than he trusts other human beings (see 2 Sam 24:14).

The two poems in these additions state clearly the promise made to David and his house. David's song of thanksgiving (also Psalm 18) clearly recognizes that it is God, and not David himself, who is responsible for David's triumph. The poem idealizes David in a way in which the Court historian did not. David is pictured as saying:

> The Lord rewarded me according to my righteousness;
>     according to the cleanness of my hands he recompensed me.
> For I have kept the ways of the Lord,

and have not wickedly departed from my God.
For all his ordinances were before me,
   and from his statutes I did not turn aside.
I was blameless before him, and I kept myself from guilt.
      (2 Sam 22:21–24)

The poem ends with a reiteration of the promise which we have already read on the lips of Nathan:

He (God) is a tower of salvation for his king,
   and shows steadfast love to his anointed,
      to David and his descendants forever (2 Sam 22:51).

This understanding of covenant is repeated in David's last words (see 2 Sam 23:1–7) when David is pictured as saying:

Is not my house firm before God?
   He has made an eternal covenant with me,
      set forth in detail and secured (2 Sam 23:5).

You may remember that when Nathan told David of God's promise to establish David's house forever, Nathan told David not to replace the tent with a temple. David was not to build God a house, at least not yet.

The first step toward building God's house and establishing Jerusalem as the city of God, as the center of worship, is taken in the last scene in 2 Samuel when David buys a threshing floor in order to build an altar to the Lord on which would be offered holocausts (see 2 Sam 24:18–25). Later, David's son, Solomon, will build the temple on this land. The ark will be brought to the temple and Jerusalem will become the center of worship for the Israelites. Sanctuaries outside Jerusalem will become unlawful, so all will come to Jerusalem on pilgrimage. Jerusalem will become "the city of God," the holy city in which God has chosen to dwell with God's people.

This "monarchical" understanding of covenant will, for a time, replace the Sinai understanding until, during the reform of Josiah, the Sinai understanding is again emphasized.

So, as 2 Samuel closes, David is secure on his throne and secure in his understanding that God has chosen his house to reign and his city, Jerusalem, to be God's eternal dwelling. Although events will eventually challenge these ideas, the deeper understanding of an eternal "king" and of an eternal "kingdom" which will replace them have continued to be expressed by the images and the language that developed during the rise of David, the Lord's chosen king.

## Review Questions

1. What theological theme is illustrated by the story of the massacre of Saul's sons?
2. What theological theme is illustrated by the stories of the warriors?
3. What theological theme is illustrated by the census and the plague?
4. Why was taking a census considered wrong?
5. What theological theme is contained in the two songs?
6. Why did David buy the threshing floor?
7. Why does Jerusalem become the city of God?

## Discussion Questions

1. Do you think our present understanding of covenant has been influenced more by the Passover/Sinai experience or by the king/kingdom experience? Why?
2. Do you think building elaborate temples/churches is a good thing to do? What are the pros and cons?
3. In what way is it true that one of David's line is on the throne and the kingdom is secure forever?

# Endnote

We have now completed our first reading of Genesis, Exodus, and 1, 2 Samuel. From the point of view of events we have followed the Hebrews from the time of the call of Abraham (1850 B.C.) to the time of King David (1000 B.C.).

From the point of view of religious insight, we have heard accounts of these events and interpretations of their meaning that come from various periods in history; from the point of view of the monarchy at its height (J); from the point of view of the northern kingdom after the split (E); from the point of view of the seventh-century reform (D); and from the point of view of the post-exilic community (P).

From no point of view have we "finished the story." You may continue your study of the Old Testament and the New; you may, through the years, grow in the depth of your knowledge of scripture, but you will never, in this lifetime, "finish the story."

You will not finish the story because you are a character *in* the story. You are the male or female made in God's image. You are Adam and Eve, flawed by sin. You are Abraham and Sarah, called to walk in faith with your God to an unknown land. You are Moses, called to speak God's word as you have received it to those who need to hear the good news. You are David, chosen by God to use your gifts to accomplish God's will on earth. You are the Yahwist and the Deuteronomist, pouring over the traditions you have received, called to understand them again in the light of subsequent events and in the context of your own life. You, too, are called to re-explain our traditions so that their relevance is understood by each succeeding generation.

The story goes on in each of our lives as we, like the Israelites,

realize that we are a chosen people, that we are in covenant relationship with a God who made us and who loves us, and that the
meaning and purpose of our lives is rooted in that relationship. The
call heard by Abraham and Sarah and their descendants is our call,
too. As we read how our ancestors in faith lived out that call
through the centuries we are discovering our own Old Testament
origins.

## THE CANON OF THE OLD TESTAMENT
*(39 books in Hebrew/Protestant Bibles; 46 in Catholic Bibles)*

**PENTATEUCH:**
("TORAH")

GENESIS
EXODUS
LEVITICUS
NUMBERS
DEUTERONOMY

**HISTORICAL BOOKS:**

"Deuteronomic
History"

{ JOSHUA
JUDGES
1 & 2 SAMUEL          In Greek Bible = 1 & 2 Kings
1 & 2 KINGS           In Greek Bible = 3 & 4 Kings

"Chronicler's
History"

{ 1 & 2 CHRONICLES    In Greek Bible = "Paralipomenon"
EZRA
NEHEMIAH

RUTH
ESTHER
LAMENTATIONS

Apocrypha/
Deuterocanon*

{ JUDITH              Only included in the Greek
TOBIT                Septuagint and part of the
BARUCH               Catholic Bible
1 & 2 MACCABEES

**WISDOM WRITINGS:**

JOB
PSALMS
PROVERBS
ECCLESIASTES         ="Qoheleth"
SONG OF SONGS        ="Canticle of Canticles"

Apocrypha/
Deuterocanon*

{ ECCLESIASTICUS      ="Sirach" or "Jesus ben Sira"
WISDOM OF SOLOMON

**PROPHETS:**

Major Prophets:

ISAIAH
JEREMIAH
EZEKIEL
(DANIEL)             In Hebrew, Daniel is not a prophet

Minor Prophets:
("The Twelve")

HOSEA          NAHUM
JOEL           HABAKKUK
AMOS           ZEPHANIAH
OBADIAH        HAGGAI
JONAH          ZECHARIAH
MICAH          MALACHI

*Books that are underlined are found only in Catholic Bibles

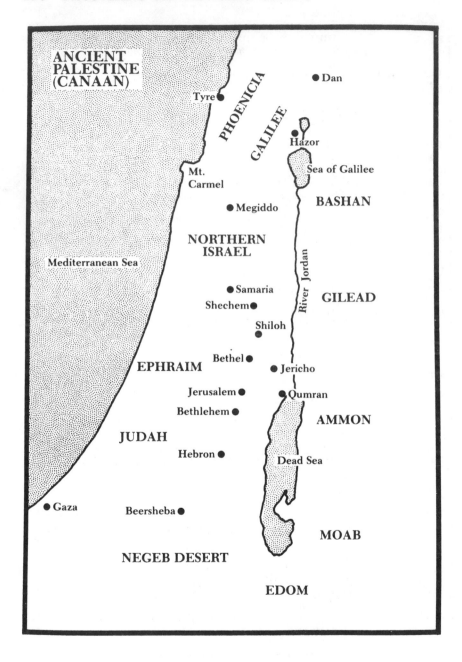

ANCIENT
PALESTINE
(CANAAN)

Dan

Tyre

PHOENICIA

GALILEE

Hazor

Sea of Galilee

Mt.
Carmel

BASHAN

Megiddo

NORTHERN
ISRAEL

Mediterranean Sea

River Jordan

Samaria

Shechem

GILEAD

Shiloh

Bethel

EPHRAIM

Jericho

Jerusalem

Qumran

Bethlehem

AMMON

JUDAH

Hebron

Dead Sea

Gaza

Beersheba

MOAB

NEGEB DESERT

EDOM

## TIMELINE

| | |
|---|---|
| 1850 B.C. | Abraham experiences God's call |
| | Isaac |
| | Jacob |
| | Joseph |
| | |
| | Slavery in Egypt |
| 1250 B.C. | Moses and the exodus |
| | |
| | Period of the Judges |
| | Saul |
| 1000 B.C. | David |
| | Solomon |
| 922 B.C. | Kingdom divides |
| | Prophets call the people to fidelity |
| 721 B.C. | Northern kingdom falls to Assyrians |
| 630 B.C. | Josiah's reform |
| 587 B.C. | Southern kingdom falls. Beginning of Babylonian exile |
| 537 B.C. | Cyrus, a Persian, conquers the Babylonians and lets the Israelites return to the holy land |
| 450 B.C. | Time of reinterpretations in the light of events |

# Glossary

*Aaron:* The person God gave Moses when Moses complained that he did not speak well.

*Abimelech:* In Genesis: the king to whom Abraham (Isaac, in one account) pretended that his wife was his sister. In Judges: Gideon's son who made himself king.

*Abner:* The commander of Saul's army.

*Abraham:* The first historical person in Jewish salvation history. Abraham lived around 1850 B.C. and is called the father in faith.

*Achish:* The leader of the Philistines whom David joined for a while.

*Ahaz:* King of Judah (the southern kingdom) from 735–715 B.C. during the time when Isaiah was a prophet. Ahaz was considered a bad king because he relied on the Assyrians for political protection rather than on God.

*Ahithophel:* The advisor who chose Absalom over David and then committed suicide.

*Amasa:* Head of Absalom's army who was later promoted by David.

*Ambiguity:* The quality or state of being ambiguous. A statement is ambiguous if it lends itself to more than one interpretation.

298

*Amnon:* David's son who raped Tamar and was killed by Absalom.

*Anthropomorphic:* Ascribing human characteristics to something which is not human.

*Apodictic Law:* Law which directs an individual person to do or refrain from doing a specified action.

*Ark of the Covenant:* The gold-plated box in which were kept the ten commandments.

*Atonement:* At-one-ment. An act of atonement is an act which brings about union.

*Babylonian Exile:* 587–537 B.C. The time when the southern kingdom was conquered and many of its citizens were taken to Babylon.

*Ban:* Those under the ban were killed. Enforcing the ban was seen as a way of acknowledging that victory belongs to God.

*Bathsheba:* The woman with whom David committed adultery. Later David married Bathsheba.

*Benjamin:* Jacob's youngest son. Joseph's younger brother.

*Bible:* The word means "a collection of books." The Bible includes the Old Testament and the New Testament.

*Book of Jashar:* A book in which David's lament appeared. The Deuteronomist used this book as a source.

*Canaan:* The land to which Abraham traveled. It is west of the Jordan River.

*Canon:* A "canon" is an instrument by which something is measured. In the context of the Bible, the canon refers to the books which are considered revelation and inspired and are therefore in the Bible. These books are the "rule" of faith.

*Case Law:* Law which directs a judge to render a given punishment in the event of a certain crime.

*Circumcision:* An operation in which the foreskin of eight-day-old males is removed. Circumcision became a sign of the covenant.

*Contextualist:* A person who reads in context. In relation to the Bible, a contextualist would ask: "What is the literary form of this book? What were the beliefs of the people of the time? How does this fit into the process of revelation?"

*Court History:* 2 Samuel 9–20; 1 Kings 1–2; also called the Succession Narrative. An insider's view of David's court.

*Covenant:* A solemn ritual agreement which could not be broken. The word "covenant" is used to describe the relationship between God and God's people.

*Covenant Code:* Exodus 20:22–23:19; The laws given to Moses after the ten commandments.

*Dagon:* God of the Philistines.

*David:* Succeeded Saul as king (ca. 1010–970 B.C.). He united the twelve tribes and defeated the Philistines. David was seen as an ideal ruler. People expected the messiah to be one like David.

*Defense Mechanism:* This is a psychological term to describe how we defend ourselves in relationship with others or even with ourselves. Defense mechanisms can be unconscious ways of responding to a perceived threat.

*Deuteronomist:* The name attributed to the editing tradition which produced the Deuteronomistic History.

*Deuteronomistic History:* Joshua, Judges, 1, 2 Samuel, 1, 2 Kings. Also called the Former Prophets.

*Dinah:* Jacob's daughter who was raped.

*E:* The Elohist editing tradition. The editing tradition which originated in the northern kingdom.

*Egypt:* The country around the valley of the Nile River, bordering the south side of the Mediterranean.

*Eli:* The priest at Shiloh when Samuel was a child.

*Elohim:* "Lord." The word used to refer to God in the Elohist tradition up until the time of Moses.

*Ephod:* Usually refers to a garment worn by the high priest.

*Ephraim:* Joseph's son who received preference over his older brother, Manasseh.

*Esau:* Son of Isaac and Rebekah. Jacob's twin.

*Etiology:* A story that explains the origin of something.

*Euphemism:* To say something in words that seem less offensive than "plain talk."

*Extant:* in existence.

*Ezekiel:* A prophet during the time of the Babylonian exile.

*Folk History:* History passed on by oral tradition rather than by written records.

*Form:* The shape of something. In literature the form is the kind of writing, or the "shape" of the whole piece. Is it a poem? a letter? a legend? One cannot understand the author's intent unless one understands the literary form in which the author is writing.

*Former Prophets:* Joshua, Judges, 1, 2 Samuel, 1, 2 Kings. Also called the Deuteronomistic History.

*Function:* The use to which something is put, or its role. In literature different kinds of writing have different functions. An editorial has a different function than a straight news story or a feature article.

*Genealogy:* The record of familial descent. In the Israelite society a person's rights and privileges depended on his membership in a clan or tribe, so genealogies were all-important. Legal paternity conferred all the rights of natural paternity, so the function of a genealogy was not always to trace a blood line. Genealogies are often repeated to further a particular emphasis or theme of the narrator.

*Gideon:* The Judge who turned down the opportunity to be king.

*Gilgamesh:* A Babylonian creation myth.

*Goliath:* The Philistine reputedly conquered by David.

*Hagar:* Maid to Sarah. She bore Abraham's son, Ishmael.

*Hannah:* Samuel's mother.

*Hebrew:* This word is used to name the Israelites, especially in their relationships with "foreigners."

*Hebrew Language:* The language in which nearly all of the Old Testament was originally written.

*Hebron:* The southern city in which David was crowned king of the Judahites.

*Historical:* An event is historical if it was witnessed and if we have oral or written accounts of the event. Not all events are historical. Some precede history, others transcend history.

*Hushai:* The advisor who remained faithful to David when Absalom rebelled.

*Image:* A mental representation of something not present to the senses. A concrete way of thinking about an abstract concept.

*Inspiration:* The state of being affected by divine influence. When we say that the Bible is inspired we mean that God affected the human authors.

*Ishbaal:* Saul's son who succeeded Saul on the throne for a short time.

*Ishmael:* The son born to Abraham by Hagar, Sarah's maid.

*Israel:* Jacob's name was changed to Israel by an angel. The nation Israel descended from Jacob's twelve sons.

*Israel:* The tribes united under Saul. After the kingdom split "Israel" was the name of the northern kingdom.

*J:* Another name for the Yahwist editing tradition.

*Jacob:* The son of Isaac and Rebekah. Twin brother of Esau.

*Jerusalem:* The city David chose as his capital. It became the center of worship, the "city of God."

*Jethro:* Moses' father-in-law. A priest of Midian.

*Joab:* The commander of David's army.

*Jonadab:* A friend of Absalom's who was in his confidence when Absalom killed Amnon.

*Joseph:* The son of Jacob by Rachel, who was sold into Egypt and later saved his family.

*Judah:* One of Jacob's sons after whom the tribe of Judah, David's tribe, was named.

*Judah:* A southern tribe. Later the name of the southern kingdom.

*Judahites:* Those from the tribe of Judah who crowned David as king.

*Judge:* A charismatic political leader in the period preceding the monarchy.

*Laban:* Father of Leah and Rachel, who tricked Jacob into marrying Leah first.

*Leah:* Jacob's first wife. Rachel's older sister.

*Leaven:* A substance like yeast which was used in making bread.

*Legend:* A symbolic and imaginative story with an historical core.

*Levi:* Jacob's son. The tribe named after Levi became priests.

*Literary Form:* The kind of writing. Examples are poetry, fable, myth, history, biography, science fiction, etc. In order to understand any book you need to know its literary form.

*Literary Technique:* A systematic way of accomplishing something in a written work. If an author wanted to make it clear that a person is acting under God's inspiration that author might use the literary technique of picturing God as talking directly to that character.

*Lot:* Abraham's nephew who went to Canaan with him. He escaped Sodom.

*Manasseh:* Joseph's son who lost preference to his younger brother, Ephraim.

*Manna:* The "bread" provided by God to the Israelites during the exodus.

*Metaphor:* A comparison that does not use the word "like" or "as." Example: "God is a mighty warrior."

*Michal:* Saul's daughter and David's wife.

*Midian:* The land to which Moses escaped when he fled Egypt.

*Monotheism:* A belief in one God.

*Moses:* The great Israelite whom God chose to lead God's people out of slavery in Egypt.

*Mount Horeb:* See Mount Sinai. The E and D traditions use "Mount Horeb."

*Mount Sinai:* The mount in the wilderness where God called Moses and where God later revealed the ten commandments.

*Myth:* An imaginative and symbolic story about a reality which is beyond comprehension.

*Narrative:* The act, technique, or way of telling a story.

*Narrator:* The "voice" telling the story. The narrator cannot always be equated with the author. The author may create a character who tells the story and is thus the narrative voice.

*Nathan:* The prophet in David's kingdom.

*Nazirite:* One set apart by vow. Samuel was a Nazirite. Nazirites did not cut their hair or drink spirits.

*Nomads:* People who are on the move rather than settled in one location.

*Onan:* Judah's son who did not fulfill his obligation to his dead brother and to Tamar, his brother's widow.

*Oral Tradition:* The traditions of the community handed on by word of mouth.

*P Editor:* The editing tradition that dates to after the Babylonian exile and is thought to have been done by the priests.

*Parable:* A parable is a story which, at base, rests on a metaphor. The comparison is between the audience and the story itself. The function of the parable is to correct and call to conversion the audience.

*Passover:* The celebration which reminds Jews of the night on which they escaped from Egypt because the Angel of Death passed over their homes during the last plague.

*Patriarch:* The male head of a family. A patriarchal society is one in which the men have all the power and women are treated as subordinates.

*Pentateuch:* Genesis, Exodus, Leviticus, Numbers, Deuteronomy. Also called "the Law" and "the Torah."

*Philistines:* The Israelites' chief enemy during the period of the early monarchy.

*Polytheism:* A belief in many gods.

*Prophet:* One who speaks for God. The prophet's spiritual gift is the ability to see the ramifications of covenant love.

*Propitiatory:* A structure on top of the ark which was considered to be God's throne.

*Rachel:* Jacob's wife. Laban's daughter. Mother of Joseph.

*Ramses II:* Pharaoh in Egypt (1290–1224 B.C.) during the time of the exodus.

*Rebekah:* Isaac's wife. Jacob and Esau's mother. Laban's sister.

*Redeem:* To set free. To redeem a person or animal was to set it free by offering something else in its place.

*Reed Sea:* The "sea" or swampy land through which the Israelites miraculously escaped the Egyptians.

*Revelation:* That which makes known God's will or truth. When we claim that the Bible is revelation we claim that it reveals the truth about God, our relationship with God, and what we should be doing to build up rather than to tear down the kingdom.

*Samuel:* Judge, priest, and prophet who facilitated the change from a tribal confederacy to a monarchy.

*Sarah:* Wife of Abraham. Mother of Isaac.

*Seer:* A person with "supernatural" knowledge.

*Septuagint:* The Greek translation of the Old Testament begun about 250 B.C.

*Shechem:* Raped Jacob's daughter Dinah.

*Shechem:* A city north of Jerusalem.

*Shiloh:* The city in which the ark of the covenant was kept until it was captured by the Philistines.

*Simeon:* One of Jacob's sons who, with his brother Levi, avenged his sister Dinah's rape.

*Simile:* A comparison that uses the words "like" or "as." Example: "God is like a mighty warrior."

*Succession Narrative: See* Court History.

*Symbol:* Something that stands for or represents something else.

*Synonymous Parallelism:* A literary device in Hebrew poetry. Two adjacent lines express the same thought but in different words.

*Tamar:* Judah's daughter-in-law who was left a widow when Er died.

*Tamar:* David's daughter who was raped by her brother Amnon.

*Tent of Meeting:* The tent was God's dwelling in which God "tabernacled" with God's people.

*Testament, New:* "Testament" means "covenant." The New Testament is the collection of Christian Greek scriptures.

*Testament, Old:* "Testament" means "covenant." The Old Testament is the collection of Jewish Hebrew scriptures.

*Theophany:* God's appearance to a person.

*Thummim:* An object kept in the pocket of the ephod used to determine God's will by the drawing of lots.

*Tone:* The pitch of a word which determines its meaning or the general effect or atmosphere created.

*Uriah:* Bathsheba's husband who was killed as a result of David's scheming.

*Urim:* An object kept in the pocket of the ephod and used to determine God's will by the drawing of lots.

*Vulgate:* The translation of the Bible into Latin done by Jerome in the fourth century.

*Yahweh:* The name by which God revealed God's self to Moses at the burning bush.

*Yahwist:* The name attributed to the editing tradition that originated in the time of the monarchy.

*Ziba:* Mcribbaal's servant who accuses him of treason.

*Zipporah:* Moses' wife and Jethro's daughter.

# Index of Biblical References

310